Capitalism in Crisis

To Glen, David and Amy

Other books by W. R. Garside

The Durham Miners, 1919–1960

The Measurement of Unemployment. Methods and Sources in
Great Britain, 1850–1979

British Unemployment 1919–1939: A Study in Public Policy

Capitalism in Crisis
International Responses
to the Great Depression

Edited by
W. R. Garside

Pinter Publishers, London
St. Martin's Press, New York

Pinter Publishers
25 Floral Street, Covent Garden, London WC2E 9DS, United Kingdom

First published in 1993

© W. R. Garside 1993

British Library Cataloguing in Publication Data

A CIP catalogue record for this book is available from the British Library

ISBN 0 86187 701 2 (Pinter)

All rights reserved. For information, write:
Scholarly and Reference Division,
St. Martin's Press, Inc., 175 Fifth Avenue,
New York, NY 10010

First published in the United States of America in 1993

ISBN 0-312-04178-0

Library of Congress Cataloging-in-Publication Data

Capitalism in crisis : international responses to the Great Depression / edited by W. R. Garside.
    p.   cm.
    Includes index
    ISBN 0-312-04178-0
    1. Europe—Economic policy.   2. Europe—Economic conditions—1918–1945. 3. Depressions—1929—Europe. I. Garside , W. R.
HC240.C33   1992
338.5'42—dc20   92-28467
                                         CIP

Typeset by Florencetype Ltd, Kewstoke, Avon
Printed and bound in Great Britain by
Biddles Ltd of Guildford and King's Lynn

Contents

List of contributors

W. R. Garside is Professor of Economic History at the University of Birmingham, England. He has written extensively on aspects of government economic policy in 20th century Britain, with particular reference to industry and the labour market. His latest book *British Unemployment, 1919–1939. A Study in Public Policy* was published by Cambridge University Press in 1990. He is currently engaged in a comparative study of British and German industrial policy in the late 1930s.

A. Booth, Senior Lecturer in Economic and Social History at the University of Exeter, England is the author of a number of pieces on British economic policy in the twentieth century. He is joint author with M. Peck of *Employment, Capital and Economic Policy. Great Britain, 1918–1939* (Oxford, 1985). He is currently researching British trade unions and productivity growth since 1945.

B. Gustafsson is Professor of Economic History at Uppsala University and Director of Economic Studies at the Swedish Collegium for Advanced Study in the Social Sciences (SCASS). His research interests have focused on labour history, the history of economic ideas, public sector growth and historical forms of economic organisation. Among his publications are *Post-Industrial Society* (editor, Croom Helm, 1979) and *Power and Economic Institutions. Re-Interpretations in Economic History* (Elgar, 1991).

H. James was until 1986 a Fellow of Peterhouse College, Cambridge University, England. He is currently Associate Professor of History at Princeton University, USA. His publications include *The German Slump: Politics and Economics 1924–1936* (Oxford, 1986), and articles on financial crises and depression. He is currently preparing a history of international financial relations since 1945.

L. Schwarz is Lecturer in Economic and Social History at the University of Birmingham, England. He has written *London in the Age of Industrialisation. Entrepreneurs, Labour Force and Living Conditions, 1700–1850* (Cambridge, 1992). He is currently working on French government economic policies after 1914.

P. Fearon is Senior Lecturer and Head of the Department of Economic and Social History at the University of Leicester, England. He has written *The Origins and Nature of the Great Slump, 1929–32* (Macmillan, 1979) and *War, Prosperity and Depression. The U.S. Economy 1917–45* (Philip Allan, 1987). His current research is on the regional impact of the depression and New Deal in the United States.

K. E. Jackson is a Senior Lecturer in Economics at the University of Auckland, New Zealand. His current research interests centre upon the economic development of the electricity and forest industries. The most recent examples of his work include a paper on 'Public versus Private Ownership of Hydro-Electric Power in Australia and New Zealand', which was presented to the 1992 Society for the History of Technology conference in Uppsala, Sweden, and a forthcoming article 'Forest Policy: The New Zealand Colonial Experience', in *Revue Française d'Histoire d'Outre Mer*.

A. M. Endres is Senior Lecturer in Economics at the University of Auckland, New Zealand. His current research interests centre upon the history of economic thought in New Zealand, 1915–50, the history of Australian economic thought and rhetoric and metaphor in classical political economy. Recent publications in these fields have appeared in *New Zealand Economic Papers, Scottish Journal of Political Economy, European Economic Review, Journal of European Economic History* and *History of Political Economy*.

D. H. Aldcroft is Professor of Economic History at the University of Leicester, England. He has written extensively on British economic history in the late 19th and 20th centuries and has research interests too in European economic development. His latest book *Education, Training and Economic Performance, 1944–1990* was published by Manchester University Press in 1992.

List of figures

List of tables

Preface

Economic histories of the inter-war period inevitably focus on the Great Depression of 1929–32. The bulk of the literature concerning this traumatic dislocation, however, lies in detailed national studies. The international dimensions of the Depression, and in particular the range of factors conditioning the economic policy response in different countries, are by no means neglected themes but discussion of them is not readily available outside of textbook surveys of comparative economic history, which by their very nature rarely capture the results of recent research. This volume is aimed at those who require an overview of the depression and recovery policies adopted in the major industrialised countries during the 1930s, but one which focuses less on the detail of policy than upon the context in which it was formulated and the attitudes which determined its characteristics. I regret the absence of a study of Italy, particularly since the macroeconomic history of that country in the 1930s has been neglected for too long; but the inclusion of papers on Australia, New Zealand and Eastern Europe alongside the expected emphasis on Britain, France, Germany and Sweden is a reminder of how much value can yet be gained by addressing fundamental questions on the basis of evidence from a variety of countries.

I am grateful for the encouragement and courtesy I received from Vanessa Harwood at Pinter Publishers and Alec McAuley at Leicester University Press. My special thanks, however, go to the contributors to this volume not only for their individual scholarship but also for their collective patience.

W. R. Garside

Introduction

W. R. Garside

Much has been written about the causes and course of the Great Depression in the early 1930s, especially in America and Europe, and about the detailed policy responses *within* major industrialised nations. Attention had increasingly been focused too on the relationship between the Depression and long-term developments in the world economy (see Aldcroft and Rodger, 1984). International comparisons are less readily available even though they offer a rich source of further investigation about, for example, the channels of transmission by which the Great Depression was propagated internationally, the role of economic institutions in conditioning responses to the economic downturn and both the formulation of policy and its effects during the Depression and the subsequent years of recovery.

This volume is not concerned directly with the detailed causes and progress of the Depression but it is useful to identify certain of its stylised features as a way of emphasising the value of such a comparative macro-economic approach. Although there is a growing consensus that both monetary and non-monetary factors account for the Great Depression phenomenon, it is clear that the shift in American Federal Reserve policy towards a contraction in monetary policy in the late 1920s provoked even more contraction abroad. The USA in other words provided the initial impulse towards the slump which was then superimposed upon the critical position other countries were already in. 'The failure of other countries to adjust to changing international competitive conditions and their consequent dependence on foreign borrowing', writes Eichengreen, 'did much to heighten the fragility of their external position, allowing the shift towards contraction in US policy to elicit an even more dramatic shift abroad' (Eichengreen, 1992, p. 223). The traumatic effects of economic depression were transmitted so rapidly because of the widespread adoption by industrialised nations of a gold exchange standard which fixed exchange rates internationally. The scale of the ensuing economic crisis soon put paid to the dominant liberal economic doctrine of economies possessing self-healing powers. At the same time the classical instruments of government intervention in the form of taxation, trade and customs duties proved incapable of turning the tide, giving rise to new ways of sustaining confidence while the search for effective remedial policies was undertaken.

Although the measures taken to combat the Depression varied from country to country, embracing at the extremes limited government involvement and state socialism, one noticeable tendency was the shift to national, political and economic autism rather than international cooperation. The paucity of coordinated action among beleaguered nations reflected in part the way they blamed others for bringing about the dire state of affairs in which they found themselves whatever the alleged cause, be it the inflationary recourse to unbalanced budgets, the sapping effects of reparations payments or the irresponsible resort to devaluation. And when attention is directed to reactions to rather than causes of the downturn of the 1930s, it can so easily appear from a modern day perspective as if an outbreak of collective mania or at the very least of ignorance and stupidity had occurred. Evidence mounts, to give but one example, of some nations striving to balance their budgets by rigid economies in expenditure and the imposition of additional taxes when their very actions were strengthening the tendencies at work for revenue to decline even further, rendering budgetary balance almost impossible.

But the principal industrialised countries were driven by a logic which defies such easy ridicule. If, the argument implicitly ran, individuals had to tighten their belts when spending exceeded earnings then so should countries. Governments otherwise would either have to borrow or inflate their currency. Borrowing would compete with investors' funds, drive up interest rates and thereby hinder the prospects of recovery. Inflationary finance would also drive up rates, penalising lenders and those on fixed incomes as well as damaging confidence at home and abroad. Although it was conceded that governments might be obliged on occasion to run a budget deficit by force of circumstance, the negative effects on consumer and investor confidence of adopting such a course as a deliberate act of policy were to be strenuously avoided. It would be preferable instead to undertake painful adjustments to allow the seeds of recovery to sprout. Thus governments might have to cut back on spending, wages might have to fall to allow goods to be sold profitably, and unemployment might have to be endured if the basis of sound finance and the legitimate role of the state were to be protected and lasting economic, to say nothing of social and political, stability secured.

These presumptions and attitudes did not of course exist in the same form or operate with equal weight in all industrialised countries nor did they necessarily remain unsullied within particular countries as the 1930s developed. They remind us however of the crucial influence which attitudes and expectations, entrenched institutional opinion and the legacy of past policy successes and failures can have on the formulation and execution of economic policy. Consequently it is important to understand why particular countries reacted as they did to the economic crisis of the 1930s and to examine how far any similarities and differences thus found can be explained by matters of common concern or preoccupation.

This volume is a contribution to such a perspective. It provides an overview of the manner in which economic policy in various countries during depression and recovery was constrained by prevailing institutional, political and financial environments and, to an extent, by the range and sophistication of alternative economic strategies. It contrasts the reactions of those public authorities which felt obliged to defend existing orthodoxies because of the pressure of vested interests or the perception of what past experience suggested were alternative options with those of other governments which remained determined either to break with the past or to build upon recent innovative policies, often for political rather than economic motives.

Even if we accept from the outset that the differing nature and timing of depression and recovery in our chosen countries renders detailed comparisons somewhat suspect, identifiable features of the decade do emerge clearly from these studies. It was not a period of fiscal revolution. Sweden's celebrated flirtation with Keynesian-type fiscal expansion following upon a brief period of slump proves less significant so far as general progress in the 1930s is concerned than does the impact of devaluation and external influences on the demand for exports. Initial responses to the Depression in America, Britain, Germany, France, Eastern Europe and Australasia shared a common emphasis upon the search for a balanced budget for the sake of sustaining confidence at home and abroad, frequently involving reduced government expenditure, tight control of credit and rising taxation. So long as the countries stayed on the gold standard domestic policies were shaped by a stern refusal to contemplate devaluation, which in turn merely reinforced internal deflation as officials slavishly avoided low interest rates or deficit spending for fear of encouraging gold outflows. Sweden, for example, was as orthodox in this regard as other countries until she followed Britain off gold. The passionate desire to retain the value of one's currency led gold standard countries to persist with high interest rates and to eschew public works spending unless it was self-liquidating, given the lingering belief in the adequacy of the exchange rate system to provide stability.

The limitations placed on public policies in Europe and elsewhere by the external constraints of the inter-war gold standard are, of course, well known. Fiscal conservatism was rife, however, even when freedom from gold permitted more flexible and adventurous policies. The slump did little to diminish the cautious and limited pragmatism of the British. If anything it taught the National Government how to appear to be reacting to changed opportunities without it having to abandon the policies which would ensure the continuation of the status quo, not least with regard to the international value and influence of sterling and the continuation of anti-interventionist sentiments. In the absence of any sustained and effective demand for a more radical stance from the populace as a whole, the balance of interest group power in Britain was not fundamentally shaken by the Depression, permitting policy to be Treasury-dominated down to 1938 and beyond.

Roosevelt's New Deal followed upon America's rejection of the sanctity of the gold standard in 1933. Whereas France clung to gold as a defence not only of economic but what it believed to be social and political stability too, America seemed as determined as did the Swedes and the Nazis to secure lasting economic recovery. As in Britain, attention became focused on ways of raising prices but the *de facto* policy of federal deficits which emerged was not part of an explicit programme of national recovery based upon a firm commitment to government spending as the leading edge of recovery. Roosevelt disliked budget deficits and his late embrace of Keynesian-type policies in 1938 was heavily influenced by the political advantage to be thus secured: only two years before he had made a determined effort to balance the budget; tight money had gone hand in hand with reduced government expenditure and raised taxes.

Nowhere is the influence of politics more clearly demonstrated than in Germany. Brüning's rejection of credit creation and rigid adherence to the principle of balanced budgets was based in part on his desire to convince outsiders of the depth of the crisis facing his country. The hope was that Germany might thereby be relieved of reparations obligations and thus begin to recover something of its past economic and political stature. Hitler's fiscal programme, moreover, was more conservative than is commonly recognised. Budget deficits were not vigorously pursued; on the contrary it was essential in the eyes of the regime for the stability of the mark to be retained and for dangerous financial experiments to be avoided. Many of the preoccupations and prejudices forged during the previous administrations found their way into official policy-making in subsequent years. What emerged with vengeance was the ability of the Nazi regime to subordinate the country, workers, producers and investors alike to the supremacy of the state. By rejecting the regulation of the economy by market forces in favour of the dictate of the state, the Nazis were able to pursue in a highly politicised fashion and with the benefit of isolationism those policies which they felt would best secure lasting popular support. Full employment was a direct result but the principal stimulus to deficit spending came from rearmament, which was itself a direct expression of the overriding philosophical and political goals to which the country was subjected.

One characteristic shared by the countries under review, irrespective of the extremity or paucity of their political transformation, was their overriding fear of inflation. Germany and France entered the 1930s with the scars of inflation and the fear of financial chaos deeply etched as a result of their experiences during the previous decade. As a consequence each vehemently rejected devaluation as an early source of relief from the Depression fearing uncontrolled inflation, with France adhering to such a stance until, in 1936, she could resist no longer. Eastern European countries likewise shared a deep fear of repeating the inflationary experience of the 1920s. Similar if less extreme fears of inflation haunted the Hoover administration in the USA and in Australia and New Zealand officials waited during the Depression for an export-led recovery, nervous of any expansion of internal demand, especially on the wages front. Nor did international fears of inflation disappear in later years. Hitler's fiscal expansion after 1935 was financed in an orthodox, anti-inflationary manner. And the ease with which Australasia, Britain, France and Germany could embrace the need for reductions in real wages as a means of securing sustained recovery reflected the gap that existed between those who could envisage a positive role for spending and raised demand and those for whom deflation of internal costs and the rejection of any planned spending programmes were crucial to economic rejuvenation, particularly where a revival in the export sector was being sought. This aspect of the 1930s is particularly intriguing given the link that exists between cautious monetary policy (based on the fear of inflation) and the pace of economic recovery. If tight money had exacerbated economic conditions in Sweden and the USA during the early years of the Depression, it was the expansion of their monetary base (and to a lesser extent that of the UK) which proved crucial to recovery in later years. But there was little systematic expansion of monetary policy elsewhere. As a result, the currency depreciations which took place in the 1930s were beggar-thy-neighbour in effect, permitting the stimulation of internal demand and the encouragement of capital flows from abroad. Such reserve gains, however, forced further internal retrenchment in those countries still on gold. The gap between those countries which could contemplate currency depreciation and those which could and would not was clearly exposed (Eichengreen, 1992).

The themes outlined above reflect some though by no means all of the issues taken up in this volume. In the essays that follow there is additional discussion of the influence of vested interest groups (particularly within agriculture), the significance of the political setting in which public policy was formulated, the impact on policy of nationalism and the drives towards self-determination (in the cases of Germany and Eastern Europe, for example) and of the symbiotic relationship between policy activism and a country's historical legacy, not least in terms of what responses to economic decline and social distress were thought to have best worked in the past and ought properly to be resurrected, whatever the change in circumstance.

These essays are offered as an exercise in what Charles Maier has called 'historical political economy'. This characterisation regards economic ideas and behaviour 'not as frameworks for analysis, but as beliefs and actions that must themselves be explained. They are contingent and problematic; that is, they *might* have been different and they must be explained within particular political and social contexts.' It presupposes that societies in some sense want what turns out to be. To say, for example, that a society in the past chose unemployment or fascism can amount to no more than saying that at the time the groups willing to accept such an outcome prevailed over those that resisted it and were more willing to risk the next step forward than to face the consequences of resisting such a step. The historian asks therefore: what set of interests were served by such expressions of collective preference and what alignments and divisions characterise societies under stress (Maier, 1987, pp. 6–7)? Further research on the comparative macro-economics of the 1930s will provide fuller and more informative answers to such a question and if this book prompts such investigation it will have more than served its purpose.

References

Aldcroft, D. H. and Rodger, R., 1984, *Bibliography on European Economic and Social History*, Manchester, Manchester University Press.
Eichengreen, B., 1992, 'The Origins and Nature of the Great Slump Revisited', *Economic History Review*, 45: 213–39.
Maier, C., 1987, *In Search of Stability. Explorations in Historical Political Economy*, Cambridge, Cambridge University Press.

1 The search for stability: economic radicalism and financial conservatism in 1930s Europe

W. R. Garside

The depression policies and recovery strategies adopted by different nations during the 1930s resulted from a complex and interrelated set of influences, both national and international. Depending on the perspective adopted they can be viewed as a function of the administrative, fiscal, coercive and judicial arrangements of given states; as the result of pre-existing legacies of public policies; as the outcome of pressure group activity, whether by working-class organisations or coalitions of business, farmer and labour interests; as a product of entrenched economic dogma or as a consequence of the constraints imposed upon nations by the international economic environment in which they operated.

As one would expect, none of these approaches is sufficient in itself to explain the complexity of depression and recovery experience across nations, though each affords valuable insights. Nor are they mutually exclusive. One study of Swedish, British and American experience in this period focused, for example, 'on the ways in which . . . state structures and policy legacies affected the possibilities for new economic ideas to be formulated and applied to innovative government policies and influenced the political orientations and capacities of conflicting parties and coalitions of social groups' (Weir and Skocpol, 1985, p. 119). No attempt is made here to prioritise any of these approaches or to suggest that such a task could easily be undertaken. Each perspective has had a respectable airing in the literature (see especially Evans, Rueschemeyer and Skocpol, 1985). The intention instead is to examine the extent to which policy responses within France, Germany and Sweden in the 1930s, however autarkic and uncoordinated, were in fact determined and modified by a common set of preoccupations, economic, political, financial or otherwise. As such it provides a modest illustration of a number of issues that warrant further research on a comparative basis.

Deflation and the exchange rate

The Great Depression was an international phenomenon and there is little doubt that its traumatic effects were transmitted so rapidly because of the widespread adoption by industrialised nations in the 1920s of the gold exchange standard. The fixed exchange rates and adherence to the rules of classical orthodoxy to which this system gave rise offered hope of a self-regulating mechanism sufficient to safeguard balance of payments equilibrium and currency stability. Unfortunately it also imparted a deflationary bias to national economic policies as governments were obliged to maintain high interest rates and a tight fiscal stance for fear of losing reserves. Fixed exchange rates and high capital mobility under the restored gold standard linked prices and interest rates internationally, ensuring that when the USA succumbed to depression the deflation quickly spread throughout Europe. Restrictive monetary policy in the United States induced restrictive monetary reactions in those other gold standard countries unable to insulate themselves from the fall in international prices. Unilateral reflation was inhibited by the strain it would impose on a country's balance of payments so long as fixed exchange rates were in place. Any nation undertaking such action was likely to suffer rising imports, capital outflows, a loss of reserves and an assault on the exchange rate. Outside of abandoning gold, a measure of internationally coordinated reflation would have been required to prevent a single country suffering the consequences of relaxing the external constraint (Eichengreen, 1991; 1992). Ideology effectively ruled out alternative policy reactions, particularly devaluation, so long as the international community clung to the belief that order and stability sprang from the monetary discipline imposed by the gold regime.

Countries such as France and Germany benefited from an undervalued currency following the post-war restoration of gold but the misalignment of parities elsewhere put intense pressure on domestic prices, wages, output and employment. The international monetary system provided arrangements for formal exchange rate management but permitted a considerable amount of national autonomy in the conduct of policy. This put a premium on international policy coordination without providing any mechanism for bringing it about (Eichengreen, 1985, p. 171). As a consequence, nations developed whatever strategies they could to accommodate economic adjustment in the later 1920s while attempting to honour their gold standard obligations. Domestic monetary policies, geared towards protecting the value of the currency, began to generate destabilising impulses which were to prove critical both in transmitting depression and in affecting the capacity of countries to adapt to the resultant deflationary shock.

Although misaligned exchange rates before 1931 created problems of internal and external balance in the majority of the gold standard countries there was a marked reluctance to consider any radical departure from the existing policy regime. Talk of tariff protection found more ready favour than that of devaluation. Given the absence of any mechanism for reconciling the competing objectives of national monetary authorities the stage was set for the collapse of fixed rates. Post mortems on the 1931 financial crisis frequently emphasise those systemic features of the international monetary regime which prompted and aggravated the slump in its early years, particularly the unwillingness of the United States to take a leading role in managing the system, the failure of central banks to play the 'rules of the game', the intrinsic instability of the gold standard and the absence of international cooperation (Aldcroft, 1977; Kindleberger, 1973). What is equally clear, however, is that policy-makers themselves thwarted stability and reflation, slavishly avoiding low interest rates or deficit spending for fear of occasioning gold outflows (Eichengreen, 1985). The scramble to liquidate foreign assets in the wake of the slump heightened the difficulties countries faced in attempting to defend their gold standard parities as the stock of international reserves fell, obliging national authorities to limit the growth of their money supply, thereby adding to the severity of the downturn. It was France and the USA, however, which exacerbated this deflation by using their favourable parity position to absorb a disproportionate amount of gold reserves, obliging foreign central banks to raise their discount rates and restrict domestic credit in an effort to defend their own gold parities. Reflation in other words was compromised not solely because of structural or institutional rigidities associated with the gold exchange system but as a result of the deliberate pursuit by some countries of misguided monetary policies which imposed deflationary pressures on the world economy, and especially on those countries with weak currencies (Eichengreen, 1990, p. 246).

Fixed exchange rates tightened the external constraint before 1931 at a time when countries were often unable, because of their recent historical experience and their perception of how the economy worked, to envisage any remedial action other than deflation. France, for example, was so traumatised by the 'battles for the franc' in the years before 1926 that it remained hesitant through-out the following decade even to contemplate devaluation as an alternative to domestic deflation. Discretionary monetary policies before 1927 had prompted inflationary credit creation, predisposing the official mind towards stabilisation and against monetary refla-tion. The country stubbornly clung to gold after the 1931 crisis, almost as an act of national honour. Although an expensive country in a relatively cheap world before 1936, France refused to commit the 'immoral' act of devaluation, viewing it as a real threat to lasting prosperity and social order. It is generally accepted that this refusal to alter the value of the franc stifled economic activity for much of the 1930s as efforts were concentrated on reducing the budget deficit and lowering domestic prices to compensate for currency depreciations abroad. France pleaded with Britain and the United States at the World Economic Conference in 1933 to stabilise their exchange rates in an effort to encourage coordinated reflation but to no avail.

It was not France's defence of its currency's gold value that was so remarkable in the early 1930s; after all, other countries were engaged in similar if often unsuccessful efforts. It was the persever-ance with which the defence was conducted, long after the battle had become not simply futile but clearly injurious to economic recovery (Mouré, 1991, pp. 5, 8). The slump created fewer immed-iate difficulties for France than did the measures other countries took to adapt to the changed competitive situation. The Depression only struck late in 1930 but immediately threatened to create demands for cheap money to stimulate recovery and reduce the cost of borrowing. But defence of the franc Poincaré was regarded as the bulwark against inflation and currency destabilisation. High inter-est rates were necessary therefore to protect gold reserves even if investment was discouraged and deflation intensified. 'Monetary stability', the Bank of France reported in 1933:

is not only the most effective means of preparing for the return of lasting prosperity. It alone, it seems to us, can with continuity promote the just and orderly development of human society. To this principle France will remain faithful. Our country instinctively repudiates the facile and adven-turous experiences which are contrary to its deepest interests and to the genius of its character. (quoted in Kooker, 1976, p. 125)

This high tone clashed with the reality of budgetary finance. The French Treasury was fully aware by 1935 that the balanced budget upon which market confidence depended could not be achieved without devaluation. But devaluation threatened a capital outflow. It was when the political consequences of further deflation became acute by the end of 1935 that the possibility of devaluation, having been quietly nurtured in some quarters, was conceded. Even when devaluation came in September 1936, it was not so much a significant departure from previous policy as a necessary if delayed retreat for the purposes of regaining stability (Mouré, 1991, p. 289). The financial accommodation struck with Britain and America under the Tripartite Agreement for the purpose of rescuing France from its economic turmoil came only after those two countries agreed not to force down their own currencies in the aftermath of French devaluation, a reflection less of the harmonious financial cooperation which France had earlier demanded than of a desire by those countries for a measure of political partnership in the face of resurgent German militarism.

France's reaction to the international monetary situation in the wake of the Depression was clearly influenced by the legacy of her immediate past. Her pre-1927 experience with inflation convinced her that monetary expansion was associated with financial and political chaos. It was excessive credit-creation by central banks refusing to play by the rules of the gold standard game that had fuelled speculation in the previous decade, thereby ushering in the Depression. Speculative excesses had therefore to be purged by liquidating enterprises that had previously over-extended themselves (Eichengreen, 1992, p. 230). Competitive devaluation was outlawed. In France's eyes convertibility was not 'an antiquated form of slavery but a necessary social discipline' (Kooker, 1976, p. 117). Recovery would come, not by engaging in dangerous adventurism, but by educating other countries against the abuse of credit and the dangers of budgetary imbalance. It was relatively easy, of course, for France to adopt a high moral tone in the early years of the Depression, cushioned to some extent by the absence of mass unemployment and sufficient hoarded gold reserves to encourage continued belief in the prestige of the franc. The paralysis of policy to which adherence to strict orthodoxy gave rise, however, severely weakened France's capacity to transform her economic condition for the greater part of the 1930s.

German memories of inflation were of course even more pronounced and haunted the policy-makers' psyche even in the midst of tumbling prices. Although it is clear in hindsight that the severity of the Depression was worsened in Germany by the limitations imposed on monetary and fiscal policies by the fixed exchange regime, it is equally certain that devaluation as a declared object of policy had no effective constituency within the country. Neither had deflation for that matter. 'The economic distance between the Brüning deflation and hyperinflation was huge', writes Temin, 'it would have allowed room for expansion to leaders less fettered by gold standard ideas' (Temin, 1989, p. 63). But fettered they were during the depth of the slump, primarily because of the fear of inflation. 'It was', Borchardt claims, 'beyond the imagination of the German people to depart from parity against gold' (Borchardt, 1984, p. 496). Germany possessed only limited sovereignty with regard to her currency. Reparations commitments in the early 1930s stipulated that the Reichsmark should be left unaltered. There was widespread fear moreover that manipulation of the currency would lead to a catastrophic fall in the exchange rate, wrecking Germany's credit-worthiness, especially among foreign creditors, with all the risks of a flight of capital. Devaluation, it was believed, would be fatal to any future expansion since the resultant shock to confidence would outweigh any suggested benefits to trade and industry.

Sweden, like France, was not seriously affected by the world depression until late in 1930. By clinging to the gold standard until 1931, Sweden also was condemned to a tight control of credits, deflation and heavy unemployment. During the 1920s the majority of economists and politicians had favoured a deflationary policy involving lowered production costs, including wages, to assist the return to a pre-war parity. Even Social Democrats believed that the gains from a return to gold, by way of a stable currency and a capacity to compete with appropriately adjusted wages and prices, would more than outweigh any temporary sacrifices endured in the process. The country proved very willing, however, to depart from gold once the international situation deteriorated in 1930. Sweden's inflow of short-term capital during 1930 and the early part of 1931 suffered a rebuff later in 1931 as capital began to seek refuge elsewhere in the wake of bank and currency crises in Germany and Austria. The resulting currency crisis forced Sweden off the gold standard one week after Britain had succumbed in the face of a heavier capital outflow.

Little more need be said to reinforce the point that policy-makers in our chosen countries were heavily influenced by the legacy of their immediate past and, during the very early years of the Depression at least, by a lingering belief in the adequacy of established international financial arrangements to provide a bulwark against instability, social as well as economic. Some economists have stressed in recent years the significant contribution an internationally coordinated system of currency devaluations could have made to economic recovery in the 1930s. Countries which devalued or imposed exchange control in the wake of the Depression, it is noted, recovered more quickly than those which clung to the gold standard. Their abandonment of fixed exchange rates raised prices relative to costs, boosted exports, stimulated investment and profitability faster than was possible through any internal adjustments and, by enabling countries to gain control over the money stock, encouraged expansionary monetary policies to be implemented without fear of the effects on interest rates, reserves or the balance of payments. Such devaluations, it is further maintained, were not only effective but critical to recovery because the lack of agreement among national policy-makers had made it impossible to achieve sufficient international cooperation to implement reflation without abandoning gold (Eichengreen and Sachs, 1985; Newell and Symons, 1988). The systematic inauguration of a new policy regime centred around devaluation, sufficiently robust to change expectations and raise confidence, might indeed have induced an earlier and stronger recovery among a greater number of countries than actually occurred (Temin and Wigmore, 1990). But it would have to have been widely championed and capable of attacking received orthodoxy on a broad front. In truth, such an assault was never likely before 1931. France, Germany and Sweden showed how deflation, unemployment and tight monetary policies could and would be endured in the early years of the slump if countries remained convinced that defence of existing practice held out the prospect of soundly based recovery free of the threat of uncontrolled inflation and the manipulations of unscrupulous financial interests. Earlier decisions on the primacy of international finance had dictated the immediate impact of the world depression in these countries by ruling out reflationary initiatives. Their differing experiences in the aftermath of the collapse of the gold exchange standard is, on the face of it, easily explained. Domestic fiscal policy came to play a more recognisable part in the economic recovery of Germany and Sweden as each was able to pursue internal expansion free of the external constraint, through strict forms of exchange control in the case of Germany and via a floating currency in Sweden. France on the other hand condemned herself to continued stagnation by refusing to abandon gold, devalue and expand her money stock in a seemingly stubborn act of economic folly. However, although the contrasting fortunes of these countries after 1933 cannot be denied, it would be misleading to view the subsequent progress of Germany and Sweden purely in terms of the reflationary fiscal expansion made available in the absence of the gold standard. Such an approach can cloud the particular circumstances, political, economic and ideological, in which recovery policies were designed and implemented. It is to these considerations that we now turn in an effort to understand better the influences shaping official policy.

Adjusting to decline: policy-making in the 1930s

Sweden is often regarded as being in the forefront of enlightened policy-making in the aftermath of the slump with its ready acceptance of unbalanced budgets for the sake of sustaining aggregate demand and employment. Until 1931 Sweden's financial traditions then had been typically orthodox; state borrowing was used only for productive purposes calculated to yield sufficient profit to cover interest charges (Wigforss, 1938). Having suffered reduced exports, falling output, rising unemployment and low aggregate demand before abandoning gold in 1931, Sweden proved determined thereafter to preserve domestic purchasing power, revive exports and secure employment. During 1931/2 the Social Democratic Party (SDP) agreed both to finance its 70 million kroner deficit by further borrowing, and to borrow a similar sum yet again for productive investment. But it was the budget for 1933/4 which demonstrated the SDP's determination to avoid reducing desirable expenditure in favour of financing the Depression by means of loans and by following a policy of price stabilisation. The principle of securing an annually balanced budget was formally abandoned in favour of seeking balance over a number of years, the explicit aim of which was not to redistribute government expenditure merely to provide 'relief' works, but rather to expand it over the course of the trade cycle, financing public works at market rates of wages. It is the apparently clear choice to stimulate aggregate demand and improve employment that makes the country's policy response appear bold, innovative and conspicuously free of the pragmatic gradualism clearly evident in other industrialised nations.

Although the relative strength of Sweden's economic recovery cannot be denied, it is by no means certain that it reflected nascent Keynesianism in the ascendency. The reality is rather more complex. Budgetary policy was geared to the problem of cyclical unemployment and did not constitute a commitment by the state to the maintenance of permanently full employment. Counter-cyclical policy was but one of numerous factors which influenced the timing and spread of economic recovery from the summer of 1933. The active fiscal policy proved to be a source of stability and growing confidence but it did not get under way until strong external forces were already at work to buttress the expansion of home demand. Exports in particular benefited from a significant devaluation of the crown against other currencies, inside and outside of the gold bloc, and from a lack of retaliation abroad, the effects of which reinforced the domestic market against foreign competition and stimulated the positive impact of public works spending (Ohlin, 1935; Uhr, 1977; Winch, 1966). Sweden's supposed 'fiscal revolution' in the mid-1930s proved in itself to be too little and too late so far as sustaining economic recovery was concerned. Budget deficits were bigger during the 1920s than they proved to be during the 1930s, and during the latter decade they had begun to grow before the Social Democrats came to power in 1933 (Jorberg and Kranz, 1989, pp. 1094–5).

Sweden's exceptional situation in the mid- to late 1930s is intriguing not because it provides overwhelming evidence of the successful implementation of first-stage Keynesian policies but because it mirrors the amalgam of circumstance, historical legacy and expediency which lie at the heart of other countries' responses to the Depression, albeit in different forms. It was extremely fortunate for the Social Democrats, free from taint of having been in office during the worst of the Depression, to be able to intervene *after* the collapse of the gold standard when their policy contributions were able to offer effective support for recovery impulses then under way. With unemployment insurance effectively blocked in Sweden in the 1920s, substantial efforts had already been devoted to developing public works initiatives. It was relatively easy in the mid-1930s therefore to call for improved and extended job creation programmes at market rates of wages when the state had already won a degree of proven capacity in this field. Moreover, the close relationship which existed between economists and state officials enabled fiscal initiatives to be made more explicit and to attract an air of 'scientific' legitimisation greater perhaps than might otherwise have been the case (Jorberg and Kranz, 1989, p. 1099; Winch, 1989). With falling prices bearing heavily upon agriculture there was also an urgent need at the time to guarantee prices in order to sustain purchasing power in that important sector. From that position it was but a short step for the Swedes to stabilise domestic purchasing power through a declared policy of price stabilisation. Neither the policy to revive demand generally through credit expansion and state-financed public works nor the strategy of price support was alien to a reformist party disposed to carry out changes in the interests of the working class. The Social Democratic Party was not seeking some utopian release from the failings of capitalism. It sought to adopt radical policies as a means of reforming capitalism from within. The private sector could thereby be stimulated while exports recovered under the impact of depreciation.

That said, it is important not to exaggerate the radicalism of Sweden's response to the Depression. Though stabilisation of domestic prices and an expansionary fiscal policy were clearly evident from 1933, they were of limited practical importance. The increase in government spending amounted to little more than 1 per cent of

GNP in the years 1932 to 1934. Support for the agrarian sector increased the cost of food to workers to the detriment of other forms of consumption. Many of the unemployed received traditional forms of aid, including poor relief, rather than assistance from government employment measures (see Chapter 3). The revival of the Swedish economy, according to one observer, was the result of 'external factors, and hence luck, rather than of any "new" principles of economic policy' (Lindbeck, 1975, p. 23). Although prevailing ideas of labour market intervention and underbalancing of the budget made it possible in the mid-1930s for the government to recommend an expansionist policy as a matter of principle rather than as a dangerous temporary expedient, it is clear that the Social Democrats' budget policy thereafter 'became increasingly and prematurely cautious, betraying less than full confidence in the policy innovations for which they claimed credit. The result was that full employment was not as closely approximated during the 1930s as it might have been' (Martin, 1979, p. 99). Although the architects of Swedish fiscal policy adopted a radical approach with a marked degree of intellectual conviction, derived in part from policy inheritance, parliamentary opposition proved an ultimate frustration, preventing them from going far beyond a contracyclical budget. The 1933 crisis loan was largely paid out of taxes permitting an overall budgetary balance in 1935 (Winch, 1989, pp. 122–4).

The apparent contrast between pre- and post-slump policies was even more vivid in Germany. Plans to increase public works expenditure to break the grip of deflation were afoot during the Brüning, von Papen and Schleicher administrations but they foundered in the prevailing climate. In the early 1930s economists at the Institut fur Konjunkturforschung, especially its director Ernst Wagemann, were advocating an active business cycle policy based upon public works. Robert Friedlander-Prechtl, a mining executive, was calling as early as 1931 for a 2 billion RM road-building programme to create some 4.5 million jobs, by setting in motion 'secondary, tertiary, and quaternary waves' of employment. In like manner Heinrich Drager advocated a year later an annual expenditure of 5 billion RM on dams, roads, housing and other public works to utilise the vast amount of unused capacity and thereby create additional jobs without inflation (Garraty, 1978, pp. 203–4). A principal advocate of revisionist economic policy was the German Trade Union Federation (ADGB) which had long championed the causes of high employment or at the very least adequate subsistence income for the unemployed and their families. Following a sharp rise in unemployment in 1928/9, the unemployment insurance scheme came under intolerable strain and when its salvation proved doubtful the ADGB launched a bold job-creation plan to counter abnormal unemployment. It demanded the immediate re-employment of 1 million workers over one year on projects initiated by the government and financed by long-term credits at a cost of 2 billion RM, the expenditure to be partly offset by reduced outlays on unemployment benefits and from increased tax revenues. The 'WTB Plan' owed its inception to three federation officials, Woytinsky, Tarnow and Baade, and was given intense publicity by the organisation during April 1932. But it failed to overcome the fear shared by the Brüning, von Papen and Schleicher administrations, and by other trade unions for that matter, that direct intervention to manage capitalism would destroy the foundations of future economic stability (Schneider, 1975).

Brüning's savage deflationary policies during the early years of the slump, involving reduced public expenditure and downward pressure on prices and wages, have been defended as the only options available at the time (Borchardt, 1991). Responding to depression by cutting social security benefits and resisting spending programmes financed by new money reflected an earnest desire to balance the budget and avoid inflation, a response which gained widespread support within and outside of government. But the economic context should not overshadow the political factors affecting Germany's reaction to depression in the early 1930s. Brüning persisted in his policy of deflation at all costs because his overriding aim was not so much to tackle the economic crisis as such, but to use the crisis to achieve certain longer term political goals. These included an end to reparations, an objective which took precedence over boosting the economy through credit creation, and an earnest desire to re-establish a starting position for Germany equivalent to what it had been in 1913. By 'deliberately deepening the crisis' rather than defeating it he would be able to convince the Western powers that the schedule of reparations payments was unviable from an economic and financial point of view. The dismissal of job creation programmes and the rigid adherence to balanced budgets were to an extent therefore as much a product of foreign policy aims as of staunch financial orthodoxy (Mommsen, 1991, pp. 124–30). Beyond this, however, lay a further important constraint. German deflationary intentions brought deflationary results. This was the outcome not so much of a greater political will to balance the budget as much as the fact that the country faced a financial crisis in the strictest sense of the term, with expenditure exceeding revenue and with creditors refusing to extend any further lending. Lack of credit, therefore, compelled the government to succeed in at least seeking a balanced budget by expenditure cuts, tax increases, the running down of reserves and the sale of assets. There was an important distinction in Brüning's time between a budget deficit *per se* and a budget deficit coupled with a chronic inability to finance it. Germany's cash reserve problem could not be so easily resolved as in other countries by recourse to the market via the tender of treasury bills or the issue of bonds. The country depended on recourse to the Reichsbank which is why fiscal deflation was pushed to such severe limits. A counter-cyclical policy of reflation in these circumstances would have demanded a radical departure from accepted practice on the part of the central bank, necessitating a return in Germany to policies likely to generate inflation (Balderston, 1982, pp. 494–8).

Nor were these the only constraints on the emergence of a more radical fiscal policy. There was little political, intellectual, industrial or trade union pressure in Germany before mid-1931 for a pro-active policy. The first deflationary steps of the Brüning administration, involving forced reductions in wages and prices, met with little resistance from the more established academic economists who initially viewed the crisis as little different in essence to previous ones in Germany's economic history (Garvey, 1975; Hudson, 1985). Many employers wanted to free themselves of state arbitration in collective bargaining and accepted deflation as a means of dismantling the Weimar system of industrial relations, which they felt had imposed too high a level of real wage costs in relation to profits and productivity (Weisbrod, 1990). Trade unionists for their part had become a force for order, fearful both of a right-wing takeover and of any untried and potentially inflationary experiments which could threaten the status quo and the interests of their employed members (Pollard, 1990). The inflationary experience of the 1920s, moreover, had prohibited the Reichsbank from advancing substantial credit to the state, leaving expansionary plans to be financed through the capital market with all the perceived risks of rising interest rates and the crowding out of private investment (Borchardt, 1991).

The arrival of full employment in Germany during 1933 to 1936, on the other hand, is traditionally associated with the *economic* miracle achieved by the Nazis through an active policy of deficit spending and state intervention on an unprecedented scale. The transformation in the conduct of economic affairs cannot be denied even if it is now acknowledged that many of the spending plans of the regime were merely pragmatic improvisations of measures initiated, in principle at least, by previous administrations (Barkai, 1990). The conventional emphasis upon construction, housing and road-building programmes, understandable as it is, can none the less obscure a range of political, historical and ideological factors which are helpful in explaining the Nazis' response to economic decline. The infamous WTB Plan illustrates this well. Government officials, trade unionists and employers remained lukewarm as we have intimated but the Nazis readily embraced the Plan. They were anxious to find practical means of realising their more comprehensive political and social ideals. Although an active counter-cyclical policy embracing state intervention and deficit spending was viewed in some other countries as a necessary if temporary step towards stimulating private capitalism in a time of crisis, the Nazis turned these unconventional arguments 'into permanent features of economic dirigisme serving the primacy of politics' (Barkai, 1990, p. 67). Nazi economic policy succeeded because it could draw upon a legacy of virulent anti-liberalism under which the economy would be made subject to the primacy of political and social goals as defined by the national leadership. It mattered little whether Nazi policies were new or not; they were able to withstand criticism because their potency was derived from an ideological conviction that economic policies should be integrated with an overall concept of the role of the state. For Hitler economic problems were not insuperable constraints; they were issues to be overcome by political will. Production, consumption and the distribution of income would be influenced not by a blind assault on private ownership but by a form of organised capitalism under which capitalists could enjoy a measure of status and accumulate profits so long as they accepted the primacy of politics, in other words control from above in the interests of national power and stability. Able to secure absolute political control and with time in which to carry out their tasks, the Nazi regime could exert administrative and financial pressure without the parliamentary consent of vested interest groups which had previously retarded similar plans (Barkai, 1990, pp. 48, 67, 161–9; Maier, 1987, pp. 84–104).

The fact that Nazi economic policies in the 1930s were not Keynesian in any strict sense merely reinforces these points. Hitler's regime maintained high interest rates, controlled the growth of demand by redistributing income to those with a higher propensity to save, enforced wage stability at depression rates until the late 1930s, and sought to regulate the secondary effects of rising expenditure to turn the economy in the direction favoured by the government. There was no presumption here that private industry would take up the initiative after a short period of government pump-priming. During its first year the Nazi administration conformed to fairly orthodox views and to conservative principles of finance, viewing public expenditure for the creation of jobs as little more than a temporary expedient necessary until such time as 'natural' recovery provided work for all. Only when the regime was politically secure was Hitler prepared to depart from a previous preference for tax incentives for the private sector towards more ambitious spending plans for the state (Silverman, 1988, pp. 185–95; see also Chapter 4). Expenditure on work creation amounted to just over 1 per cent of GNP during the period 1932 to 1935. Government expenditure did rise from 18 per cent of national income in 1928 to 27.5 per cent in 1938 but this was accompanied by the emergence of a command economy embracing controls over prices, wages, the money market, foreign exchange and overseas trade, and by compulsion on private industry to sustain internal investment from undistributed profits (Overy, 1982). Government intervened to ensure price stability while industrial managers were cajoled by incentives and penalties to ensure that investment resources were used in accordance with the state's needs. It is necessary, therefore, to view the dramatic fall in unemployment from the mid-1930s in light of the overriding characteristics of the Nazi regime. Autarkic policies were a natural outgrowth of the political premises of Nazism.

Hitler certainly benefited from gaining power after the depth of the Depression had been reached and after the disparity between real wages and productivity had narrowed substantially. Thereafter a combination of civil works and rearmament expenditure, the latter especially from 1936, is commonly regarded as the basis upon which recovery proceeded. However, although no one doubts that preparing for war was a top political priority for the Nazis, the allocation of resources for rearmament and the solving of unemployment were by no means foregone conclusions. Large-scale rearmament was as much a consequence as a cause of recovery and benefited from a unique and wide-ranging economic system of nationalist etatism. Deficit spending was just one, albeit one very important, component of a whole set of economic and institutional measures which rejected regulation of the economy by market forces in favour of the dictum of state supremacy in all spheres of life, including the economy. Resources could have been directed more to civil rather than military consumption but the state's freedom to create money was determined by a political leadership that wanted an expansionist war. Nazi economic policy, therefore, incorporated those tools that best suited its ideology and philosophy. As unemployment fell in the early days of the regime without inflationary pressure confidence in the government and the economy increased, enhancing the stature of the Nazis among the public, businessmen and academics. Full employment was to some extent an autonomous objective, a means of stabilising the regime as well as recruiting public support. Reducing unemployment became an essential precondition, rather than an economic necessity, for engaging in large-scale rearmament. Thus the immediate need to help agriculture and industry eventually gave way to economic priorities being dictated by 'a mixture of short-term pragmatic manoeuvering with fanatical adherence to ultimate goals' (Barkai, 1990, pp. 9–10; 222–7, 247; Overy, 1987, p. 278). Autarky and economic regimentation were promoted for defence and military victory, not for profit or social welfare.

The paralysis of policy in France during the greater part of the 1930s stands in stark contrast to the energetic pursuit of a highly charged political vision within Nazi Germany. France too, however, was subject as much to political partiality as to economic analysis. Its persistent economic stagnation and unadventurous government policies arose in large part from a tortured if passionately held view as to what remedial actions were feasible and acceptable. As a country wedded to gold, France pursued contractionary fiscal policies down to 1936 with ghoulish fervour, the authorities repeatedly forced to cut public expenditure and to raise taxes in order to suppress domestic spending and defend convertibility. Parliament had proved unable to preserve the balance in public finances achieved in 1928 and there was already a budget deficit in 1931 as revenues began to collapse because of the economic crisis. Officials believed that vigorous cuts in government expenditure and raised taxes would prove sufficient to bring French domestic prices in line with foreign ones. Although existing spending commitments to pensioners, civil servants and creditors stifled any easy adjustment, the government viewed budgetary stability as one of the principal foundations of economic and social order. It was essential, therefore, to control the threat that declining public confidence would pose to the franc. The result was enforced deflation combined with an expensive monetary policy which delivered France into continued stagnation and a paralysis of policy. Tighter control of expenditure was accepted in principle in 1932. When it was combined with fears of a resurgence of inflation it produced such a strident belief in fiscal probity as to preclude any counter-cyclical spending. But although government expenditure was reduced by nearly 6 million francs during 1931 to 1935, it proved insufficient to produce a balanced budget or to restore confidence (Mouré, 1991, pp. 45, 189–90). Any more adventurous policy to end the crisis would not be entertained without a balanced budget, but the worsening of the crisis rendered the achievement of budgetary balance almost impossible. Involuntary deficits arose as public indebtedness, especially with regard to unemployment relief, increased faster than revenue income. The stock of money fell at a time of heavy public borrowing from the private sector to finance increased deficits, starving potentially productive sectors of necessary funds. If the French authorities had let the franc float in the second half of 1933, the economic climate may well have been transformed (Saint-Etienne, 1984, p. 38). But reducing prices and costs via devaluation, as we have already indicated, was never an option. Although the disparity between French and foreign prices continued unchecked between 1933 and 1936 deflation was still regarded as a necessary discipline however much rising unemployment, firm closures, falling exports and diminished fiscal revenues signalled the need for a change in policy. The desire to recapture a sound budgetary balance was powerful, fed by memories of how bankers and politicians had acted in the 1920s. Deficit financing ran the threat of the financial community holding short-term bills rather than the public, increasing the risk that if the left came to power bankers and investors could operate to undermine the authority of the state (Lee, 1989, p. 164).

The interests of the French nation were increasingly sacrificed to the interests of vested groups. Deflation served the rentier well enough while the peasantry were mollified by artificially pegged agricultural prices. Giant firms are alleged to have restricted output to maintain prices and profits rather than invest and innovate (Kemp, 1972, pp. 174–5). If deflation was the reaction of the right, there was little effective resistance from the left before 1936. Socialists lacked sufficient ideological coherence to back their hunch that planned deficits in a depression might not prove to be as disastrous as many feared. They were faced, moreover, by the stubborn application of orthodox policies by a succession of ministers in a fractious parliamentary system which rendered caution a virtue.

France's deflationist policy came to a peak in 1935 when the continued refusal to seek competitive advantage through devaluation gave way to a 10 per cent reduction in all public expenditure and compulsory reductions in the price of certain goods, such as coal and bread. The impact on public opinion was rapid and graphically demonstrated by the election in June 1936 of a Popular Front government under the premiership of Leon Blum. Composed of Radicals and Socialists and supported in Parliament by the Communists, it was charged with ending stagnation by a deliberate expansion of working-class (and especially peasant) purchasing power, the inauguration of loan-financed public works and a reduction of the working week to forty hours without any reduction in money wages.

The 'Blum Experiment' demonstrated the difficulties France faced in forcing adaptation to depression even when the object was expansion rather than deflation. The assumptions behind the recovery package were themselves suspect. With working hours reduced, employers anxious to produce the same output were expected to increase their demand for labour from among the unemployed, thereby boosting consumer demand. Increased labour costs would be met from greater capacity utilisation and productivity gains. The possibilities that such gains might reduce the opportunities for the unemployed to obtain work or might encourage an investment strike from industrialists facing higher costs without the guarantee of higher prices were never seriously considered.

In a desperate effort to end the wave of strikes which greeted its arrival, the Blum administration increased money wages and promised a minimum of two weeks paid holiday per year, all within a framework of collective agreements, itself a major concession in France. French costs, already high because of the devalued franc, were raised even further. These developments occurred against a rising feeling abroad that France would be forced to devalue the franc. This she did, from a position of relative weakness, in October 1936. Instead of recovery with monetary stability, the nation faced devaluation amidst stagnation (Barkai, 1990, pp. 138–9). Neither the devaluation nor the policy of raising purchasing power, however, was able to overcome economic decline. Confidence weakened further as capital fled the country. Although industrial production revived and unemployment fell towards the end of 1936, inflation rose only to be further increased by the implementation of the forty-hour week during 1937. Shorter hours and higher pay were given precedence over economic recovery; the effect of high real wages was to wipe out the expansionary gains from devaluation. By the spring of 1937 industrial production was falling, government expenditure rising and a budget deficit looming at a time when the franc was under heavy pressure. The bank rate was raised and such mobile capital as had not already fled the country did so. Unable to gain support for special powers to deal with the financial crisis Blum resigned (Kemp, 1972, pp. 123–8; Temin, 1989, pp. 124–5). Thereafter rearmament expenditure provided more profitable conditions than had hitherto prevailed and a further devaluation of the franc by some 34 per cent offered the hope of economic betterment. Unfortunately even an attack on the forty-hour week during 1938 and the growing needs of rearmament failed to overcome the underinvestment of previous years and the bottlenecks in production created by an inadequate supply of skilled labour (see Chapter 5).

The failure of the Blum administration and the frustrated efforts thereafter to institute the foundations of a stable domestic recovery are closely bound up with the early rejection of devaluation, the continued disparity between French and foreign prices and the inflationary impact of the expansionary measures. But the post-deflationary experience of France cannot fully be understood solely in terms of economics any more than can the policy stance of the early to mid-1930s. Blum's first administration may have seen the restoration of confidence in the franc and gains to the working class as a bedrock of economic and social stability but this did little to instil confidence among employers and the bourgeoisie who sought to avenge themselves against the trade unions and the government. The conditions for recovery were as much psychological as economic. Any remedy had to provide property owners with adequate assurances that revolutionary changes were not imminent. The continuous drain of capital overseas from 1935 reflected deep distrust among industrial and financial interests. Capitalists feared that if the Popular Front's programme proved successful and popular, and if the overt sympathy towards the trade unions hardened, it would give way to even more radical interventions (Bleany, 1985, p. 64). No class or group was willing to sacrifice its perceived interests. Blum's first government had neither placated private capital nor obliged it to invest in the future of the country. The situation demanded either exchange controls to force capitalists into submission or the creation of conditions in which the profit motive would function. Blum's government waivered between these two positions because it feared that either policy would create civil discord, which would only weaken France further, and alienate the Radicals without whom it could not govern. The administration's insistence on radical social reforms and deficit spending with little regard to the budget or to the effects on business confidence went hand in hand with a refusal to suppress strikes or to impose such policies that may have offered some hope of success, including exchange control.

This brief review of responses to depression in three countries during the 1930s emphasises the fact that we cannot view the formulation of policy, as an economist might, as an exogenous factor. Differing historical experiences, social and political structures, and perceptions of what constituted the basis of prosperity and stability are but some of the variables that influenced both the formulation and the effects of policy in these chosen countries. The reactions of officials frequently expressed social and ideological preferences as well as the extent to which a ruling political party felt obliged to honour existing commitments, economic or otherwise. They reflected also the degree of political support for a realignment of policy, and the pattern of business or bureaucratic influence.

Rejecting monocausal explanations of action should not, how-ever, drive observers to limit their scope of enquiry to pure prag-matism on the one hand or circumstantial determinism on the other (Winch, 1990, p. 68). Policy decisions which might appear with hindsight to be mistaken – if not clearly disastrous – need to be understood in a much broader context, not for the sake of excusing contemporaries but as a way of reminding ourselves of the gap that did and does exist between the stylised pursuit of the best available options and the frequent desire of policy-makers to legi-timise and justify their actions and ideas by whatever means might secure them social and political acceptability. French, German and Swedish experience in this period also reminds us of the danger of over-estimating the political, intellectual and popular support that could possibly have been marshalled in favour of what might now be regarded as more acceptable policy responses – expansionist spending or devaluation for example – at the very time such choices were needed. Moreover, official policy was critically affected on occasions not by the capacity of officials to apply sophisticated economic reasoning to the fundamental changes occurring around them so much as by the order in which such events happened, as the Swedes found when they came to determine policy after the crisis had reached its depth, after the gold standard had gone and while the forces of revival were already making themselves felt (Winch, 1989, pp. 116–20). And in making comparative judgements on policy responses, we ignore at our peril the perception a nation held of its role in the international economy, of the appropriate relationship that did or should exist between the state and the capital market, and of the extent to which fiscal and monetary experimentation should be pressed before it threatened economic, social and political stability.

References

Aldcroft, D., 1977, *From Versailles to Wall Street 1919–1929*, London, Allen Lane.

Balderston, T., 1982, 'The Origins of Economic Instability in Germany 1924–1930. Market Forces versus Economic Policy', *Vierteljahrschrift Für Sozial und Wirtschaftsgeschichte*, 69 (4): 488–514.

Barkai, A., 1990, *Nazi Economics. Ideology, Theory, and Policy*, Oxford, Berg.

Bleaney, M., 1985, *The Rise and Fall of Keynesian Economics*, London, Macmillan.

Borchardt, K., 1984, 'Could and Should Germany Have Followed Great

Britain in Leaving the Gold Standard?', *The Journal of European Economic History*, 13 (3): 471–97.

Borchardt, K., 1991, 'Constraints and Room for Manoeuvre in the Great Depression of the Early Thirties: Towards a Revision of the Received Historical Picture', in K., Borchardt *Perspectives on Modern German Economic History and Policy*, Cambridge, Cambridge University Press.

Eichengreen, B., 1985, 'International Policy Co-ordination in Historical Perspective: A View from the Interwar Years', in W. H. Buiter and R. C. Marston (eds), *International Economic Policy Co-Ordination*, Cambridge, Cambridge University Press.

Eichengreen, B., 1990, *Economic Stability. Essays in the History of International Finance*, Cambridge, Cambridge University Press.

Eichengreen, B., 1991, 'Relaxing the External Constraint: Europe in the 1930s', in G. Alogoskofis, L. Papademos, and R. Portes (eds), *External Constraints on Macroeconomic Policy: The European Experience*, Cambridge, Cambridge University Press.

Eichengreen, B., 1992, 'The Origins and Nature of the Great Slump Revisited', *Economic History Review*, 45 (2): 213–39.

Eichengreen, B. and Sachs, J., 1985, 'Exchange Rates and Economic Recovery in the 1930s', *Journal of Economic History*, 45 (4): 925–46.

Evans, P., Rueschemeyer, D. and Skocpol, T., 1985, *Bringing the State Back In*, Cambridge, Cambridge University Press.

Garraty, J., 1978, *Unemployment in History. Economic Thought and Public Policy*, New York, Harper & Row.

Garvey, G., 1975, 'Keynes and the Economic Activists of Pre-Hitler Germany', *Journal of Political Economy*, 83: 391–405.

Hudson, M., 1985, 'German Economists and the Depression of 1929–1933', *History of Political Economy*, 17 (1): 31–50.

Jorberg, L. and Kranz, O., 1989, 'Economic and Social Policy in Sweden 1850–1939', in P. Mathias and S. Pollard (eds), *The Cambridge Economic History of Europe Volume 8*, Cambridge, Cambridge University Press.

Kemp, T., 1972, *The French Economy, 1919–1939*, London, Longman.

Kindleberger, C., 1973, *The World in Depression 1929–1939*, London, Allen Lane.

Kooker, J., 1976, 'French Financial Diplomacy: The Interwar Years', in B. M. Rowland (ed.), *Balance of Power or Hegemony?: The Interwar Monetary System*, New York, New York University Press.

Lee, B., 1989, 'The Miscarriage of Necessity and Intervention: Proto-Keynesianism and Democratic States in the 1930s', in P. Hall, (ed.), *The Political Power of Economic Ideas: Keynesianism Across Nations*, Princeton, Princeton University Press.

Lindbeck, A., 1975, *Swedish Economic Policy*, London, Macmillan.

Maier, C., 1987, *In Search of Stability. Explorations in Historical Political Economy*, Cambridge, Cambridge University Press.

Martin, A., 1979, 'The Dynamics of Change in a Keynesian Political Economy: The Swedish Case and Its Implications', in C. Crouch (ed.), *The State and Economy in Contemporary Capitalism*, London, Croom Helm.

Mommsen, H., 1991, 'Heinrich Brüning as Chancellor: The Failure of a Politically Isolated Strategy', in H. Mommsen, *From Weimar to Auschwitz*, Cambridge, Polity Press.

Mouré, K., 1991, *Managing the Franc Poincaré, 1928–1936*, Cambridge, Cambridge University Press.

Newell, A. and Symons, J. S., 1988, 'The Macroeconomics of the Interwar Years: International Comparisons', in B. Eichengreen and T. J. Hatton, *Interwar Unemployment in International Perspective*, Dordrecht, Kluwer Academic Publishers.

Ohlin, B., 1935, 'Economic Recovery and Labour Market Problems in Sweden: II', *International Labour Review*, 31 (5): 670–99.

Overy, R., 1982, *The Nazi Economic Recovery, 1932–1938*, London, Macmillan.

Overy, R., 1987, 'Unemployment in the Third Reich', *Business History*, 24 (3): 253–81.

Pollard, S., 1990, 'German Trade Union Policy 1929–1933 in the Light of the British Experience', in J. Kruedener, *Economic Crisis and Political Collapse. The Weimar Republic 1924–1933*, Oxford, Berg.

Saint-Etienne, C., 1984, *The Great Depression, 1929–1938: Lessons for the 1980s*, Stanford, Hoover Institution Press.

Schneider, M., 1975, *Das Arbeitsbeschaffungsprogram des ADGB. Zur Geswerkschaftlichen Politik in der Endphase der Weimaren Republik*, Bonn-Bad Godesberg.

Silverman, D., 1988, 'National Socialist Economics: The *Wirtschaftswunder* Reconsidered', in B. Eichengreen and T. J. Hatton (eds), *Interwar Unemployment in International Perspective*, Dordrecht, Kluwer Academic Publishers.

Temin, P., 1989, *Lessons from the Great Depression*, Cambridge, Mass., MIT Press.

Temin, P., 1991, 'Soviet and Nazi Economic Planning in the 1930s', *Economic History Review*, 44 (4): 573–93.

Temin, P. and Wigmore, B., 1990, 'The End of One Big Deflation', *Explorations in Economic History*, 27 (4): 483–502.

Uhr, C., 1977, 'Economists and Policymaking, 1930–1936: Sweden's Experience', *History of Political Economy*, 9: 89–121.

Weir, M. and Skocpol, T., 1985, 'State Structures and the Possibilities for "Keynesian" Responses to the Great Depression in Sweden, Britain, and the United States', in P. Evans, D. Rueschemeyer and T. Skocpol, *Bringing the State Back In*, Cambridge, Cambridge University Press.

Weisbrod, B., 1990, 'Industrial Crisis Strategy in the Great Depression', in J. Kruedener, *Economic Crisis and Political Collapse. The Weimar Republic 1924–1933*, Oxford, Berg.

Wigforss, E., 1938, 'The Financial Policy During Depression and Boom', *Annals of the American Academy of Political and Social Society*, 197: 25–39.

Winch, D., 1966, 'The Keynesian Revolution in Sweden', *Journal of Political Economy*, 74 (2): 168–76.

Winch, D., 1989, 'Keynes, Keynesianism, and State Intervention', in P. Hall, *The Political Power of Economic Ideas: Keynesianism Across*

Nations, Princeton, Princeton University Press.
Winch, D., 1990, 'Economic Knowledge and Government in Britain: Some Historical and Comparative Reflections', in M. Furner and B. Supple, *The State and Economic Knowledge. The American and British Experience*, New York, Cambridge University Press.

2 The British reaction to the economic crisis

Alan Booth

The slump hit the British economy hard, especially in those industries and regions which had borne the brunt of the economic problems of the 1920s. But the slump also presented British policy-makers with opportunities. Since World War I Britain had struggled to lead the rest of the world back to liberal internationalism. Britain had pushed for balanced budgets, independent central banks, freer world trade and restoration of the gold standard. But the days when Britain could police the international economy had long gone. The liberal order collapsed in 1931/2. Yet the slump also brought release. British policy-makers could pursue domestic goals, unfettered by international considerations. There were obvious domestic problems to tackle. Unemployment had been above the average for the developed world for a decade. It was widely accepted that the staple export industries needed overhaul. There were many plans for a more domestically oriented economic strategy. A British 'New Deal' had been proposed even before the slump had hit. There were other, more radical blueprints put forward in the 1930s. New ideas emerged from all quarters of the political spectrum.

However, the full potential of the situation was not grasped. Despite the collapse of the liberal international order, economic and social policy in the 1930s retained much of the caution and anti-interventionist sentiment it had displayed for a century. Furthermore, cautious pragmatism was popular with the electorate and public opinion more generally in the 1930s. According to the best guesses, the Labour Party would not have won the general election due in 1939/40. Nor was there any great demand from the business community for more expansionary policies despite depression.

It would not be unreasonable to explain the unwillingness to grasp the opportunities of the 1930s as a systemic failure rather than lack of courage or vigour by any specific individual, group or institution. Social scientists have therefore turned to a variety of explanatory devices which operate at the aggregate level to explain the lack of innovation. Economists were wont for many years to blame the hold of outmoded economic ideas on the policy process (see Stewart, 1967). Attention was next turned to the hangover of liberal ideology; British policy-makers of the inter-war years continued to be highly influenced by ideas and approaches which were more suited to the conditions of the nineteenth century (see Skidelsky, 1975a). The most recent attempt to explain Britain's lack of response to the slump has come in a fascinating comparative study by historical sociologists (Weir and Skocpol, 1985). They argue that the critical feature is the historical pattern of development of the state. For two decades before 1931, the British state's method of coping with unemployment had been by compulsory insurance. Both the political and administrative systems were much better equipped to develop insurance further than innovate more radical policies. Each of these approaches can be criticised in detail, but they all have the considerable virtue of seeking to explain why state and society together were so hesitant to see the opportunities of the early 1930s grasped by innovative policies.

Also relevant must be the ideas of those who have sought to explain long-term political stability. Of particular note is the work of Paul Addison who charts the decline 'of one established order in politics and the rise of another: Attlee's consensus replaces Baldwin's' (1975, p. 9). Addison's 'established order' or 'consensus' is produced by interaction between party leaders and mass public opinion. At the top, party leaders tend to reach a consensus about what will be attractive to the electorate.[1] For much of the time public opinion will be relatively stable. In key periods, however, components of public opinion can change and Addison suggests that shifts in or special prominence for expert opinion can have noticeable effects on wider public sentiment. The political leaders who first detect and exploit these movements in popular opinion will force other leaders to adjust their mix of policies or presentation to the electorate. Thus, the special conditions of World War II brought about temporary shifts in public opinion which were underwritten by the pronouncements of experts who had been drawn into Whitehall. Party competition thereafter took place on the new ground laid out by wartime experts.

As compelling as Addison's hypothesis is in explaining the relative stability of political debate in the middle quarters of the twentieth century, it raises more questions than it answers about established orders in British politics. Where, for instance, did

Baldwin's consensus originate? If the special circumstances of war and the contribution of impartial experts were so important to shifts in consensus, why was it that Attlee's consensus was replaced by Thatcherism at a time of peace and against the better judgement of impartial experts on Thatcherite economics, the most innovatory element of the new order? Why, moreover, do parties allow themselves to be diverted from the political centre ground?

To help answer these questions and embellish rather than replace the approach offered by Addison, we can turn to the 'politics of power' and the 'politics of support', two relatively simple but extremely helpful concepts formulated by Andrew Gamble (1974). The former recognises the way that the nineteenth century liberal order of limited government and individual rights has adapted to the increasing complexity of economic activity and the constant emergence of new social needs. The facade of the liberal order has been preserved by co-opting every important interest into the process of policy-making and formulation, while maintaining a highly centralised system for actually taking decisions (Gamble and Walkland, 1984, p. 8). In the nineteenth century, policy-makers developed the concept of voluntarism. Governments turned to private groups and individuals for help in formulating and executing policy. In the early twentieth century, class conflict and international rivalry posed questions which voluntarism could not contain. The British system developed instead a pronounced 'corporate bias' and drew the major organised interest groups into the policy processes. By the middle of the century, the most important corporate groups acquired the status of governing institutions (Middlemas, 1979). The effect of sharing the authority of the state has meant that whole areas of policy are not for party determination. The 'politics of power' recognises that what goes on outside parliament is at least as important as party political manoeuvring in the making of certain policies. Experts and organised interest groups have shaped policy in profound ways.

The 'politics of support' on the other hand recognises that the British political system rests on the cornerstone of party organisation. Parties have class and ideological dimensions which are not necessarily compatible with the requirements of the politics of power. Mass parties are necessarily coalitions of interest, and party programmes inevitably reflect shifting emphases within the mass party. What has resonance within the party at any one time may not be in tune with the requirements of the politics of power. Political parties by their very nature will always contain factions which seek to change policy. The 'politics of support' thus describes the process of policy-making within parties. The ability of activists to reshape party policy will depend upon the power of the leadership, the effectiveness of existing policy and the ability to mobilise the wider political party behind a change of direction.

Armed with these insights into the policy process, we can now begin to ask why the apparent opportunities of the early 1930s were not exploited. The proper starting point of an explanation of long-run political stability is not, of course, in the slump itself but in a much earlier period.

The politics of power and the politics of support in the 1920s

For generations British historians have argued about the nature of policy in the late nineteenth and early twentieth centuries, particularly about the usefulness of *laissez-faire* to describe the policy regime. This is not the place to enter this historiographical thicket, but we can say that at this time the core of economic policy consisted of liberal internationalism. The main focus was the network of markets which extended far beyond the boundaries of the nation-state and the main preoccupation was to see that the national economy adjusted to world conditions as smoothly as possible. It suited the British pattern of 'gentlemanly capitalism' with its focus on international commercial and trading activities.[2] British industry remained very parochial in its outlook as it had been since mid-century (Melling, 1991) but the export staples were very content with this external orientation. What about the workers? They had cheap food and rising real wages. At the same time, growing imperial and national rivalry meant that British government could not be indifferent to the domestic casualties of liberal internationalism.[3] National political cohesion and economic potential vied with the demands of world markets for the attention of British policy-makers. Thus the flow of 'social' legislation to repair the damage wrought on the domestic population by unregulated market forces began to increase and take on a class dimension. The need to help the unemployed in ways which did not encroach too far on the market system became the focus of this supportive policy-making (Brown, 1971; Harris, 1972). The welfare reforms of the early twentieth century were a very sophisticated attempt to retain a liberal market order while both incorporating the respectable working class into the national polity and promoting greater efficiency in British industry. The interests of an increasingly assertive working class had been to some extent accommodated within a policy regime which allowed British commercial interests access to market opportunities throughout the world. A stable politics of power had been established.

This consensus did not survive World War I. British government entered the war believing that the market mechanism would suffice and ended it directing much of British economic life. The war saw the full flowering of a national political economy in Britain;[4] production and the preservation of national solidarity behind the war effort were the ultimate goals. Although wartime governments tried to preserve class harmony there were also forces driving a wedge between the interests of labour and capital (Waites, 1987) with the result that there was no consensus on the course of policy after the war. Thus there were no firm decisions in reconstruction policy (Abrams, 1963).

The politics of power was in a state of flux. Simplifying heroically, we can identify at this time four groups with a claim on economic strategy: the City of London, industrialists, organised labour and the government itself. These groups were in no way monolithic, as will become clear. The goal for the City was the restoration of liberal internationalism, particularly resumption of the gold standard and capital exports. Industrial employers were split between those who wished to continue the wartime pattern of consensual bargaining in a post-war imperial bloc and those who wanted to reverse wartime gains by labour and revert to managerial prerogatives. Organised labour also had its moderates wanting to preserve the wartime tripartite system and radicals who pressed for revolutionary change. At the political–administrative level, the post-war coalition appeared to promise reform but the driving force within Whitehall was the Treasury's effort to regain its control over the bureaucracy by committing ministers to sound finance and the gold standard; if a liberal economic policy were restored, Treasury control could return. These widely differing goals could not be reconciled by consensus.[5] Policy was determined by conflict, which polarised classes and weakened moderates on all sides. The government's role was critical; it made concessions when under duress, but in the crisis period ministers conspired with employers to destroy the organised radical working-class elements.

From this period of conflict all sides emerged with some gains. The labour movement gained the shorter working week as a 'peace dividend', major extensions of unemployment insurance, granted in 1920 to avert the threat of revolution from unemployed ex-servicemen, and confirmation of the enhanced status of labour's industrial and political organisations. The demands for workers' control and nationalisation were thoroughly defeated. For the City, there was a commitment to restore the gold standard and to regain London's position as the centre of international finance. However, no precise date for restoration was given. Industrialists were freed rapidly from state controls and a high tax regime. Within the bureaucracy, the Treasury regained control over civil service establishments and public spending by nudging the government back to balanced budgets and the gold standard thus neutralising radical impulses from within Whitehall (Lowe, 1978a). The Bank of England, which had its own reasons for wanting a quick restoration of gold, was very supportive in dealings with ministers.

It is not difficult to see in this a new politics of power, a 'post-war settlement' similar to that forged by agreement during and after World War II. The main features (the gold standard, tight control of state spending and the withdrawal of government from industry and recognition by government of labour's gains since 1914) dominated policy for the 1920s and, it will be argued below, for the 1930s as well. A measure of the success of this new politics of power was its legitimation by ideological support. The main political parties quickly fell behind its broad principles. Baldwin, MacDonald and Chamberlain developed 'the politics of safety first'; in Addison's words they conspired 'to prevent anything unusual from happening' (1975, p. 14). The Liberal Party could not adapt, in large part because of the personality and record of Lloyd George, whose reputation for unorthodoxy, experiment and shady dealings was ill-suited to the new conditions. Both Labour and the Conservatives squeezed Liberal support effectively by embracing fiscal and monetary rectitude to demonstrate their 'responsibility' and fitness to govern.

There was an unforeseen problem for this politics of power. In the new conditions in the world economy of the 1920s, the costs of adjustment were borne heavily by the old staple, export-oriented industries. Coal, cotton, ship-building and iron and steel endured heavy unemployment and industrial relations problems as they sought to reduce their costs to prevailing world market levels. The restoration of the gold standard, a critical element in the politics of power after 1920, produced enormous problems for these industries, and especially for coal. The failings of 'safety first' provided fertile ground for luxuriant development of the politics of support.

The new programmes contained much common ground.[6] Almost all sought to tackle business depression by concentration of production into larger more efficient units to secure scale economies and make wage cuts unnecessary. For the labour displaced by this process and for the persistent hard core of unemployment there would be public works. The Empire also figured prominently as part of the solution, either by taking more British manufactures or by absorbing more British unemployed workers. By the very nature of the politics of support, each version was specially geared to the political need of the party within which it originated. Thus, the alternative strategy of the Labour left placed particular emphasis on nationalisation and the maintenance of a 'living wage'. That of the radical backbench Conservatives was keen to promote cartelisation to enable industry to maintain profitability. The Liberal Party, unable to align itself fully behind the politics of power since 1920, now looked to expert opinion not only to give the party new ideas but also to shift public opinion. The resulting programme combined an appeal to the working class (major public works to reduce unemployment), a reassurance to property holders (no new taxes except for those on property speculators and reorganisation of industry without nationalisation) and a restatement of traditional Liberal shibboleths (commitments to free trade, the gold standard and the international perspective).

New economic policy ideas abounded. But how would the architects of the politics of safety first react? MacDonald tried very hard to condemn the new ideas but could not keep more ambitious promises out of the Labour Party policy documents of the late 1920s. Baldwin was less moved. His government, which had already supported rationalisation with vigour, promised an extension of 'safeguarding' (that is, further protection for specific industries rather than a general tariff) and relief from local taxation. The Conservatives rejected a big public works programme and preferred to promise 'safety first', in contrast to the experimental pledges of Lloyd George (Williamson, 1982).[7] But the government was rattled by the subtle shifts in popular opinion. It commissioned the civil service to produce what can be described only as party political propaganda in the guise of a White Paper; a detailed demolition of the Liberal programme by ostensibly impartial civil servants (HMSO, 1929).

Thus by the late 1920s British political economy had reached a critical point. The 'politics of power' or 'the established political order' allowed only limited pragmatic adjustment in economic policy. The two leaders with the biggest stake in this order, Baldwin and MacDonald, were trying hard to keep their parties within the policy boundaries which had been established in the early 1920s. However, mass opinion had moved. Popular opinion, fuelled by the obvious signs of failed economic policies in the 1920s and the new hopes raised by the experts marshalled by all the major parties, signalled that more expansionary, innovatory policies should be tried. Certainly the result of the 1929 general election could be so interpreted. Expansionist parties captured 60 per cent of the votes and Labour emerged with most seats. There are obvious parallels with the situation in the early 1940s analysed by Addison. However, no new political order emerged. The New Deal offered in 1929 was not realised.

All versions of the New Deal had been premissed on the revival of the world economy but as Labour took office unemployment in the export industries increased even further. The government responded not by domestic expansion but by intensifying its economic diplomacy. Labour ministers tried to persuade other governments to act as good internationalists by lowering tariffs and exporting capital. British commercial and industrial opinion was broadly behind these efforts (Boyce, 1987). But Britain lacked the clout to enforce its way and the imbalances were too intractable. The world economy pursued its downward course into depression despite the best wishes of statesmen.[8]

What happened to the promises to expand domestic demand? When unemployment began to rise in 1929, the campaign to build a broad coalition behind expansionist policies intensified, but so too did the campaign for orthodoxy consistent with the politics of power. There was a clear tension between the new public mood and the politics of power. The case of Mosley illustrates the issues. Mosley had made economic policy his main theme on joining Labour after a colourful early political career (Skidelsky, 1970; 1975b). He repeatedly called for the reorientation of monetary policy away from the maintenance of the fixed exchange rate towards the creation of expansionary domestic conditions. In 1929 he was appointed to the small team of ministers working on employment policy, and restructured his ideas around the expansionist parts of Labour's election manifesto. But Mosley was singularly unsuccessful. His programme was rejected successively by the Cabinet, the parliamentary party and the wider Labour Party Conference.

Skidelsky (1970, pp. 433–4) has explained the rejection of Mosley in terms of the weakness of Fabian socialism; the Labour Party as a whole had no real theory of how to use parliament to advance socialism. The government had nothing to do but to govern without conviction a system it did not believe in but saw no real prospect of changing. Fabian socialism certainly did have its weaknesses but there is very little evidence to suggest that those without these doctrinal blinkers would have been any more decisive. The Liberals, for example, took delight in criticising Labour, but when they were put to the test their resolve weakened. They split over the need for protection of the home market and Lloyd George offered no real leadership. His eyes were on power and the opportunity to impose the land tax he had pursued since the Edwardian period (Booth and Pack, 1985, pp. 52–4). The failure was systemic.

The real problem for the radicals lay in the politics of power and the position of extra-parliamentary interest groups with leverage over policy. The main economic problem after 1929 was the rapid fall in export revenues when import costs contracted to a lesser extent. A weak current account did not help when confidence in sterling began to ebb as markets began to appreciate that London's position depended heavily and perhaps dangerously on short-term liabilities to foreign centres. The Bank was under persistent pressure in the foreign exchange markets and opinion in both the City of London and New York was hardening in mid-1930. The view spread that the British government needed to take fundamental deflationary measures (Moggridge, 1972, pp. 136–40). Against such a background the chances of a major loan-financed public works programme were nil. The City simply would not have subscribed. Nor was there much scope for financing a large part of the cost of public works out of revenue. To curb Labour's expenditure plans the Treasury fed Snowden an excessively gloomy forecast of the public finances for Labour's first major Cabinet meeting (Howson, 1975, p. 68). The Treasury was also very vigorous in picking holes in the Mosley memorandum (Marquand, 1977, pp. 533–54). The judgement from the City, the Bank and the Treasury on expansionist policies was therefore uniformly adverse from the time the government came to office. Nor was industrial opinion supportive. Some sections of British employers had seemed interested in joining with the Trades Union Congress (TUC) in the late 1920s to urge the government to ease monetary conditions, but as the Depression began to bite employers pressed for wage reductions and cuts in public expenditure to ease corporate taxation. By 1930 they too had joined the unequivocal opposition to expansion of public spending. Even organised labour disappointed the expansionists. The TUC's power had been weakened by unemployment and when the crunch came organised labour devoted most of its efforts to defending levels of unemployment benefit to protect wage levels rather than fight for public works. Thus there was a very powerful restatement of the politics of power as the slump began to unfold. In fact the restatement was so powerful and the international economic position so apparently hopeless that the public mood hardened. The apparent majority behind innovation and expansion soon became a thumping majority behind orthodox policies (Booth, 1982). There was no real contest between the new public mood of 1929 and the politics of power, as Mosley was the first to discover.

If these problems derived ultimately from the pressure on the balance of payments under the gold standard, what would have happened if some way had been found to improve the balance of payments? Thus, Hatton (1987) has suggested what might have happened if Britain had devalued in the late 1920s. But these are only games. Moggridge (1972) has demonstrated that devaluation was simply off the agenda when Britain returned to gold in 1925.

Once that decision had been made, Mosley was the only authority of any weight to call for devaluation. Everyone else sought ways of making the gold standard work. Hatton's calculations are built upon the assumption that Britain could achieve a unilateral devaluation in an otherwise unchanged international economy. In the real world, however, Britain could abandon the traditional dollar parity only as an emergency measure, and when she did so most of her trading partners followed suit. Unilateral devaluation was not an option.

The tariff was no easier. By the late 1920s British industrialists favoured protection in sufficient numbers to encourage the Federation of British Industries (FBI) to campaign for a general tariff (Marrison, 1990). But limited measures of safeguarding had been rejected by the electorate in 1929 and general protection was politically impossible in the 1929–31 parliament. The tariff had been one of the few contentious aspects of the politics of safety first, with Conservatives always *pro* and the other two parties always *anti*, with the mass electorate in favour of free trade until the depths of the crisis.

As we have seen, in the absence of devaluation and protection, deflation was the only possible course between 1929 and 1931. Resistance to deficit-financed public works did not however rest solely upon the presumed balance of payments costs of unbalanced budgets. There was also powerful reinforcement from within the administrative system. Public works invariably required approval by local authorities in a process which embraced public consultation. Expansionists proposed to short-circuit this procedure to start work quickly. But politicians and administrators were unwilling to reshape constitutional relationships between central and local government. Major public works also implied a shift in the balance of political power within central government, with more power for the centre, with a strong Prime Minister's office and a small Cabinet of ministers without major departmental responsibilities. Both Lloyd George and Mosley talked of emergency powers to fight a 'war against unemployment'. But neither business confidence nor public opinion was prepared either for this sort of innovation or for a major loan to finance large-scale public works. Treasury officials warned that domestic and foreign capital might take flight, calling forth higher interest rates and a collapse of domestic investment. These bureaucratic influences were immensely powerful. It is true that a strong politician could have overridden such arguments, as Lloyd George had done during the war and was prepared to do again. But there was no mandate for such bold gestures.

Despite the pressures for orthodoxy, the government was not

immobile. Ministers attempted to make the most of a very bad situation by helping the export industries. Economic diplomacy was geared to that end. Labour's manifesto had promised 'rationalisation', and the government did succeed in passing a Coal Mines Act which aimed both to regulate prices and production and promote amalgamations within the districts. J. H. Thomas, the employment minister, was active in promoting rationalisation by agreement in other staple export industries and embarked on a vigorous effort to promote closer economic ties with Empire countries. At the same time, the Bank of England, fearing that Labour would resort to nationalisation, established a number of new organisations to assist industry to rationalise. Labour even tried to alter the constitutional arrangements which it inherited. Snowden, for example, established the Macmillan Committee on Finance and Industry to look for ways to make finance more freely available to industry without compromising the gold standard and the May Committee on National Expenditure to bounce the Cabinet into expenditure cuts when decision-making became deadlocked. MacDonald was still more adventurous. He brought both sides of industry and economic experts into the Economic Advisory Council (EAC) to help devise new policies and appraise policy choices (Howson and Winch, 1977). When the Cabinet was split in late 1930 over unemployment policy, MacDonald turned to the economists on the EAC to find a way out. But the experts were divided and could not help the Prime Minister to take on the Treasury.

What could have made public opinion more resolute and prepared to face up to this battering from organised interests? The system as a whole from Cabinet to peak organisations to public opinion came to favour retrenchment, if not unanimously at least in overwhelming majority. The experts who might have sustained the optimistic public mood of 1929 were, however, as divided and ultimately as pessimistic as everyone else when the crunch came in 1931. The 'New Deal' of 1929 was thus the main casualty of the rise in unemployment from late 1929 onwards. What was needed was a revision of the politics of power, but there was no mechanism for negotiating such fundamental changes. Only the economic juggernaut could change the established policy priorities, and even then the change was marginal.

The politics of power in the 1930s

In the autumn of 1931 the economic juggernaut wreaked its havoc. In quick succession, Britain was forced off the gold standard by a massive outflow of funds from London and into protection by an enormous inflow of foreign goods into Britain's ports. This was the signal for the rest of the world to retreat into much more restrictive, nationalistic policies as barriers to trade and payments spread rapidly throughout the world. There were obvious problems for the conduct of British policy. The international perspective had been dominant hitherto. But in an autarkic world, demand for British goods, services and capital was much reduced and unrestricted importing threatened the rate of exchange. Moreover, this demonstration of the impact of unregulated competition weakened confidence in the efficacy of market forces. Liberal internationalism clearly could no longer be the driving force behind British economic policy. The most obvious alternative, planned national development, seemed equally implausible. British economic growth had for more than a century looked to external markets and the British occupational and industrial structures reflected world rather than domestic patterns of demand. The restructuring necessary for a more self-sufficient economy in the inter-war years would have been enormous. However there was a third way. Part by accident, part by design, British government found a regional solution to the problems posed by the chaos in international economic affairs after 1931.

In many ways the role of sterling was the key. The City was potentially the principal casualty of the slump. Lower levels of world trade reduced City earnings and loss of faith in sterling cut back further the opportunities for profitable commercial activity. When Britain was forced off gold Treasury officials quickly realised that they would not be able to return for some time and began to consider how the currency might best be managed. One obvious strategy would have been to drive sterling down against other currencies to give British industry competitive advantage and stimulate import replacement production. But both the institutional structure of the City's markets and the closeness of its relations with the Treasury and the Bank remained intact (Ingham, 1984, p. 190). Instead of a new role for the City in the modernisation of domestic industry officials sought a second best to internationalism. During the crisis, in assessing the likely outlines of a post-gold monetary policy, a leading Treasury official argued:

One of the leading objects we ought to have in mind as soon as we can keep sterling steady at a reasonable level, is to make it easy for as many as possible of the unstable currencies to base themselves on sterling so that we may become the leaders of a sterling block which, pending our restabilisation on gold, would have the best opportunities of mutual trade *and would give sterling a new force in the world.* (quoted in Drummond, 1981, p. 10. Emphasis added)

Not only were the structural links between the City and the

Treasury still strong, but there was no political momentum behind a 'pro-industry' policy. The always tentative 'producer interest' of industrial capital and labour had collapsed in 1930 (Dintenfass, 1984). Moreover, the drift from internationalism to regionalism had begun before the slump. The minority Labour government had already been driven by the failure of international conferences into regional agreements on trade and payments (Boyce, 1987). Before 1931 the Empire had been the focus of this activity but the quotation above indicates that the slump afforded wider possibilities. A regional trading bloc consisting of the Empire and other nations with strong trading links with Britain was now possible.

It was essential to give sterling stability to make it an attractive reserve and transactions currency. Accordingly, the first priority in economic policy was not with industry but to find a support mechanism for sterling. Emergency interest rates were followed by the tariff (partly justified for the effect it would have on sterling), a public commitment to orthodox fiscal policies and the creation of a new agency, the Exchange Equalisation Account to try to iron out the fluctuations in sterling's international value by trading in currencies (Howson, 1980). Treasury officials learned a significant lesson in the months of deepest crisis. Sterling was vulnerable. Withdrawal of a substantial part of London's short-term liabilities would have provoked a panic flight of foreign and domestic capital, resulting in a German-style hyperinflation, and threatening the fabric of the economy and society. These fears were genuine and widely held outside the Treasury. The practical significance of giving sterling 'a new force in the world' was that the City could retain its external orientation. Thus, capital exports, which had been discouraged by the Bank of England in the period of financial stringency after 1925, were once more promoted in the 1930s to develop the economies of Empire countries (Strange, 1971, p. 55). The City could retain its external role, albeit on a regional rather than full international basis. The politics of power had been modified, not transformed, by the slump.

Labour was also vulnerable after 1931. Unemployment had risen and benefit rates were cut in late 1931, in part to demonstrate the willingness of the new National Government to defend the international value of sterling rather than pursue short-term domestic policy goals. But the real value of benefits remained higher than at the last major revaluation in 1927 and despite the introduction of means-testing the broad structure of insurance and the dole remained unaltered. When government attempted major changes in the mid-1930s it discovered that labour's power remained strong to resist change which weakened the position of wage-earners. Chamberlain had long wanted to reform the administration of unemployment relief. This was effected in the Unemployment Act of 1934 which detached assistance benefits (as the dole was now termed) from the insurance fund and imposed national principles for the operation of the household means-test to replace widely differing local practices. However, some recipients were faced with cuts in benefit levels. Fierce political controversy resulted, with the unemployed taking to the streets and forcing the government to withdraw (Garside, 1990). Labour's ability to defend the gains it had won was therefore unquestioned, and governments knew that they could manipulate the benefits system only at their peril. An awareness of the disruptive power of the labour movement may have been a factor in the failure of the anticipated attack on wage levels to materialise in the early 1930s. Many wage agreements tied pay to movements in the cost of living index, but after a large fall in 1930/31, the index was relatively stable, as were real wages. Despite the slump there was no general attack on labour conditions.

The levels of wages and employment were indirectly supported by the adoption of general protection. Hitherto, Conservative governments in the 1920s had planned to use safeguarding for industries willing to rationalise themselves. But the government had found the industries with which it was negotiating impossibly divided and incapable of reform from within. The advent of general protection removed from government the only weapon it had to nudge industry to greater efficiency. Government thus had two polarised alternative strategies. It could become more directly involved in the internal workings of British industry or leave everything to trust and the good will of industrialists. The latter had many advantages from the government's point of view. Under the terms of the post-war settlement governments had allowed 'home rule for industry' and the negotiations over safeguarding in the late 1920s had indicated that industrialists had lost none of their suspicion of government. It was always going to be politically easier to allow industrialists to make their own decisions. Ministers and officials, like almost everyone else, continued to believe that the key to economic recovery lay in a rise in prices. Industrial collusion behind the tariff would help prices up. But protection and collusion would also enable firms to set output and prices at levels consistent with existing wages and employment. If, on the other hand, government sought immediately to impose more efficient methods on industry, the likely first result was a rise in unemployment for which the government could be blamed. The optimum solution was for the government to do what it could to enable industry to raise prices in the short term (the substantial devaluation of the early 1930s clearly helped) while in the longer run to exert whatever pressure it could to raise industrial efficiency. In this way, the line of demarcation between government and industry could be maintained, at least on the surface, and industrialists would not be under pressure to force their workers to take cuts in wages or conditions of employment.

The tariff was thus constructed in a way which both maintained the distance between government and industry and gave industrialists maximum scope for collusion. A new body, the Import Duties Advisory Committee, was established as a buffer between government and industry. Government continued to pursue rationalisation but without having protection to offer as a quid pro quo. Ministers and officials held a consistent line in their dealings with industrialists in coal, cotton, steel, shipping and ship-building: cuts in surplus capacity and reorganisation were essential and the government would do what it could to help. Thus, when the majority of cotton-spinning firms agreed to raise a levy on existing spindles to finance the scrapping of excess capacity, the government passed the Cotton Spinning Industry Act of 1936 to force the small minority of dissidents into the scheme. These contacts were kept informal and unofficial as civil servants wanted neither to interfere in industry nor pre-empt the role of parliament in making policy. The pattern of working through producer associations was counter-productive for the health of the export industries. Industrial diplomacy implied a relatively strong central body in the industry with which contacts could be made. However the more powerful the central body of industrialists, the less effective was persuasion by ministers and officials (Tolliday, 1986, p. 104). In the end, industrial policy placed higher priority on the preservation of the appearance of demarcation between government and industry and the avoidance of redundancy for which government might be blamed than on efficiency. The industrial structures which government was indirectly supporting had been regarded as anachronistic in the mid-1920s but that was the cost of a pragmatic, consensual industrial policy.

Although liberal internationalism gave way in the 1930s to active, but pragmatic, economic management there were many continuities in the politics of power from the 1920s. The City's market structure survived both the collapse of the international economy and demands for regulation 'in the national interest' (see below). The independence of industry from the state could not be openly flouted and the defensive power of labour had to be acknowledged. The pressures which had built the politics of power in the early post-war period had not changed but adapted to active but pragmatic management. The goal was economic recovery and the route was via higher prices. The central department in this new strategy was the Treasury which significantly began to establish medium-term goals for policy.[9] The main features were the estimation of future levels of prices, wages, exports and unemployment. This can be styled the macro-economic management of the 1930s and represented a significant erosion by the Treasury of the Bank of England's traditional responsibilities for sterling and interest rates, though changes had already begun in the previous decade (Howson, 1975; Moggridge, 1972). Micro-economic management in the 1930s was delegated to industry itself with government creating the conditions to make delegated management effective. The politics of power was almost unchanged from the 1920s.

Monetary policy illustrates the way new tactics supported the old strategy. In the 1930s critics of government policy fought for two changes; cheaper money and the use of City capital to reorganise British industry. The Treasury and the Bank had both wanted cheaper money in the 1920s and both quickly came to see the suspension of the gold standard as an opportunity to lower the whole complex of interest rates. The Treasury had particular need of lower rates. During World War I the size of the national debt had mushroomed and the relatively high interest rates necessary in the 1920s to get back to and stay on gold had resulted in the emergence of a huge deadweight burden of debt service on the national budget. Between 1929/30 and 1932/3 total debt service was the equivalent of more than 8 per cent of GDP (Middleton, 1985, p. 102). The Treasury needed lower interest rates if it stood any chance of meeting the cost of the higher levels of unemployment without unbalancing the budget. One of the key steps in cheaper money was to convert War Loan to a lower coupon, and this in turn rested upon the Treasury's ability to overcome the sense of crisis in sterling after the devaluation of 1931. Conditions were stabilised in mid-1932 and conversion of War Loan went ahead to allow a reduction in the whole range of interest rates. One of the main justifications for cheaper money was the stimulus which would be given to industry, and Treasury officials took great comfort from the signs of economic revival after 1932. Indeed, Treasury officials opted to allow sterling to sink a little in 1935 rather than raise interest rates at what appeared to be a critical time in the business upswing. This was indeed a remarkable shift in priorities from the gold standard days but there were limits. For technical reasons the Treasury wanted to shift as much of its borrowing as possible from short-dated floating debt to longer term bonds. To persuade the market to take bonds longer term, rates had to rise to make them more attractive. Keynes complained that higher long-term rates would damage industry, but to no avail. Similarly, the Treasury was preparing to raise the Bank Rate in late 1936 to avert a crisis of market confidence despite the probable effect on British industry. In short, the Treasury tried to make funds more freely and cheaply available to industry but was not prepared to run risks with its management of the money markets. Safety first was the rule.

There were fewer successes for those who called on the government to create new institutions to finance the re-equipment of British industry. It is true that the Bank of England had set up the Securities Management Trust and the Bankers' Industrial Development Company to effect 'a marriage of finance and industry' (Best and Humphries, 1986, p. 233). But as has been noted the aim had been defensive, to head off an exaggerated fear of intervention in the affairs of private industry by the new minority Labour government and to protect the interests of those banking houses which had provided credit for businesses already in difficulties (Garside, 1990, p. 217). The experiment failed to effect a marriage between industry and finance but did help to frustrate demands from Mosley and others for more active measures to hasten industrial reorganisation. There was in fact no significant change in orthodox banking and commercial practices in the 1930s. The politics of power gave governments little scope to experiment in this area despite the obvious needs of industry for capital to re-equip and reorganise.

The politics of support and other stabilising forces in the 1930s

The politics of support had much less significance on the conduct of economic and social policy after the slump than in the years 1929 to 1931. Party politics were of rather less significance after 1931 anyway. The events of that year, with politicians desperately trying to retain national solidarity in the face of potentially disruptive forces, tended to emphasise country rather than party. In the first half of the decade the main development of the politics of support occurred within the Labour Party but had no resonance outside. With the departure of MacDonald, Snowden and Thomas, Labour lost the main conduit through which it had absorbed the politics of power. The remainder of the Party, sensing the collapse of capitalism and angry at the 'bankers' ramp' which it believed had ejected it from office, explored a positive socialist strategy in the early 1930s. Labour promised nationalisation of industry and financial services, socialist planning, a transitional programme and large-scale redistribution. This programme was fully endorsed at the time by such subsequent pillars of the establishment as Attlee,

Cripps and Dalton. The Party became very introspective; more concerned with ideological purity than with reaching out to the wider electorate. When it became clear that British voters had not become radicalised by the slump but had settled down on the dole, the new party leadership, and in particular the trade union bosses, began to reassess policy and to incorporate new ideas from economics and elsewhere (Durbin, 1985). The new programme certainly looked forward to the new politics after 1945 but had almost no effect on politics or policy in the 1930s.

The National Government, as a purely parliamentary organisation, did not have a mass party organisation within which a politics of support could develop. Even when the government became more obviously Conservative after 1935 party debate on policy was very muted. The government was impregnable and its critics responded by campaigning outside parliament. Presumably they calculated that there was more chance of shifting public opinion than influencing ministers in parliament. The most striking attempt to map out a radical, non-socialist alternative to government policy came from the Next Five Years (NFY) Group. It put forward an economic and a foreign policy programme which could be implemented within a single parliament, five years. Its policies included more planning and a large-scale programme of public works. Planning certainly had a strong appeal in the 1930s. The successes of the planned economies in the 1930s confirmed what many believed instinctively: market forces could not go unregulated after the chaos of the slump. A strong faith in the positive benefits of scientific progress also tended to swell support for planning. Despite these advantages neither the NFY Group nor the wider planning movement had any success in shaping government policy before 1939. The NFY Group was politically inept, scarcely surprising since most of its leaders were drawn largely from outside politics. The planning movement as a whole suffered as it became clear that the totalitarian regimes which had gone furthest towards the planned economy had also moved furthest from the individual political freedoms which had been so central to British political culture. Not the least of the problems for radical opinion was that from mid-decade economic reform tended to take a back seat to the need to shift foreign policy. A call for more vigorous opposition to the dictators was not the best accompaniment to a campaign for more vigorous planning.

Thus the opposition to the National Government could not create a mass movement behind an alternative agenda. Labour, having 'run away' from the problems of the economy in 1931 into a class-based ideological programme, lost the confidence of a significant section of the electorate. The centre ground had been captured effectively by Baldwin, MacDonald and Chamberlain; there was very little for radicals to work with. There was no great pressure on the government to adopt radical policies. British policy-makers edged forward into the much more disturbed conditions in the world economy in the 1930s without major political frictions at home and without the need for substantial new policy initiatives to cement new interest group alliances.

Three more general factors underwrote the stability of the politics of power and the weakness of the politics of support in the 1930s to ensure that limited pragmatism continued to dominate policy-making in Britain. The first was the flexibility of the political system and above all its willingness to include legitimate claims from the working class. It would have been easy in the context of the 1931 crisis for the government to signal an onslaught on the conditions of labour. The majority of professional economists certainly saw high real wages as the cause of unemployment (Casson, 1983), and British governments could have exploited the weakness of the industrial and political wings of organised labour in 1931/2. There were reductions in public sector wages and, more critically, in the level of unemployment benefit but the cuts in benefit were less than the fall in prices, as has been noted, and the wage reductions were no more than those experienced by private sector workers on sliding scale agreements. When the private sector did not pick up the invitation to attack the conditions of labour, the government did not press further. There had been reductions in the coverage of unemployment benefits, but the government had dealt with 'anomalies' (in large measure, the rights of married women to benefit). The rights to benefit of the more powerful male labour movement were not threatened, nor was there any attempt to lead employers into calls for longer hours of work. The improvement in working conditions won by the labour movement in the immediate post-war period was not threatened, nor were the much enhanced political rights of labour in question after 1931. It is true that Labour had been vilified for pursuing 'class policies' but the Party's bona fides were never in doubt. Indeed, the essence of limited pragmatism in British policy was to demonstrate that the working class could be 'trusted' in the new era of mass democracy.[10]

The second stabilising factor was the failure of a new generation of leaders to emerge during the inter-war years. Politics was dominated for two decades by Baldwin, MacDonald and Chamberlain. There were more radical politicians of the same and later generations but they failed to make their mark; Lloyd George, Churchill, Mosley and Macmillan could all claim to be able to transcend the constraints imposed by the politics of power, but none fulfilled his potential between the wars. All were to some extent 'fusionists', wanting a realignment of parties or shifts in mass political culture to secure parliamentary support. Almost all were popularly regarded as untrustworthy: Lloyd George for the sale of honours; Churchill for the Dardanelles campaign and his supposed part in the repression of workers at Tonypandy; and Mosley for being the aristocrat in the ranks of the socialist party. All made major political blunders in the inter-war years. Quite simply, none was comfortable with limited pragmatism and collectively they were unable to break the mould. Outside the ranks of professional politicians a similar story emerges. The Depression failed to throw up new leaders on either side of industry. The 'statesmen of industry' certainly did come to the fore in the inter-war years but they tended to reflect prevailing attitudes rather than work to change policy in radical ways. The best example would be Sir Eric Geddes who worked on ambitious plans for peacetime economic planning and corporatist arrangements in 1918–20, then emerged as the external authority to enforce retrenchment and orthodoxy on the Cabinet in 1921/2, and was finally transformed into the chairman of a quasi-public corporation, Imperial Airways, who campaigned constantly for higher subsidies from the government (Grieves, 1989). On the union side, the 1920s saw the beginnings of the dominance of Bevin and Citrine, but the political and industrial weakness of labour after 1921 led the unions to settle down to live with organised management while clinging to the state in a hostile economic environment (Middlemas, 1979, p. 214). Radical new ideas had nothing in which to root. Even the climate of intellectual ideas favoured those in power. The economics profession was divided over the causes of unemployment from the mid-1920s onwards and, as noted above, on the occasion when the Prime Minister appealed in 1931 to economists for new ideas, all they could supply was deep doctrinal division, notably over free trade. New ideas did emerge in the form of Keynes's General Theory in 1936, but even at the outbreak of war the economics profession remained in bitter dispute over its central message.

Finally, limited pragmatism was not without its successes. Apart from years of international crisis (1920–2, 1929–32, 1937) or domestic dislocation (1926), unemployment was on a downward trend. Limited pragmatism appeared to be working, the more so since unemployment does not appear to have been as great a problem as the unemployment insurance (UIS) figures suggested. It was always known that the UIS figures were a poor guide to the extent of unemployment among the work-force as a whole, and it has been suggested that the actual level of unemployment may have been only 60 to 65 per cent of those given by the UIS data (Metcalf et al., 1982). So, outside the years of world economic slump and recession, when conditions were beyond the power of any British government to manipulate, unemployment was not such an unprecedented problem.[11] Moreover, policy was not as fixed as some have argued and policy-makers were adept at spiking the guns of critics by adopting watered versions of radical policies. Broadly, the alternative strategies favoured by radicals fell into two groups. In the 1920s, critics wanted more vigorous expansion (lower interest rates, major public works schemes) but after 1931 more planning (industrial policy, import regulation) was demanded (Booth and Pack, 1985). But governments before the slump could demonstrate that public works schemes were in operation and were beginning to outrun the ability of the local authorities, who were mainly responsible for planning and executing the work, to suggest additional projects (Middleton, 1985). In the 1930s, the Treasury reduced interest rates and kept the Bank Rate at low levels. The National Government's attempt to portray itself as a supporter of 'planning' was helped by the vagueness of the term. In the 1930s, governments did what they could to regulate imports (the tariff and the Ottawa talks) at the time when public opinion seemed to be most decisively for 'planned trade'. Rather later, government involvement in rationalising the old staple export industries became public after Macmillan and others had mounted a vigorous campaign for an industrial policy which gave greater support to planning by industry. Governments which eschew the bold gesture in times of crisis have to be very careful about their public relations. Baldwin, Chamberlain and MacDonald could always claim to be implementing the sensible aspects of alternative strategies. That was the very essence of safety first.

Realisation that British inter-war governments did introduce new policies is a useful corrective to the conclusions of a comparative survey of anti-depression policies in Sweden, the UK and the USA by Weir and Skocpol (1985). They have pointed to the power of bureaucratic and institutional forces within the state machine, noting in particular the significance of British pioneering of state social welfare policies and the vigorous debate about social insurance in the 1920s. As a result, governing and opposition parties became skilled in the politics and administration of the scheme and devoted little energy to alternative policies. When unemployment began to rise again and bureaucrats began to resist the new idea of large-scale public works for the unemployed, Labour ministers could at least claim to be persevering with the tried and trusted remedy of unemployment insurance and the dole. Thus, state structures played a massively important part both in the focu of political debate and in the choice of policy to combat rising unemployment. This is fine as far as it goes, and much of the discussion of the importance of bureaucratic influences is consistent with what has been argued above. But the thrust of Weir and Skocpol's argument is that all radical impulses in British economic policy were muffled by bureaucratic inertia in the inter-war years. But they make nothing of the subtle changes which did take place in British economic policy, especially in industrial policy, and the breadth of the support for limited pragmatism throughout the British body politic. After all Mosley, who probably came closest to upsetting the cautious approach, was rejected by forces beyond the boundaries of the state. If the massed ranks of Labour activists did not fall in behind new policies, from where would the support for alternatives come? The importance of 'the state' as a barrier to certain types of economic strategy will of course depend on how 'the state' is defined. There should be no doubt, however, that the key shifts before and after the 1929 general election were in civil society, not the state, and reflected popular concern about the impact of rising unemployment on policy.

Conclusion

Despite its reputation for orthodox rigidity in both inter-war decades, British economic policy demonstrated an ability to adapt to the new conditions which confronted policy-makers after World War I. Slow, pragmatic change was nothing new to the inter-war period and there is nothing to indicate any major acceleration or deceleration in the pace of that change as a result of the slump in the early 1930s. Those seeking more dramatic initiatives had a major barrier to cross; the boundaries within which policy was formulated had been settled in the first post-war slump in a period of intense social and political unrest and subsequently had been legitimated by the ideology of safety first. A new agenda implied either a further period of social and political conflict or a major effort to shift opinion. However, for the majority neither economic conditions nor short-term prospects were at any time so bad to induce rebellion from right or left. The British economy achieved rates of economic growth which if not spectacular were historically respectable and unemployment, particularly in the 1930s, was neither as bad as in those countries with which Britain was apt to compare itself nor as bleak as the UIS statistics suggested (save for particularly depressed industrial areas). Despite this difficult environment, the efforts to induce change by persuasion did have some impact, notably at the end of the 1920s. Britain did have its 'New Deal', but it was a programme which came before rather than after the slump. It was designed to spread anticipated prosperity more broadly rather than cope with the ravages of depression. It was prompted by the reappearance of social conflict in 1926 rather than a conviction that unemployment was imposing unbearable costs. It died as unemployment began to rise. The slump did not have the same effect. It neither devastated the British economy nor upset the balance of interest-group power. It also cut away the political ground in which an alternative policy could be formulated. There were radical campaigns in the 1930s but none could penetrate the major economic interest groups nor mobilise effectively on a mass scale. No doubt alternative policies could have improved economic and social conditions but Britain lacked the means to devise and campaign effectively for ameliorative measures.

Notes

1 In the present century, one can think of 'the politics of safety first' between the wars, 'Butskellism' in the years between *c.* 1945 and *c.* 1975 and there appears to be convergence between 'Majorism' and the opposition parties at the present time.

2 'Gentlemanly capitalism' is defined by Cain and Hopkins, 1987.

3 An internationalist political economy recognises the nation-state but its central preoccupations are with the network of markets which extend far beyond the boundaries of the nation-state. A national political economy places more emphasis on capitalism as a system of organised and increasingly collective and interdependent production. Its priorities are with safeguarding productive capacity and securing collaboration between the major classes rather than with the market framework (Gamble, 1981, pp. 132–40, 168).

4 Keith Middlemas (1979, pp. 51–67) would identify the government response to the industrial relations crisis of 1911 as the origin of policies coloured by concerns of national political economy.

5 The best demonstration of the failure of consensus is the fate of the National Industrial Conference (see Lowe, 1978b).

6 Material on the alternative strategies of both inter-war decades is taken from Booth and Pack, 1985.

7 Phillip Williamson's (1982) article is by some way the best introduction to the political economy of Britain in the late 1920s.

8 Kindleberger (1973) has argued that the world plunged into recession because no country was able to support the world financial system in key respects: the British government lacked the resources to back the good intentions of its statesmen.

9 In an exercise undertaken at the request of Chamberlain and known as 'Old Moore's Almanack' (Howson, 1975, pp. 94–5).

10 His biographers have argued strongly that Baldwin was determined to ensure that the new franchise after 1918 worked successfully by giving the working class no legitimate cause for dissatisfaction with the working of the system (Middlemas and Barnes, 1969). Similarly,

Lowe's (1986) magisterial study of the Ministry of Labour argues that this new department of state took Whitehall into new areas of policy to cope with the problems of policy-making in the new environment of pluralism after 1918.

11 Levels of unemployment before World War I are almost impossible to ascertain with any degree of precision but it is almost certain that the levels experienced in slump years exceeded those prevailing in most 'non-crisis' inter-war years (Garside, 1980). Precedents for very high localised unemployment had been set in Ireland on various occasions in the nineteenth century and in the handloom weaving districts of Lancashire in the 1820s.

References

Abrams, P., 1963, 'The Failure of Social Reform, 1918–1920', *Past and Present*, 24: 43–64.

Addison, P., 1975, *The Road to 1945*, London, Jonathan Cape.

Best, M. and Humphries, J., 1986, 'The City and Industrial Decline', in B. Elbaum and W. Lazonick, *The Decline of the British Economy*, Oxford, Clarendon Press.

Booth, A., 1982, 'Corporatism, Capitalism and Depression in Twentieth Century Britain', *British Journal of Sociology*, 33.

Booth, A. and Pack, M., 1985, *Employment, Capital and Economic Policy: Great Britain, 1918–1939*, Oxford, Basil Blackwell.

Boyce, R. W. D., 1987, *British Capitalism at the Crossroads, 1919–1932: A Study in Politics, Economics and International Relations*, Cambridge, Cambridge University Press.

Brown, K. D., 1971, *Labour and Unemployment, 1900–1914*, Newton Abbot, David & Charles.

Cain, P. J. and Hopkins, A. G., 1987, 'Gentlemanly Capitalism and British Expansion Overseas II: New Imperialism, 1850–1945', *Economic History Review*, 2nd series, 40: 1–26.

Casson, M., 1983, *Economics of Unemployment: A Historical Perspective*, Oxford, Martin Robertson.

Dintenfass, M., 1984, 'The Politics of Producers' Co-operation', in J. Turner (ed.), *Businessmen and Politics: Business Activity in British Politics, 1900–1945*, London, Heinemann.

Drummond, I. M., 1981, *The Floating Pound and the Sterling Area, 1931–9*, Cambridge, Cambridge University Press.

Durbin, E., 1985, *New Jerusalems: The Labour Party and the Economics of Democratic Socialism*, London, Routledge & Kegan Paul.

Elbaum, B. and Lazonick, W., 1986, *The Decline of the British Economy*, Oxford, Clarendon Press.

Gamble, A., 1974, *The Conservative Nation*, London, Routledge & Kegan Paul.

Gamble, A., 1981, *Britain in Decline: Economic Policy, Political Strategy and the British State*, London, Macmillan.

Gamble, A. and Walkland, S., 1984, *The British Party System and*

Economic Policy, 1945–83: Studies in Adversary Politics, Oxford, Clarendon Press.

Garside, W. R., 1980, *The Measurement of Unemployment. Methods and Sources in Great Britain, 1850–1979*, Oxford, Basil Blackwell.

Garside, W. R., 1990, *British Unemployment, 1919–1939: A Study in Public Policy*, Cambridge, Cambridge University Press.

Grieves, K., 1989, *Sir Eric Geddes: Business and Government in War and Peace*, Manchester, Manchester University Press.

HMSO, 1929, *Memoranda on Certain Proposals Relating to Unemployment*, Cmd. 3331.

Harris, J., 1972, *Unemployment and Politics, 1886–1914*, Oxford, Oxford University Press.

Hatton, T., 1987, 'The Outlines of a Keynesian Solution', in S. Glynn and A. Booth (eds), *The Road to Full Employment*, London, Allen & Unwin.

Howson, S., 1975, *Domestic Monetary Management in Britain, 1919–1938*, Cambridge, Cambridge University Press.

Howson, S., 1980, *Sterling's Managed Float: The Operation of the Exchange Equalisation Account, 1932–39*, Princeton Studies in International Finance, 46, Princeton, Princeton University Press.

Howson, S. and Winch, D., 1977, *The Economic Advisory Council: A Study of Economic Advice in Depression and Recovery*, Cambridge, Cambridge University Press.

Ingham, G., 1984, *Capitalism Divided? The City and Industry in British Social Development*, London, Macmillan.

Kindleberger, C. P., 1973, *The World in Depression, 1929–1939*, London, Allen Lane.

Lowe, R., 1978a, 'The Erosion of State Intervention in Britain, 1917–1924', *Economic History Review*, 2nd series, 31: 270–86.

Lowe, R., 1978b, 'The Failure of Consensus in Britain: The National Industrial Conference, 1919–1921', *The Historical Journal*, 21: 649–75.

Lowe, R., 1986, *Adjusting to Democracy: The Role of the Ministry of Labour in British Politics, 1916–1939*, Oxford, Clarendon Press.

Marquand, D., 1977, *Ramsay MacDonald*, London, Jonathan Cape.

Marrison, A. J., 1990, 'Businessmen, Industries and Tariff Reform in Great Britain, 1903–1930', in R. T. P. Davenport-Hines (ed.), *Business in the Age of Depression and War*, London, Frank Cass.

Melling, J., 1991, 'British Industrialists and the State, 1850–1930', paper given to research seminar on problems of the state, University of Exeter, May.

Metcalf, D., et al., 1982, 'Still Searching for an Explanation of Unemployment in Inter-War Britain', *Journal of Political Economy*, 90: 386–99.

Middlemas, K., 1979, *Politics in Industrial Society: The British Experience of the System Since 1911*, London, Andre Deutsch.

Middlemas, K. and Barnes, J., 1969, *Baldwin: A Biography*, London, Weidenfeld & Nicolson.

Middleton, R., 1985, *Towards the Managed Economy: Keynes, the Treasury and the Fiscal Policy Debate of the 1930s*, London, Methuen.

Moggridge, D. N., 1972, *British Monetary Policy, 1924–1931: The Norman

Conquest of $4.86, Cambridge, Cambridge University Press.

Skidelsky, R., 1970, *Politicians and the Slump: The Labour Government of 1929–31*, Penguin, Harmondsworth.

Skidelsky, R., 1975a, 'The Reception of the Keynesian Revolution' in M. Keynes (ed.), *Essays on John Maynard Keynes*, Cambridge, Cambridge University Press.

Skidelsky, R., 1975b, *Oswald Mosley*, London, Macmillan.

Stewart, M., 1967, *Keynes and After*, Penguin, Harmondsworth.

Strange, S., 1971, *Sterling and British Policy: A Political Study of an International Currency in Decline*, Oxford, Oxford University Press.

Tolliday, S., 1986, 'Steel and Rationalisation Policies, 1918–1950', in B. Elbaum and W. Lazonick, *The Decline of the British Economy*, Oxford, Clarendon Press.

Waites, B. A., 1987, *A Class Society at War: England 1914–1918*, Leamington Spa, Berg.

Weir, M. and Skocpol, T., 1985, 'State Structures and the Possibilities for "Keynesian" Responses to the Great Depression in Sweden, Britain and the United States', in P. R. Evans et al., *Bringing the State Back In*, Cambridge, Cambridge University Press.

Williamson, P., 1982, 'Safety-First: Baldwin, the Conservative Party and the 1929 General Election', *Historical Journal*, 25: 385–409.

3 Unemployment and fiscal policy in Sweden during the 1930s: myths and reality

B. Gustafsson

According to a widely held opinion the economic policy initiated and pursued by the Social Democratic government in Sweden during the 1930s was the first historical example of the new active fiscal policy advocated by Mr Keynes, but never realised in any other Western country until after World War II. From then on Sweden acquired an international reputation for being 'the archetype of the welfare state' (Verney, 1955, p. vii). Within the Swedish context there has been much debate over this issue since the 1930s. Those who were sympathetic towards social democracy tended to accept the received view, while liberals and conservatives were inclined to negate it, referring to the upswing of the business cycle in late 1933 as the main cause of increasing employment. One early spokesman of the latter group was the renowned liberal economist and economic historian Arthur Montgomery, who already in 1938 pointed to the spontaneous forces behind the recovery (Montgomery, 1938). Looking back on this debate it is curious to note the extent to which the participants were referring not so much to what government was actually doing (still less to the results of governmental action) but rather to the intentions and the decisions of government spokesmen or – still more – of prominent economists. It is as if the mere declaration of an intention was sufficient evidence for something having taken place in fact.

With the publication of Karl-Gustaf Landgren's dissertation on 'the new economics' in Sweden in 1960 the scientific discussion took a new turn. Landgren held that the new economics in Sweden was mainly indebted to Keynes in respect of theory and to the Swedish Social Democratic Minister of Finance, Ernst Wigforss, in respect of policy measures. He found very little of the new economics among Swedish economists. Only Bertil Ohlin succeeded, according to Landgren, in sketching a theory of output as a whole similar to that of Keynes (Landgren, 1960). Landgren's views were vigorously disputed by Otto Steiger in his dissertation, 'Studien zur Entstehung der Neuen Wirtschaftslehre in Schweden – Eine Antikritik' published in 1971 (Steiger, 1971). In contradiction to Landgren, Steiger claimed that 'the new economics' in Sweden was an indigenous product, the theoretical origins of which could be traced to the Swedish economist Knut Wicksell. He agreed with Landgren that the economic policy measures advocated in the 1930s were strongly backed by Wigforss. But while Landgren perceived Keynes's shadow behind Wigforss, Steiger stressed a Social Democratic policy tradition with historical roots in Marxism and, more important for practical policy, in British Fabianism, especially the Minority Report of the Webbs in 1912. Steiger's attempt to regard Wicksell as the historical originator of the new economics of the 1930s has itself come under attack (Gustafsson, 1973). But as to the relative weight of Keynes and the indigenous Swedish Social Democratic economic policy tradition respectively, in shaping the government policy programme of the 1930s, no agreement could be found; the matter was complicated by the fact that Wigforss himself was not quite clear about which of those influences had been the most important.

The discussion, while throwing light on the origins and the theoretical and ideological aspects of unemployment policy in the 1930s, had little or nothing to contribute to the more important issue of what really happened and with what results. In 1969 the economist Villy Bergström, in a historical survey of economic policy in Sweden, claimed that it was the 1920s rather than the 1930s that witnessed (unintended) deficit financing. It was, moreover, extremely difficult to assess the supposed impact of government fiscal policy because of the intricacies of the budget (Bergstrom, 1969, p. 134). Other studies have questioned the assumed importance of the 'new economics' in Sweden during the 1930s[1]. The purpose of this chapter is to re-examine Swedish unemployment and fiscal policy in the 1930s in an effort to establish the extent to which policy activism was in any way remarkable or innovative.

Unemployment policy

The reason Swedish unemployment policy in the 1930s has been regarded as innovative is twofold: first, an alleged increased emphasis on public works in the open market, the nature of which differed noticeably from the relief works practised earlier; second, the acceptance of the need to pay market wages on public works rather than a level of remuneration below that granted to the lowest paid unskilled worker. But neither the state's commitment to public works expenditure nor its willingness to contemplate market rates of wages was a novel outcome of the 1930s Depression. During the depression of 1908/9 parliament granted money for canal and railway construction work amounting to 18 per cent of the state budget in order to boost employment and demand. At this time the level of wage rates was not in dispute and market wages or wages close to market wages were frequently paid on public works schemes. When a special unemployment commission was established in 1914 because of increasing unemployment in the wake of the outbreak of World War I, the issue of wage rates in public works was still uncontroversial. The commission rejected an attempt in 1915 to depart from 'the evidently correct' principle of paying market wages.

The changes in unemployment policy which received so much publicity with the coming to power of the Social Democrats in 1933 cannot be represented as a radical breakthrough in policy. They amounted in essence to a rejection of reactionary responses to unemployment which had characterised the previous decade. The 1920s did little to promote the enlightened thinking evident early in the century. A neo-liberal tendency to roll back the influence of labour had gained increasing strength during the decade and it proved difficult for government to expand public expenditure or to raise taxes. Attitudes to unemployment, moreover, altered significantly. The unemployment commission, led by a forceful conservative public servant Otto Järte, insisted that relief works should not compete with regular public works but be geared towards unskilled workers. Remuneration would be set at a level below the lowest wage rate normally paid to unskilled workers while unemployment relief paid in cash would be lower still.

This policy stance was based on the idea that the prevailing level of unemployment was only a lapse from the full employment norm of the pre-World War I period. Although the unemployment crisis of 1921/2 was short and dramatic, the economy was not restored to full employment. A more serious structural unemployment crisis emerged as a result of three factors: demographic change, which swelled the labour force with young workers; the drift of workers from agriculture to urban employment; and the rationalisation of industry propelled by the return to the gold standard.

The policy of the unemployment commission was not adequate to deal with this situation. On the contrary it worsened it, since the setting of low wage rates encouraged local government to transform regular public works into relief works, which merely created additional unemployment. To be sure, in the short run some profited from this policy. The low wage rates on relief works put a brake on the outflow of labour from agriculture while the choice of work projects (mainly road building and wood works far away from population centres) did not compete with private investments. But the policy had few longer term benefits. There were limited multiplier effects and little incentive at the prevailing level of wages for workers to maximise their effort. In addition the rapid turnover of labour combined with the geographical spread of work projects raised costs to a level some 15 per cent higher than comparable projects performed in the open market. Workers who remained on relief works gradually lost their former skills; those who ceased working on such projects merely drifted towards poor relief, forcing an increase in local government expenditure in areas often least able to bear the burden.

Thus, conditions for a change of unemployment policy matured well before its official reversal with the coming to power of the Social Democrats in 1933. The Conservative government, for example, suggested in 1929 that relief works should 'successively and naturally be replaced by public works in the open market and at wage rates prevailing in the market'. The Social Democrats built on such sentiments, moving a bill on unemployment in 1930 which stressed the inefficiency of relief works, their negative impact on the costs of poor law expenditure and their tendency to impede the steady transfer of skilled labour back into the normal labour market. In like manner the Liberal government of 1931 suggested a prompt return to pre-war policy with the inauguration of public works in the open market at market wage rates (so-called *beredskapsarbeten*) as a complement to relief works.

The labour market policy of the 1920s was thus being slowly eroded before the advent of the Social Democratic government in January 1933. What the Democrats did was to attempt to expand the scope of *beredskapsarbeten*. While parliament had successively granted increasing sums for public works in the open market from 1929/30 to 1931/2 (88, 103 and 142 million Swedish crowns respectively), the new Social Democratic government requested 195 million for 1933/4 (subsequently reduced to 180 million). At first sight, the employment effects of public works expenditure after 1933 seem creditable. Contemporary estimates put the additional creation of jobs at more than 40,000 in late 1934 and 1935 – after this employment was reduced parallel to the upswing of the business cycle. But these figures include not only workers who were unemployed but also workers who had previously been employed but who preferred to leave their regular jobs for employment on public works. Many of the unemployed, moreover, were given work on schemes which to all intents and purposes were conventional relief works (unskilled work in agriculture and wood work for example). As Table 3.1 shows, the employment of unemployed workers in what might be called the new public works only reached about 15,000 at its height in 1935. Unemployment policy during and after the Depression was based in practice on traditional relief works and, still more, on cash relief. During the depth of the Depression, moreover, the second largest category of unemployed workers were those who did not receive any support at all. This appears quite clearly from Figure 3.1, which summarises the effect of unemployment policy from January 1933 to January 1935. It should be noted that the reduction of total public employment after 1934 occurred in spite of the fact that unemployment among trade union members still was 18 and 15 per cent in 1934 and 1935 respectively.

Table 3.1 Number of unemployed in relief works and public works in Sweden 1930–38

År Year	Relief works	Public works	Total	Change of employment		
				Relief works	Public works	Total
1930	4,065	?	4,065	–	–	–
1931	13,817	?	13,817	+ 9,752	–	+ 9,752
1932	31,539	?	31,539	+17,722	–	+17,722
1933	44,861	3,221	48,082	+13,322	+ 3,221	+16,543
1934	44,208	11,802	56,010	– 653	+ 8,581	+ 7,928
1935	29,781	14,974	44,755	–14,427	+ 3,172	–11,255
1936	16,065	11,394	27,459	–13,716	– 3,580	–17,296
1937	7,829	8,159	15,988	– 8,236	– 3,235	–11,471
1938	6,038	6,329	12,367	– 1,791	– 1,830	– 3,621

Source: Gustafsson, 1974

Note: The employment in public works before 1933 (according to the new definition of public works introduced in 1933) has never been estimated. This explains the absence of data for employment in public works 1930–32.

The employment of workers in public works refers only to workers who earlier were unemployed, not to workers who shifted employment from earlier occupations to public works. Figures for earlier unemployed and earlier employed workers, respectively, are to be found only for 1933 and 1934. The distribution between these two categories for 1935–1938 has been estimated on the basis of the figures for 1934. The figures referring to employment in relief works in 1938 also includes those employed in the new type of public works introduced in 1934 (the so-called *beredskapsarbeten*). Before that year those workers were included in the category of public works.

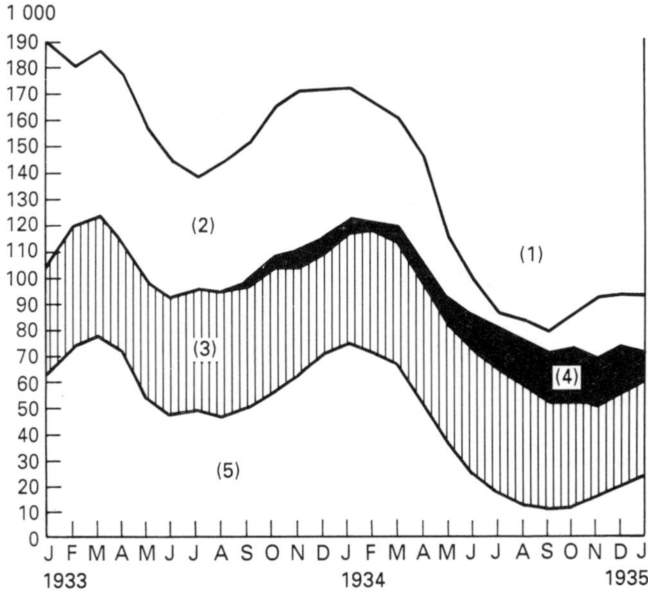

Figure 3.1 The scope and effects of various employment policies in Sweden 1933-35

Key (1) = officially registered seeking assistance
　　　(2) = not assisted applying for assistance
　　　(3) = employed in relief work
　　　(4) = employed in public work
　　　(5) = assisted by cash contributions

Note The number of earlier unemployed workers in public works was on the average 50 per cent of total employment in public works
Source: Gustafsson (1974)

In fact mass unemployment did not disappear in Sweden even after the Depression in spite of the business upswing. Unemployment among trade union members was not lower between 1936 and 1940 than it had been between 1926 and 1930, i.e. 11 per cent. Unemployment among non-unionised labour was even higher. Mass unemployment disappeared only with World War II, when a substantial share of the labour force was drafted into the army.

Why then did Sweden not experience a real expansionist employment policy during the course of the 1930s? One may point to several causes. In the first place the financial resources allocated to unemployment policy were clearly insufficient. What was made available was poorly utilised and appropriations were themselves reduced as soon as business showed signs of recovery. This point will be elaborated upon below. It is sufficient to note here that in

1933/4 only 69 per cent of the money borrowed by government was actually spent and within the spending budget only 59 per cent of the financial resources was aimed at increasing public employment. Second, new unemployment was successively created during the 1930s because of a rapid increase in the substitution of capital for labour (Aberg, 1969, p. 114). Third, there was lacking an organisation for implementing the new public works policy, which caused substantial delays in the process of planning and execution of decisions. Lastly, even within the Social Democratic government there were voices warning that the moderate programme was in fact too expansionist.

Fiscal policy

The prominence of public works policy in Sweden during the 1930s – modest and somewhat traditional as it was – has usually been perceived as a moment in a larger set of policies: the utilisation of fiscal policy as an instrument for business cycle policy designed to even out fluctuations and to increase the level of economic activity. In this connection one usually refers to a series of more or less coordinated decisions: the allegedly new fiscal policy from 1933, the introduction of investment funds in 1938 as well as the tax reform of the same year and the establishment of the governmental Business Cycle Institute (*Konjunkturinstitutet*) in 1937.

If fiscal innovation was paramount in Sweden's response to depression one might have expected that the government would have decreased taxes in order to stimulate consumption and spending. Nothing of the kind occurred. Taxes as a percentage of national income increased from 10.4 per cent in 1930/31 to 13.0 per cent in 1938. They reached a maximum of 13.8 per cent in 1933 the very worst Depression year. To some extent this trend is explained by the spontaneous decline of income during the Depression. But it also followed from the deliberate increase of indirect taxes in order to compensate for the declining returns from income and property taxation. During the Depression the share of indirect taxes in total state tax income increased from 33 per cent in 1930/31 to 41 per cent in 1933/4. While the return from income and property taxation decreased in absolute terms from 165 to 143 million crowns during these years, the return from indirect taxation increased from 195 to 251 million crowns. The implication of this is that fiscal policy (as far as tax policy is concerned) closely implemented the age-old Treasury view of 'balancing the budget. In exchange for the political support of the farmers' party for their own fiscal policy programme, the Social Democrats had introduced a comprehensive price-support programme for agriculture. But since this agreement (popularly called the 'cow-swop') at the same time implied rising prices for foodstuffs, it is clear that the higher propensity to consume of low income earners could not have been stimulated. On the contrary it was repressed with ensuing negative multiplier effects.

The introduction of the investment funds as well as the tax reform of 1938 were aimed mainly at consolidating (big) business. Investment funds implied that business firms which funded 10 to 20 per cent of their profits and gave the government the authority to determine when such monies should be invested (i.e. during downturns), did not tax for this share of their profits and even earned a low interest on the money while funded. The tax reform of the same year, which had been devised by the Liberal government under Mr Ekman in 1931, abolished the progressive profit tax for companies, made it proportional and lowered it substantially, especially for big companies.

Taxation apart, it is frequently suggested that Sweden benefited from three innovative approaches to fiscal policy and labour market disequilibrium. They can be stylised thus:

(1) According to conventional economic thinking unemployment could be effectively avoided only by lowering the general wage rate, since unemployment indicated that the supply price of labour was higher than the demand price. By lowering wages profitability would be restored, investments stimulated and unemployment would gradually disappear. According to the new view, represented first and foremost by the Social Democrats, wage cuts would, on the contrary, worsen depression by lowering effective demand. Therefore they suggested an increase of the level of economic activity by means of public works.

(2) The traditional view, moreover, maintained that the state budget should be in balance with annual expenses covered by the income of any year. Representatives of the new view, on the other hand, recommended deficit financing during depression in order to increase effective demand. Such a fiscal stimulus would increase the level of economic activity and the growth of income as well as taxes so that the budget deficit would disappear. Put another way, the budget should be balanced over the time-span of the business cycle rather than every year.

(3) Conventional economics further claimed that unproductive government expenses should not be financed by loans, since that would decrease the net value of government assets. But according to the more radical approach suggested in (2) above,

fiscal policy would actually restore the value of state assets since increasing investment would increase the stock of capital. Furthermore, the argument ran, an unchanged value of state-owned assets was by itself no overriding goal for fiscal policy as long as the state debt was owned by the citizen of the country.

Let us take a closer look at these contrasting views of fiscal policy. It is true that most economists – with the exception of Bertil Ohlin, prominent member of the Liberal Party – were convinced that unemployment was caused by a too high general rate of wages and that, consequently, unemployment could only be cured by wage cuts. It is likewise true that the Social Democratic Minister of Finance, Ernst Wigforss, who was well acquainted with the writings of Keynes, strongly opposed this view in his theoretical and political writings. But as a representative of the government, Wigforss took a much more cautious view, either because he was obliged by his official position to adopt a different view than he did in his personal writings or because of political expediency.

Before the advent of the new Social Democratic government in January 1933, the theoretical presumptions of budgetary policy were inspired by Gustav Cassel, a die-hard believer in neoclassical macro-economic theory. From 1933, Gunnar Myrdal, a Social Democrat, achieved greater prominence. His long appendix to the budget proposal of 1933 has been viewed as the theoretical embodiment of a new view (Myrdal, 1933). It is doubtful, however, whether this document can be regarded as a clear-cut expression of the new macro-economics. On the one hand, Myrdal quite clearly emphasised the importance of public works in order to increase effective demand. But as to wage policy Myrdal was ambiguous. He did not seem to realise that, in an economy with over-capacity of labour and capital equipment, the demand effect of wage cuts would outweigh their cost-reducing effects. He thought that wages were 'too high from the point of view of profitability' and that therefore 'some wage cuts in private business' would be 'the most efficient instrument for promoting a business upswing'. He recognised that wage cuts were 'a double-edged instrument' and warned of the social conflicts that they could bring forth. Finally, he suggested increased taxes on wage-goods as an alternative strategy to wage cuts. The ensuing lowering of consumption would 'make room for public works giving a stronger stimulus to the depressed capital-goods industries and a stronger increase in the demand for labour'. Myrdal seemed to argue, in other words, that investment could be increased only at the expense of consumption. The increased investment would mainly be brought about by increasing public works which would be the vehicle for stimulating private investment.

As far as wage policy was concerned, therefore, the Social Democrats, representing labour and trade union interests, could not contemplate direct wage cuts in the private business sector. They could, however, reach the same goal by utilising taxation, i.e. increasing the money price of wage-goods, thereby cutting real wages. Wigforss admitted as much in a speech to the Association of Economists (Nationalekonomiska föreningen) in 1933:

I can only say that it is self-evident for anybody who accepts the present level of wage rates and who wants to induce people to work at these wage rates that he should be willing, nay forced to accept the increase of prices that possibly would be the effect thereof. (Wigforss, 1954, pp. 25–7)

The conflict between spokesmen of the old versus the new line, respectively, was thus not whether there should be an adjustment between costs and prices in order to promote a business upswing but rather, as Wigforss emphasised in the same speech, which method of adjustment should be used. Wigforss and the Social Democrats declined to lower real wages by reducing money wages but accepted a lowering of real wages by raising prices. Both methods, of course, depart from a common acceptance of high wages being a cause of unemployment. The difference is that the latter method, which Ellis, referring to Keynes, once called 'a Machiavellian device' (Ellis, 1949, p. 475), has a stimulating effect on long-run profit expectations. The traditional view in other words was turned away at the door but was let in by the back entrance. We have already noted that wage-goods increased in price due to the combined effect of increasing indirect taxation and the 'cow-swop' with the farmers' party. Wages increased less than cost of living, wholesale prices and output during the rest of the 1930s and the wage share also decreased.

Turning to the second alleged new main aspect of fiscal policy, the balancing of the state budget, it is noteworthy that there were indeed deficits during the Depression years 1931 to 1935. But there is no substantial difference in budgetary practice when we compare the years 1931/2 with the years 1933/4. The age-old budgetary principle of not infringing upon the net value of state assets was closely preserved during the 1930s. Although it may have been intended for placating the political opposition – the Social Democrats were at this time not yet firmly seated in the saddle – Wigforss confirmed that the new budget of 1933 did not represent 'any deviation from prudent and reliable methods of financing'. And he was right. The so-called 'ordinary expenses' of the budget were cut down even more drastically than had been suggested in the proposals of the official committee seeking economies in government expenditure; one-fourth of government borrowing was covered by increased taxes; the amortisation period was short, seven years, and in practice the borrowed money was paid back in four years, which implied that the new expenses for public works did not differ much from tax-financed expenses. The budget proposal for 1934/5 had the same general orientation.

The main difference in fiscal policy orientation between the years 1931 and 1933, when the Liberal Ekman government was in power, and 1933 to 1935 was technical. There had been deficits during the years 1931 to 1933, but at that time the deficit was covered by transferring funded money to the so-called tax budget. (The funded money was taken from a special fund for excise duties on spirits. But since this was a touchy subject for the Liberal Party with a very strong temperance faction, this move was hardly publicised!) When this funded money was no longer available in 1933, the budgetary shortfall was covered by transferring the deficit to the so-called loan budget.

Let us, lastly, try to estimate the effects of fiscal policy in Sweden during the 1930s. After all this is the most interesting point, irrespective of the claims and intentions that have been made by the historical actors. Since the 1930s were characterised by unemployment and under-utilisation of capacity one may assume that changes in national income were mainly determined by changes in total demand. Fiscal policy influenced total demand in two ways. When government consumption, investment and transfers increased, demand increased and when taxes and other public revenues increased, demand decreased and vice versa. Using a very simple model to calculate the effects of fiscal policy, we will assume that changes in government consumption and investment exerted a direct effect on demand and that changes in government income and expenditure surpluses exerted an indirect effect on demand.[2] Figure 3.2 shows the effects of fiscal policy on changes in GNP from 1924 to 1938 at current prices. What emerges is that:

(1) With the exception of some few years fiscal policy exerted a very restricted influence on changes in GNP. This observation applies not least to the Depression years of 1931 to 1933.

(2) Fiscal policy exerted an expansionary effect during nine of the fifteen years, a contractive effect during five years and was neutral during one year.

(3) During the years of economic crisis and depression in the early 1930s fiscal policy had expansive effects but did not decisively shape the course of GNP changes. The fiscal policy effects were about as large in each of the years 1931, 1932 and 1934, and somewhat less in 1933. If we compare the years 1931/2 with

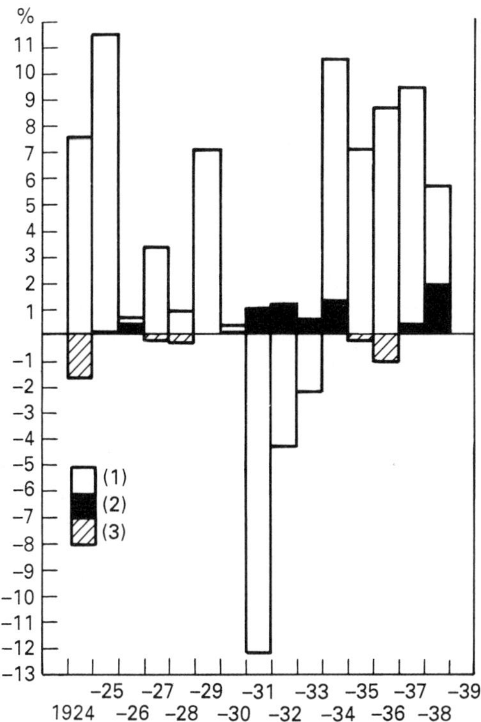

Figure 3.2 Effects of fiscal policy in Sweden 1924-38

Key (1) = yearly change of GNP in current prices
      (2) = expansive effect of change in GNP due to fiscal policy
      (3) = contractive effect of change in GNP due to fiscal policy

Source : Gustafsson (1974)

1933/4 the expansive effects were in fact somewhat larger during 1931/2 (2.1 per cent) than during 1933/4 (1.7 per cent).
(4) After the years of crisis and depression, fiscal policy once again
     became contractive in 1935 and 1936.

Of course, these results should not be over-interpreted. But they fit
well with those Erik Lundberg reached in 1938 with the help of a
still more simplified model, namely that fiscal policy exerted 'its
most stimulating effect during the budgetary year of 1931/32'
(Lundberg, 1938, p. 73).

In conclusion one may very well ask whether and to what extent
that much renowned 'new economic policy' of Sweden during the
1930s really did represent a unique case at all. What later became
known as 'the Swedish model' was to some extent conceived during
the 1930s, e.g. in various publications by Alva and Gunnar Myrdal

(Myrdal and Myrdal, 1938). But in the main this 'model' belongs to the post-World War II period. The Scandinavian countries in the 1930s were considerably more ambitious in their policy goals than other Western European countries partly perhaps because of the stronger leftist bent of their governments and the relative absence of class consciousness and division compared say to Britain, France and even Germany and Italy. But within the Scandinavian context it does not seem as if the Swedish experience was unique. True, there are indications that Swedish fiscal policy was somewhat more ambitious than that of Norway, although the case still does not seem to be sufficiently researched. But a comparison with the Danish case is instructive. In 1939 Jörgen Dich made an explicit comparison between Denmark and Sweden with regard to the expansion of public purchasing power measured by changes in public liquid resources and public borrowing. He found that the expansion of public purchasing power started in both countries at the same time (1931/2). One notable difference, however, is that the governmental effort in Sweden had already reached its maximum in 1931/2, while it increased continuously in Denmark peaking in 1933/4.

With some justification Dich could conclude:

Sweden's way through the crisis, and thereby not least its expansive crisis policy has, as a consequence of the publicity effort of Sweden's economists, become famous. Not many are aware of the fact that those efforts made in Sweden were carried through in Denmark to a greater extent and with a greater efficiency than in Sweden. However, we do not envy Sweden for having become famous for a policy which was carried through first and foremost in Denmark. But perhaps it would also pay Danish democracy to devote some more effort to publicity? (Dich, 1939, p. 148)

Notes

1 First and foremost I have in mind the unfortunately still unpublished investigations by Eskil Helmersson, who made an intensive counter-factual study of the fiscal policy of the early 1930s. He found that the differences in ambition between various political programmes for fighting unemployment were marginal (Helmersson, 1972).
2 The derived model is: $dK = 2dG + dE - dT$, where dK is the total demand change induced by the variables on the right hand, dG being the change in public consumption and investment, dE the change in transfers and dT the change in tax income (see e.g. Hansen, 1969).

References

Aberg, Y., 1969, *Production och Produktivitet i Sverige, 1861–1965*, Uppsala.

Bergstrom, V., 1969, *Den Ekonomiska Politiken i Sverge*, Uppsala.

Dich, J., 1939, *Arbejdsloshed-sproblemet i Danmark, 1930–1938. Social-ministeriets Okonomisk – Statistiske Undersögelser nr 4*, Kopenhavn.

Ellis, H. S., 1949, 'The State of the "New Economics" ', *American Economic Review*, 39: 465–77.

Gustafsson, B., 1973, 'A Perennial of Doctrinal History: Keynes and the "Stockholm School" ', *Economy and History*, 16: 114–28.

Gustafsson, B., 1974, 'Perspektiv pa den Offentliga Sektorn under 1930-talet', in *Krisir och Krispolitik i Norden under Mellankrigstiden*, Uppsala.

Hansen, B., 1969, *Fiscal Policy in Seven Countries, 1955–1965*, Paris.

Helmersson, E., 1972, *Svensk Krispolitik under 1930-talet*, Mimeo, Department of Economic History, Uppsala University.

Landgren, Karl-Gustaf, 1960, *Den 'Nya Ekonomien' i Sverige. J. M. Keynes, E. Wigforss, B. Ohlin och Utvecklingen 1927–1939*, Uppsala.

Lundberg, E., 1938, *Meddelanden fran Konjunkturinstitutet, Serie A*.

Montgomery, A., 1938, *Hur Sverige Övervann Depressionen, 1930–1939*, Uppsala.

Myrdal, G., 1933, *Konjunkturer och Offentlig Hushållning. Appendix III to the Budget Proposal 1933: 1*, printed in the yearly series of Swedish Parliamentary Papers ('Riksdag-strycket').

Myrdal, A. and Myrdal G., 1938, *The Population Question*, Harvard.

Steiger, O., 1971, *Studien zur Entstehung der Neuen Wirtschaftslehre in Schweden – Eine Antikritik*, Berlin.

Verney, D. V., 1955, *Public Enterprise in Sweden*, Liverpool.

Wigforss, E., 1954, *Minnen, vol. III*, Stockholm.

4 Innovation and conservatism in economic recovery: the alleged 'Nazi recovery' of the 1930s

Harold James

How different was Nazi economic policy from the strategies adopted by the presidential governments of the Weimar Republic? Often we make over-convenient assumptions about the 1930s: that in a system in which economics has become highly politicised, a new political system translates simply into a new economics; or that because Hitler said he was doing something new he really did innovate; or that political totalitarianism solved an economic problem.

The myth of a peculiarly Nazi 'economic recovery' had already been generated in the 1930s, and since then has served a wide diversity of political interests. At the time, it was termed the *Wirtschaftswunder* (Priester, 1936). The Nazis themselves needed to boast about their economic success. Weimar governments had, they claimed, failed to deal with the problems of an over-indebted and bankrupt countryside or with the crisis phenomenon of mass unemployment. A struggle for the survival of the German peasantry and a 'battle for work' became key ingredients in a Nazi propaganda campaign of considerable effectiveness.

Other observers had a different political argument, but reached the same conclusion: Nazi economics was working. Keynes saw the Nazi 'success' in dealing with evidence that market capitalism, unless regulated and managed through the actions of a politically liberal state, would succumb to the superior power of totalitarian economies. To him, the successes of Hitler and Stalin constituted a proof that the world needed economic management if democracy were to survive. Economic liberals drew the opposite conclusion. During the 1930s, and also after World War II, Wilhelm Röpke and Walther Eucken attacked the interventionist economy as inherently totalitarian. What more convenient way of discrediting economic interventionism than to show that it had been created by Nazi Germany? In international economics, Harry Dexter White made the same argument: at Bretton Woods in 1944 he tried to discredit the management of trade and financial flows, and Keynes's proposals for a new international economic order, by describing all this as 'the Schachtian system'.

Uncovering and exposing myth is an important part of the historian's task. The surprising conclusion provided by a study of the development of fiscal policy, of trade and currency strategy and of views of the appropriate mix between public and private activity is that 30 January 1933 did not mark a major turning point in Germany's inter-war economic history. Rather there existed substantial continuities between the course taken by Weimar's presidential governments and that of the Nationalist–Nazi coalition under Hitler's chancellorship.

Fiscal conservatism and work creation

Part of the confusion about the nature of Nazi economic policy stems from the ambiguity of the Nazi programme before 30 January. The Party was pulled in opposite directions, partly because of its socially highly heterogeneous support, and partly for the simple logical reason that promoting economic recovery conflicted with the goal of not appearing irresponsibly and dangerously adventurist. In the course of 1932, the Party's platform shifted frequently and dramatically. It often simply assumed that the Party would be able to overcome the existing 'system'. Hitler and his movement had pledged themselves to conduct a 'battle for work' (*Arbeitsschlacht*). In the electoral campaigns of 1932, the most explicit Nazi statement on work creation came from Gregor Strasser in his Reichstag speech of May 1932, which promised 10 billion RM spent on roads, agricultural improvements, and the resettlement of urban workers in the countryside. These measures were supposed to generate up to 2 million jobs, but the programme was soon attacked as being too inflationary, and in October 1932 a new programme only specified a spending of 3 billion RM.

The Nazi dilemma – of how to be expansionary without being inflationary – was by no means unique to that party. Almost every political actor in Depression Germany – political parties, labour unions, civil servants and ministers – faced a similar problem: some kind of action in the face of the economic crisis seemed a political necessity. Merely saying that nothing could be done, that the world Depression or allied reparations bore the blame for an insoluble predicament, looked like political ineffectiveness.

Political actors were expected to 'do something'. At the same time political action was perceived to run the risk of endangering established interests, or of threatening a new expropriation of workers and the middle classes through inflation.

The discussion about job creation in these terms went back to 1931. Already before the banking crisis of July 1931, which immediately weakened the economy further, employment projects looked like a way of dealing at least with the political consequences of economic crisis. In the course of 1932, discussion of job creation schemes had become a political commonplace. The trade unions in April 1932 drew up a major reflationary proposal at an Extraordinary Congress in order to be able to demonstrate to their members that they had adopted an activist approach. The Weimar governments, and even the fiscally highly orthodox Brüning regime, also believed that it was desirable politically to 'do something', though the actual outcome of that action might be uncertain.

In 1931 the Brüning government had instituted a commission to study unemployment as well as possible measures to reduce its extent and impact. Some of the Brüning ministers – especially the Labour Minister Adam Stegerwald and the Finance Minister Hermann Dietrich – pushed hard for work creation measures. In April 1932 the Cabinet agreed to 'economic pump priming' (*Wirtschaftsankurbelung*) to the extent of (a rather modest) 135 million RM. In the last months of the Brüning government unemployment policy acquired a major political significance. However, before the Brüning schemes could begin to operate, the government had been dismissed by von Hindenburg. Von Papen's larger scale approach developed on the foundations laid by his predecessor. The chief element was an indirect stimulus to job creation: the payment of tax credits as a subsidy to employers who would hire new workers (linked with permission to pay wage rates below the negotiated level). Only a relatively small sum – 167 million RM – was devoted to direct job creation. The Papen package led to 15,169 new jobs in textiles and 12,638 in mining: in other words, the immediately visible impact was slight in a country with over 6 million registered as being without a job (Wolffsohn, 1977, pp. 62, 101). Papen's successor von Schleicher turned to direct job creation in place of the subsidisation of private business, with 500 million RM allocated.

The link between political popularity and the ability to create jobs through government action had been established already before 30 January 1933. From 1933, the Nazi regime tried to make a propaganda success out of work creation measures. Support for house construction and renovation (extending a scheme already introduced by von Papen) involved 332 million RM in subsidies and 667 million RM in loans. Tax concessions for motor vehicles (10 April) encouraged a rapid recovery for automobile production. In July 1933 a general reduction of the corporation tax load followed. Direct work creation measures (chiefly in the so-called Reinhardt Programme) amounted to a total of over 5 billion between 1932 and 1935 – though it should be borne in mind that this represents only about 1 per cent of GNP for this period, in quantitative terms not a substantial stimulus (Grebler, 1937; Overy, 1982; 1987; Schiller, 1936).

The schemes for work creation were supplemented by direct administrative regulation of the labour market: from 1933, young males were sent to work in agriculture, and if they refused they lost their entitlement to unemployment benefit. Females were encouraged to leave the work-force through marriage loans (but even though the Depression had increased the share of females in employment the number of women employed – though not the proportion – still rose after 1933). A voluntary labour service (*Arbeitsdienst*) had been established already by Brüning in the emergency decree of 5 June 1931 as a way of supporting 'unemployed workers' through land improvement, the creation of rural settlements and small allotments, local road-works and sewer construction. This scheme remained in operation after 1933, even though Hitler had written to Papen that it had 'no value either economically or in any other way' (Köhler, 1967, p. 250). In June 1935 Labour Service became compulsory.

The Nazi work creation programmes bore a similarity to conservative proposals during the Depression, advocated by figures such as the Lord Mayor of Leipzig, Carl Goerdeler. This vision saw economic policy primarily in terms of socially corrective policy – bringing workers back to the land and away from the trouble spots of the big cities. It had little in common with the schemes proposed during the course of 1932 by the left and the labour movement, in which an important part of the policy had been the expansionary effect of creating employment with public funds at the current wage rate.

The period of voluntary labour service under Nazi rule could hardly be reckoned as a large-scale experiment or as a radical innovation. The *Arbeitsdienst* paid low rates for highly labour-intensive projects of the ditch-digging or road-building kind. Between 1932 and 1935 the number of men working in the *Arbeitsdienst* actually fell. Another category of workers taken into state-run projects – 'emergency workers' – had a similarly limited effect on the labour market. The number of workers employed in this way reached a peak in 1934, but the scheme was then cut back and in the winter of 1934/5 only a trivial 6 million RM out of the Reich budget was spent on the project, (Overy, 1987, p. 261; Wolffsohn, 1977, p. 48).

The relatively meagre resources directed towards work creation contrasted oddly with the propaganda image of a regime that would get Germany to work. Two contrasting political pulls operated: on the one hand, the need to demonstrate success in the battle for work; on the other, the widespread fear of budgetary expansion and inflation. The traumatic effects of the post-war inflation produced a deep scar on the German collective memory which influenced both decision-making and popular debate. During the Depression, accusations of being inflationary formed a stock-in-trade of almost every political movement.

At the Harzburg rally of the National Opposition (October 1931), as the Nazis and the old right moved closer together, the former president of the central bank (Reichsbank) Hjalmar Schacht accused the Brüning government of preparing a new inflation. Hitler in April 1932 explained that inflation would be produced by the currently ruling parties: 'the specialists in inflation are sitting in the parties which now rule the state'[1]. On the other hand, the parties of the left – Sozialdemokratische Partei Deutschlands (SPD) as well as Kommunistische Partei Deutschlands (KPD) – charged that the right wanted a repeat of 1918–23 in order to strengthen the position of the big farms and trusts, and to wipe out their debt at the expense of Germany's small savers. This charge led to the swings and shifts in the Nazi economic programme in 1932. Hitler felt that the Strasser re-employment programme offered ammunition to the left in the mutually reciprocated propaganda war of inflation smear stories, and forced the withdrawal of this platform. Fear of doing anything that might be considered inflationary remained a powerful motive in 1933, both in the election campaign, and in announcing the success of work creation. In 1934, when claiming successes in the battle for work, Hitler still needed simultaneously to explain with emphasis that 'the German Mark has remained stable' (Domarus, 1965, p. 448).

Another argument for fiscal conservatism came from the German bureaucracy. Among officials in the Finance Ministry and the Reichsbank a widely held interpretation suggested first, that the major government anti-cyclical programme of 1925/6 had not been very effective in generating employment; and second that the Depression was a result of the high level of government deficits in the mid- and late 1920s. In consequence, tackling the Depression required fiscal constraint rather than abandon. But this was an interpretation not confined simply to Treasury civil servants. In 1931 Hitler is claimed (by Otto Wagener) to have objected to large work creation schemes on these grounds, as well as because of the inflation argument. He attacked the Nazi economic specialist Bernhard Köhler who had been arguing that the state should print money to deal with the slump: 'That's exactly what previous governments have done. *They* pour money for unemployment relief down the drain' (Turner, 1978, p. 332). 'Keynesianism', or expansionary fiscal policies, might endanger the propaganda image of a party espousing respectability and stability.

This caution presented problems within the National Socialist movement. The Nazis – as a catch-all protest party that purported to offer patent solutions to any and every problem Germany might face – certainly attracted a generous sprinkling of fanatics who saw currency experimentation as a panacea for economic difficulties. Köhler or Gottfried Feder (who had drawn up a reflationary or inflationary scheme which involved the progressive demonetisation of money in order to encourage spending) or even the highly eccentric pair Max Roosen and Werner Kertscher (who tried to assassinate the central bank president in 1932 in order to call attention to their currency views) found in the Nationalsozialistische Deutsche Arbeiter-Partei (NSDAP) a suitable vehicle for their proposals. They remained marginal men, however, and in the course of 1933/4 the Party and the government redefined themselves in an increasingly conservative way.

For a time, the economy's future lay open and discussion blossomed as the Nazi theorists attempted to make their point. The great opportunity for a fundamental restructuring of the economy along lines of state socialism or corporatism or monetary experiment was the great Bank Inquiry of 1933/4. This presented the chance for which many would-be experimenters were so eagerly waiting. The Inquiry had the task of investigating reforms for a financial sector that in 1931 had broken down completely; it would be easy to implement any proposals since the bank crisis had left a considerable part of the financial system in the hands of the state. Already on 13 July 1931, the day the Darmstädter Bank's collapse became public knowledge, the Ministry of Justice began to investigate legislation to limit the purchase and ownership by a company of its own shares – a manipulation that had contributed to the outbreak of the bank crisis (Born, 1967, p. 152). The Brüning government then started to intervene systematically in the banking sector: removing bank directors responsible for mistaken policies, appointing a State Commissar for Banking as the price for public aid, imposing audit requirements for banks, and regulating interest rates. The Inquiry's purpose was to systematise, and perhaps extend, the Brüning measures concerning Germany's banks.

At the Inquiry, the Nazi 'experts' at first set the tone: Wilhelm

Keppler, for instance, explained that in a proper order, banks and 'capital' were supposed to 'serve' the people and the economy, but that finance had made itself into the 'master of the Economy', not the servant. He wanted municipally owned savings banks to expand their activity at the expense of the private banks. Yet these views were quickly set aside.[2]

The Nazi theorists were allowed to state their theories, and these were then ignored. Indeed Reichsbank President Hjalmar Schacht was quite keen to boast that this was precisely his plan.

Dr Schacht replied that the whole object of the Inquiry in his view was to let all the people with new theories talk themselves out, and to bring them face to face with competent experts, who would give the real answers to their theories. Dr Schacht would confine himself in the main to asking questions. The Chancellor [Hitler] seemed to him absolutely sound and was always prepared to take good advice. Dr Schacht believed in fact the party theorists would have no great influence in this affair.

'My strong point', concluded Schacht in speaking of the Bank Inquiry, 'is my modesty. You see, I shall let the others do all the discussion and take all credit, and I shall see myself that all the right measures are put through.'[3]

Schacht's account corresponded to the actual conduct of the Inquiry. In one of the sessions, the chairman, Vice-President Dreyse of the Reichsbank, noted: 'I can establish that the discussion has ended with a complete victory of the bankers and bank directors.' Another banker expressed his delight that 'the tasks of bankers were recognized in the new Reich'.[4]

The 'right measures' that Schacht spoke of were indeed implemented by the new Bank Law of 5 December 1934, which regulated the *ad hoc* bank supervision erected under the terms of the emergency decree of 19 September 1931, and laid down reserve provisions for major loans. The limitation of dividends to 6 per cent (law of 29 March 1934) was intended to bring down interest rates (and make bonds and state paper relatively more attractive than shares, rendering the public financing of the state debt easier). It was a more sophisticated and better thought out version of the interest reduction laid down in the Brüning emergency decree of 8 December 1931. Whereas the Brüning decree had increased the confusion and uncertainty of Germany's financial markets, the March 1934 law did indeed stabilise – and then increase – bond prices (and cut interest rates). It hardly needs to be pointed out that the new measure could not be seen as the outcome of a Nazi war on capitalism.

The same fear of dangerous experimentation also marked the initial Nazi approach to fiscal policy: the result was pragmatic, cautious and surprisingly orthodox. The Brüning government had increased the general deflationary pressure by putting up taxes – and had in the process made itself great enemies. Yet the Nazis on the whole left taxes at the high levels set during the Depression: with the exception of the tax reductions provided in the work creation programme (for house construction) and for automobiles. State Secretary Reinhardt of the Reich Finance Ministry actually argued that there should be no major tax reform until the first Nazi priority – the reduction of unemployment – had been accomplished[5]. There would be no large-scale bonfire of Brüning's tax decrees. From a modern, or a Keynesian, perspective this appears a bizarre order of priorities, but there existed among Nazi policy-makers no concept of providing an economic stimulus through a general reduction in tax burdens (as opposed to specific fiscal stimuli).

Conservatism prevailed when it came to the issue of how to fund public deficits. Once more the legacy of the past left a suspicion of unsound finance – with the public, with the financial community and with the civil service. Such government deficits as did emerge after 1933 were carefully camouflaged. Deficits appeared as 'anticipations of future revenue' in the accounts. The work creation programme for instance was largely paid for through tax certificates (*Steuergutscheine*), paper which might be used at a future date to settle Reich tax liabilities, and which in the meantime could be discounted by the banking system. These certificates had been used in Papen's September 1932 programme as a subsidy to those employers who hired extra workers. Schleicher used them to raise the 500 million RM for public works. After 1934 a new concealment device was employed, the subsequently notorious Mefo-Bill, (a bill supplied by a company, Metallurgische Forschungsgesellschaft mbH, to armaments suppliers, which could be discounted by the central bank but which did not appear to be a liability of the German government). This again was a consequence of the regime's obsession with avoiding the appearance of strain on the budget, as well as in order to keep secret the extent of rearmament.

Even allowing for all these concealment devices, the fiscal expansion of the early years of Nazi rule was initially rather limited. Work creation measures had accounted for just over 1 per cent of GNP. The macro-economic picture of the budget is equally unexciting. Government deficits altogether represented 2.2 per cent of GNP in 1933/4, 3.6 per cent 1934/5, and then 5.2 per cent in 1935/6. As Arthur Lewis pointed out in 1949, this rise of the public sector borrowing requirement from a relatively modest level to increasingly inflated proportions over the course of the 1930s means that Nazi economics cannot be taken as an experiment in Keynesianism:

Unfortunately the German experiment ceased to be helpful just as it was
becoming interesting. What interests economists in this sort of situation is
whether, after heavy government expenditure has set recovery in motion
in this way, private investment will start to grow cumulatively, and so
make it possible for government expenditure to be curtailed without the
system collapsing once more ... From 1935 the German economy ...
becomes only an illustration of the workings of a war economy, detailed
examination of which, now that we have all had the same kind of experience, is tedious for any but the specialist. (Lewis, 1949, p. 96)

When large deficits appeared, they followed as a consequence of
rearmament, rather than from the intention of giving a fiscal
stimulus. In 1936, military spending more than doubled (on the
army and navy it rose from 1735.7 million RM to 3596.4 million
RM, for the air force from 1035.7 million to 2224.7 million).[6]
Already before 1936, military spending (some of which was camouflaged as work creation) had been a substantial element in recovery. From 1934, rearmament had had some impact on employment,
so that, for instance, by 1936 the German air industry employed
more workers than did automobile manufacture (Overy, 1987,
p. 272). After 1936, the political restraints on military spending
were lifted entirely.

But even after the swelling of the fiscal stimulus in 1935/6, and
the turn towards a war economy in 1936, the deficits were financed
in a relatively orthodox and anti-inflationary way. The pressures
exerted by a public worried about the security of savings bank
deposits continued to influence the government. It treated the
purchase of state paper as a sort of daily financial plebiscite about
the regime: recalling the events of 1916, when German citizens had
suddenly stopped being willing to buy Reich loans. Until the end of
1938 in fact private purchases of government loans continued, and
only after this did the share of government debt held by the banking system rise dramatically.

This interpretation of Nazi fiscal policy as substantially orthodox
– even as carrying over many of the deflationary dogmas of the
Depression era – may seem surprising to those weaned on a historical literature which emphasises the concealment devices, semi-
secret spending and rearmament. It was, however, an interpretation of the Schacht period (1933–6) that was widely held at the
time. Contemporary observers found it hard to say precisely what
was innovative about Nazi approaches to economic policy. For
instance, in March 1935 a Bank of England memorandum stated
that Schacht was contemplating an 18 per cent budget cut. 'Is he in
fact contemplating a form of deflation which seems quite beyond
the imagination of all post-war democratic politicians, yet which is
well within the scope of National Socialist thought, which is in fact

in complete harmony with their economic ideology, namely budget deflation on a large scale?' In fact, of course, the Nazi regime never came near to enacting such a dramatic austerity campaign, not least because it was frightened of the social and political destabilisation that such a step would entail. But later that year, Pinsent, the Financial Secretary of the British Embassy in Berlin, was still quoting Schacht as saying that 'under present conditions the standard of living in Germany must fall': and Schacht's attempts in late 1935 and 1936 to restrict the import of consumer foodstuffs (and especially fats) did amount to a squeezing of general living standards.[7]

How do we account for economic recovery in the face of all this conservatism in policy? Part of the recovery doubtless was an illusion, created in 1933 by imaginative use of statistics. The unemployment figures were cut at a stroke in July 1933 by 619,000: emergency relief workers, members of the Labour Service, those employed in Land Help or in public relief. Even the manipulation of employment figures can, however, account for no more than around 200,000 additions to the employment series (Silverman, 1988).

By now historians and economists, who for over fifty years have wrestled with the problem of accounting for the 'Nazi economic recovery', have concluded that there can be no single explanation, and that a large number of causes played a role.

The price control mechanism for agriculture by means of the Reich Food Estate (*Reichsnährstand*) in 1933 helped to halt a price decline that had threatened to plunge Germany's farmers into bankruptcy, and also to bring down the credit system. But the institution of price support coincided with the lowpoint and then a recovery in world food prices, with the result that a Nazi political apparatus reaped some of the acclaim that might more properly have gone to the international commodity market. From 1935, price controls in agriculture had an opposite effect: prices were held down, increasing the disposable income available to urban workers.

Motorisation was a deliberate National Socialist strategy, fostered by the abolition of the tax on new automobiles (10 April 1933), and, most famously, by the public construction of highways (*Autobahnen*). The Nazis undoubtedly exaggerated the employment-creation effects of this. In 1933 the maximum number of people employed in constructing *Autobahnen* was 3,900; in 1934 8,863; in 1935 115,675; and in 1936 124,483. Including all those employed in supplying the construction sites (the secondary work creation effect) as well as the administrative machinery organising the building drive, no more than 250,000 were estimated to have been employed on the *Autobahnen* at any one time (Ludwig, 1974, p. 333; Overy, 1975).

How far the 'motorisation' of Germany in the 1930s, and in particular the indisputable rise on car production and sales, was a consequence of government policy is also debatable. Relative to Britain or France, Germany was underdeveloped as a market for automobiles in the 1920s. Partly this was because of the excellent railway system, which made alternative transport less attractive. Also, tax policy in the 1920s had curbed automobile sales, in part because such sales entered into the computation of Germany's capacity to pay reparations under the 'prosperity index' provided in the Dawes Plan. The growth of the 1930s may have been in part simply a making-up of a deficit in automobiles incurred in the previous decade, although the catching-up process clearly benefited from sympathetic government policy.

The most convincing case that government action led to recovery has been made for building and construction. Public spending on housing – one of the major investments of Weimar governments – had been cut back in response to the fiscal crisis that afflicted all levels: communal, state and central.The new regime reversed these cuts, and gave tax concessions for house renovation and the breaking up of old large apartments into smaller units. According to one calculation, employment in building (including road-building, also a favourite for Nazi spending) increased by 276 per cent from February 1933 to February 1934, while in iron and steel the corresponding rise was only 20 per cent (Lee, 1988, p. 141).

The combination of government spending, altered taxes, and an existing housing shortage (in marked contrast to the position in the USA) allowed a rapid rise in the German building industry. By 1936, spending on construction had overtaken that of any year in the 1920s[8] (Overy, 1982, p. 49).

On the other hand, it is difficult to account adequately for the early stages of recovery with this explanation. In 1934, when the recovery was already under way, building was at 74.8 per cent of the 1928 level, while textiles stood at 99.7 per cent, and foodstuffs at 97.1 per cent. Producer goods output was 76.1 per cent of 1928, consumer goods 93.0 per cent. The most dramatic rise of all was in automobiles (136.3 per cent) (Wagemann, 1935, pp. 49–50). The figures of producer goods recovery look very much more impressive, it is true, if presented as recovery figures, from the depression low, since the collapse in output had been most severe there.

Of course, if the Nazis had cared less about building, recovery would have been slower, but it looks implausible to take construction as the driving force on the road out of depression. In addition, retrospective critics of the Brüning government who claim that the large sums spent on agricultural support would have been more wisely spent on building (Lee, 1988; Witt, 1982, pp. 400–401), miss both a political and an economic point. Such a diversion of funds would have been unacceptable to the farming lobby whose political influence extended over all the major parties, as well as over Reich President von Hindenburg. It would have also been detrimental to the economy as a whole, since bankruptcies, defaults, and an endangering of the whole credit system would have been the consequence.

The most plausible view of the early stages of recovery – the first two years, 1933 and 1934 – would be as a relatively spontaneous cyclical recovery: a rise in consumption (benefiting all consumer goods, but especially automobiles); and an increase in inventories (which had been run down to unusually low levels during the Depression, in large part as a consequence of the 1931 financial crisis). 1933 was the first year since 1928 in which inventories had increased: the increase is largely accounted for by artisan business, and by trade and commerce; in industry there was still a very small net disinvestment. By 1934, all inventories were increasing (*Statistisches Handbuch*, 1949, p. 604). The prospering consumer economy suffered a major shock in 1934 when a new currency shortage led to a reordering of Germany's trade and a cutback in imports. By allocating raw materials, the supply of consumer goods was curtailed. There were also signs of quality deterioration in consumer goods. Finally after 1934 the maintenance of high (and unKeynesian) rates of taxation further deterred consumption. From 1935, public investments and rearmament took over from where the consumer boom of the early Nazi period had left off, and the Nazi *Wirtschaftswunder* turned into a display of producer goods dynamism.

Public investment had already reached 1928 levels by 1934, and in 1936 private industrial investment also passed the 1928 mark (Lurie, 1947, p. 23; *Statistisches Handbuch* 1949, p. 605). By 1938 producer goods had reached 135.9 per cent of their 1928 value, while consumer goods remained at a lowly 107.8 per cent.

Until 1934/5, then, we are dealing with a rather different phenomenon than that usually associated with the Nazi era. At first there was a surprisingly dynamic 'normal' recovery; and after that a transition to a *Staatskonjunktur*, though one that preserved many aspects of the old fiscal conservatism. The change in policy occurred while recovery was already well under way; and it took place within the framework of rather orthodox policies. The use of administrative measures to tackle unemployment, coupled with an initially highly conservative fiscal policy, remained as a legacy of the Depression era. It would be hard to find here a Nazi revolution.

Trade policy and debt

Trade policy on the other hand appeared – according to the choice of perspective – as either innovative, or else as unscrupulous and devious. The related issues of trade and international debts had presented the central international economic difficulty of the world economic crisis. They were bound up in the following way: debtors attributed their defaults to the cession of capital flows, the worsening of their terms of trade, and the international spread of protectionism. Tariff protection offered a way of halting the deterioration of trade balances and could be defended as a measure calculated to allow the prompt – or at least the continuing – servicing of debt. Finally, measures designed to control currency movements could be used to disguise trade measures and thus reduce the probability and extent of retaliatory measures.

A tightly controlled exchange policy, regulation and restriction of debt repayment, and a push towards the bilateralisation of trade were the hallmarks of 1930s economies, and of the flight away from a liberal international order throughout the whole world. But all these features were particularly pronounced in the German case. Indeed they were generally referred to – and later condemned as – 'Schachtian economics'. Such controls of foreign transactions allowed greater room for domestic manoeuvre – by providing a framework within which could be applied domestic controls – of investment, capital movements and even (through the allocation of scarce raw materials) production levels.

'Schachtianism' is a misnomer for all this. In fact Germany had started to apply all the major elements of the 'Schachtian system' before the chancellorship of Hitler and before Schacht had been reappointed as President of the German central bank. Its progenitor was not Schacht but Reichsbank President Hans Luther. The new system began as a response to the bank and credit collapse of July 1931. Foreign currency had to be registered. Foreign loans were frozen in Germany. A law on payments abroad (1 August 1931) stopped the free operation of capital markets. The law also inaugurated a novel approach to trade issues: imports were divided into three categories (essential, necessary 'to a certain extent' and unnecessary) and the classifications used to issue permits (James, 1985, pp. 215–19). This early form of 'Schachtianism' lasted only a few months, though it appears to have struck a favourable response with some industrial leaders. Later, in March 1932, a memorandum produced by the Reichsverband der Deutschen Industrie (RDI) on currency control argued strongly against the launching of a tariff war (which would hurt relations with The Netherlands and the Scandinavian countries, all major importers of German manufacturing goods). But it also stated that 'the principle of not using currency policy in the service of trade policy has been exaggerated'.[9]

The method of running trade policy through semi-secret lists of undesirable imports had in fact produced initially too much bureaucratic complication, and in October 1931 foreign exchange was instead allocated to German importers as a share of the previous year's requirements: 50 per cent from May 1932 to February 1934. After February 1934, because of a growing shortage of foreign exchange, the proportions had to be reduced. By the summer of 1934, the old scheme was in collapse. Exchange was simply allocated each day at the Reichsbank between 5 and 7 p.m. according to what happened to be available.[10] Between January and September 1934, the German balance of trade was negative (deficit: 247 million RM), and the Reichsbank lost almost all its gold and foreign currency reserves (they dropped from 317 million to a trivial 79 million RM; at the beginning of 1933 they had still been 964 million RM and in December 1930 they had stood at 2,907 million).

In September 1934 a plan based on an openly explicit acknowledgement of the bilateral principle (New Plan) was adopted in order to restrict German purchases requiring foreign exchange. The trade balance of course reflected the extent of recovery in 1933/4: as the German economy grew, it sucked in more imports. In 1935/6 further expansion threatened the New Plan in turn, and obliged Schacht to cut back further on imports, which led him into a major political struggle with Robert Ley of the Deutsche Arbeitsfront and Walter Darré of the Reich Agricultural Estate.

At these moments of conflict over policy, in 1934 and again in 1936, there existed a choice only in a very fundamental sense: between a continuing and incremental process of detachment from the world economy on the one hand, and reintegration in the international economy on the other. The latter course would mean the end of bilateralisation, the repayment of debts, and the devaluation of the mark to a realistic rate. The terms of the debate, and the nature of the choice, had already been laid down in 1931.

What were the costs and benefits of these alternative courses?

The gains from isolation

Integration into the world economy would have been useless unless other countries would also be willing to reverse their own paths to protectionism and economic nationalism. Why should Germany be expected to give a lead? Central and Eastern European states waited for the traditional centres of the world economy to show the way. In consequence, the first moment when German devaluation looked possible was 1936, after the British–French–American tripartite pact on currency stabilisation. Germany alone could not bring the world back to multilateralism.

Some German economists and businessmen looked favourably at the prospect of a hiatus from the world economy, a 'time out', as it were, a spell when they might be protected by the combination of artificial exchange rates and currency control. Businessmen from the traditionally protectionist coal and steel industries were not enthusiastic about agricultural protection, partly because of its effects on the cost of living and thus on wage demands, and partly because of the hostile reactions from exporters of agricultural goods to Germany. A very comprehensive list of the aims German businessmen hoped to achieve before their economy was reintegrated into the world is provided by the steel and engineering industrialist Paul Reusch in July 1932 in a letter to Max Warburg. Reusch had an influential voice in these matters: he was one of the German representatives on the Board of the Basel Bank for International Settlements:

As I have already told you in person, I agree with your view that at present currency experiments cannot be contemplated. But once the German public budgets are set in order, once the internal situation is clarified and stabilized, once England has stabilized her currency, and, above all, once the reparations issue is settled, we should devalue as soon as possible to the same extent as sterling is devalued against gold. Only so will industry be capable of exporting again.[11]

This letter states very powerfully the case that devaluation could only be beneficial if undertaken with a balanced budget. The prerequisite for an economic recovery on conservative lines – fiscal rectitude and a destruction of the labour movement – were in place by 1933, but even after this there were few industrial voices raised in favour of devaluing. A visiting British banker in October 1933 found only one German openly in favour of devaluation – the export manager of the Vereinigte Stahlwerke.[12]

Domestic political considerations were paramount in keeping Germany on the isolationist tack. Here there was little change from Brüning to Hitler: both were highly sensitive to popular fears of inflation. A devaluation might mark the beginning of a new inflation. Inflation trauma not only obstructed fiscal expansion, it stood in the way of currency devaluation.

Hitler drew the lesson of World War I that inflations had a socially destructive effect: 'the last war was lost because of a limitless lack of understanding for the susceptibilities of the masses of small savers and housewives.' 'I have pledged my word. I will not make inflation. The people would not understand it.' (Rauschning, 1940, pp. 195–6; Turner 1978, p. 401). One of the key indicators as to whether a new inflation was taking place was the exchange rate: in 1922/3 the daily dollar quotation acquired immense significance as the chief guide to the mark's loss of value. Rumours about devaluation and inflation did indeed circulate in 1935/6: the Gestapo reports for instance give instances of Schacht's speeches being cited as evidence that the German currency 'was without real backing, only a fiction'.[13] Popular fears as well as Hitler's obsession made devaluation a highly precarious choice in domestic political terms.

There were also foreign political calculations. The large volume of foreign debt frozen in Germany after 1931 gave German policy-makers a valuable negotiating weapon. In 1932 fear for the security of commercial debt in Germany played a major part in softening up Britain and the USA for a reparations solution at Lausanne. After July 1932 and the end of reparations, foreign debt was still used in the same way – to secure, for instance, more favourable treatment of German fish exporters by the British; or, more politically, in the case of the Special Agreement of 4 July 1934 to reassure Britain about German intentions after 30 June 1934.

While political issues – concern about the pace of German rearmament, about the nature of German goals in south-east Europe, or about the treatment of German Jews – might pull the western powers together and create alliances such as the Stresa Front of 1935, economic themes had the reverse effect. Von Neurath explained in 1933 how economic measures might be used

in order to avoid under all circumstances warlike complications, which at the present time we cannot cope with . . . By means of a statement that the objectives of our policy are exclusively economic and financial we can succeed in breaking up the front that has now been formed against us because of concern about the possibility of surprise actions on the part of Germany. (Schmidt, 1981, p. 223)

Debt frozen in Germany, and the wish of foreigners to unfreeze it, formed the key element in a strategy of encouraging 'economic appeasement'. All participants in the game of currency control and debt blocking knew that Germany's foreign exchange resources were limited, and that the creditors stood in a competitive relationship with each other. The British hoped for preferential treatment of their commercial debt; Schacht held out the possibility of exporting more cotton to the USA; the Swiss were promised more German tourism and repayment on short-term debt. 'Debt divides' and 'Bilateralism breaks apart' might be taken as the slogans for German economic diplomacy during the 1930s.

The costs of autarky

Servicing loans in an orderly way may often be the best way to obtain new money. Although the Nazi leaders sometimes expressed the hope that Germany might find new international credits, they never undertook serious steps to obtain them. Indeed in the conditions prevailing on the international capital market in the 1930s, the prospect for fresh inflows of capital into Germany looked bleak. As a result, an argument based on credit as a reason for moving back into the world economy carried little conviction and played little role in German calculations.

German exporters were immediately affected by the overvaluation of the mark. After the British (1931) and then the US (1933) devaluation, German prices were 30 to 40 per cent above the world level. Part of the German response to September 1931 involved the intensification of deflation, in the December 1931 Emergency Decree, in an attempt to drive down German prices to British levels. But there were also other ways of making good the German disadvantages. Exporters received some compensation through a diversity of schemes to subsidise 'additional exports' (by taking payments in blocked marks, or in scrips, or by repurchasing foreign domiciled German bonds at a discount and then reselling them at the higher prices prevailing on the German domestic market). In the case of the bond repurchases, Germany's frozen debt actually provided one way out of the problems caused by the German failure to abandon exchange control.

The amount of the export subsidy varied wildly, depending on the firm concerned, the commodity, and the country to which the export was being made. Gerhard Kroll states that the subsidy lay anywhere between 10 and 90 per cent of the value (Kroll, 1958, p. 492). This was a highly bureaucratic process, which famously produced enormous amounts of paperwork. The scheme operated through twenty-five Price Examination Centres for Exports (*Preisprüfungsstellen für die Ausfuhr*); by the time of the New Plan, forty forms were required for each export transaction. Such bureaucratism undoubtedly irked German exporters: Göring was even able to play with the dissatisfaction of German exporters when he began his campaign to succeed Schacht as economic dictator. On the other hand, it did offer the government a gigantic element of control: there was the advantage for the state of being able to regulate very carefully business contacts with foreigners. And the defenders of the scheme could also argue that after 1933 German exports grew at a faster rate than did the general level of international trade.

Some German manufactures dependent on imported goods suffered. The industry most affected was textiles: already in March 1934 imports of raw materials for textile producers had been cut back severely in response to the worsening situation for foreign exchange. The New Plan made a further cut. An index of textile production (1928 = 100) reached 105.1 in May 1934, a reflection of the staggeringly quick recovery in some consumer goods. But it then fell, to 93.8 in October 1934 and 88.6 by August 1935. Whereas in April 1934 German wool-weaving employment was 88.4 per cent of capacity, by the end of the year the equivalent figure was 73.4 per cent (Wagemann 1935, pp. 283, 287). It was not only textiles that were hit by the foreign exchange control bottle-neck: it was politically highly significant that by 1935 there were even signs that armaments producers were unable to get the raw materials they needed.

After 1933, Schacht toyed with the idea of a devaluation that would solve all the problems of German exporters and manufacturers, and reverse the road to autarky. By 1936, he had surprised foreign observers by making himself into the public champion of the world economy. If a devaluation did not mean abandoning a fixed parity, but merely shifting from one fixed rate to another, the danger of inflation could be reduced. Thus he spoke in 1933 that: 'he had pledged himself not to go off gold, but had never pledged himself not to lower the parity . . . He thought on the other hand that merely to depart from the gold standard in Germany would almost certainly cause a panic in the German population.' In 1934 he complained to US Ambassador Dodd about the economic national-ism of the 1930s: 'The whole modern world is crazy. The system of closed national barriers is suicidal and we must all collapse here and the standard of living everywhere be reduced. Everybody here is crazy. And so am I. Five years ago I would have said that it would be impossible to make me so crazy. But I am compelled to be crazy.' In November 1935 the British Ambassador in Berlin reported: 'I learn from a reliable source that Dr Schacht would seize a favour-able opportunity to devalue the Mark to sterling level.'[14] In September 1936, the issue of devaluing became acute once the tripartite stabilisation pact had been concluded. Should Germany join the Western countries? Schacht was apparently in favour, but any move was blocked by Walther Funk, the State Secretary in the Propaganda Ministry (and Schacht's eventual successor as Economics Minister). Goebbels's diary entry records: 'Spoke with Funk. He prevented a German inflation. Schacht wanted to devalue as well. But Funk went straight to the Führer. And he intervened.'[15]

Schacht's change of mind to pursue the path of rejoining the world economy scarcely reflected the political calculation of costs and benefits. In general in the 1930s, only one state which had embarked on exchange and trade control and debt freezing reversed its policy (the exception is Austria in 1936, which was taken back into the world of the controlled economy by the 1938 *Anschluss*).

For Germany, not devaluing and remaining at the old mark parity was the logical outcome of the decision to take as the foundation of policy the popular fear of inflation. The calculation that the political gains of not devaluing and not reintegrating in the world economy outweighed the economic gains from such a course was a choice that had already been made in 1931.

The mixture of public and private

How far did the public/private mix reflect Nazi ideology? It is not hard to find in Nazi writings statements calling for a state socialism. Hitler personally believed that private business had failed. 'The role of the bourgeoisie is played out', he claimed. The captains of industry were 'gullible fools' (Rauschning, 1940, pp. 26, 44). In 1936, the Four Year Plan was accompanied by a threat that if private business failed to accomplish the national task the state might easily intervene in its place.

In the course of 1933, the institutional framework of German business life was completely reordered: the old interest organisation the Reichsverband der Deutschen Industrie was dissolved and replaced by a Reichsstand (Reich Estate). The new professional organisations excluded Jews, and thus marked the first step in the driving of Jews out of German business life.

At the same time labour politics were completely transformed by the destruction of the free (socialist) trade unions on 2 May 1933, and the subsequent surrender of the Christian and liberal unions. The economic consequences of these political steps ruled out a repeat of the wage push that had occurred in the later 1920s, and had then severely reduced the profitability of enterprise and in general weakened Weimar's economy. For instance, as late as 1935/6, when parts of the economy showed signs of overheating, real gross hourly earnings for the iron and steel industry actually fell.[16]

As the old professional organisations and the labour unions collapsed, it seemed inevitable that the state should move into the vacuum and that the state's power should grow. Yet until 1936, the Nazi state made little use of its new-found strength.

The first problem concerning the legitimate scope of political activity in the economy concerned the banking industry. As a consequence of the collapse of 1931 and the rescue attempts of the Brüning government, a large part of the capital of German banks was owned by the state: 91 per cent of the Dresdner (merged with the Danat Bank), 70 per cent of the Commerzbank, and 35 per cent of the Deutsche Bank. The Deutschnationale Volkspartei (DNVP) Economics Minister Hugenberg suggested placing both the Dresdner Bank and the Gelsenkirchen steel works (another victim of the Depression that had been rescued by the state) under the management of the Central Reich Cooperative Bank (Reichszentralegenossenschaftskasse) so that both institutions could be used to support bankrupt agricultural enterprises. Hitler refused: 'he feared that such a foundation would be criticized either as concealed state socialism or as an attempt of big capital to assert itself'. Reforms would 'take time'; nothing could be done at the moment. Hitler's response captures the tentative nature of Nazi policy in the recovery phase[17].

The Bank Inquiry of 1933/4 produced, as we have seen, few fundamental changes: it merely set a supervision for large loans, and limited the number of Supervisory Board seats that any one banker might occupy. Instead of using the banks as a base for the creation of a socialised credit sector, the financial institutions were turned back to the private sector. The Deutsche Bank bought out the Reich already in 1933 by selling off an empty building. In 1936, the Commerzbank used the bourse to secure a privatisation, and in October 1937 the Dresdner Bank had completed the process of ridding itself of Reich ownership (Pohl, 1982, pp. 398–403).

The second major clash concerning the place of private business occurred only in 1936/7. It involved the Four Year Plan, the extent of German autarky, and in particular the use of German iron ore. Now the conflict was settled in a very different and much more radical way. It was a political tug-of-war contest between business and the state which German industry lost humiliatingly. Schacht attempted – rather late in the day – to form an alliance with the steel industry of Rhine–Ruhr in his struggle with the other Nazi leaders, Darré, Ley and now particularly Göring. He believed that business would attempt to resist Göring's plans for autarky and, in particular, the schemes for the creation of a steel works, the Reichswerke Hermann Göring, with capital raised from the private steel works, and the plans for the development of German iron ores. On 5 August 1937 Schacht sent Göring an ultimatum: an increase in the domestic production of raw materials would strain industrial capacity, result in a collapse of exports, and make it impossible for Germany to undertake strategically necessary imports. 'I am unable', he concluded, 'to raise the means for projects whose extent and duration are as difficult to ascertain as their effectiveness. The provision of banknotes and book money does not mean the provision of raw materials and food. It is impossible either to bake bread with money or to cast cannons' (Kroll, 1958, p. 521). Schacht also drafted a memorandum which was presented by Albert Vögler of the Vestag to other steel industrialists. But in a dramatic meeting on 24 August 1937, and after very obvious pressure had been applied by Göring, the united front of Rhine–Ruhr business crumbled. Business gave in, Schacht was abandoned, and he had little choice except to give up the Economics Ministry (Overy, 1985, pp. 313–40; Riedel, 1973, pp. 208–26). At this stage it was clear that the conservative phase of Nazi policy-making had come to an end.

Conclusion

The verdict on the early period remains surprising. Until 1936, the evidence supports the conclusion that Nazi policy-makers had, in Knut Borchardt's phrase, limited *Handlungsspielräume* (room for manoeuvre). A rather unadventurous and conservative policy, following the lines laid down by previous governments' responses to the world Depression, coincided with a staggering economic recovery. From January 1933 to July 1935, recorded employment rose from 11.7 million to 16.9 million (Wagemann, 1935, pp. 15, 16). It is remarkable that a return to virtual full employment should occur within the confines of a policy still dominated by the preconceptions and prejudices of the Depression era. The implication is that any government could have reaped the rewards that the Nazis harvested with such propagandistic insistence; or that, as regards economic policy, 'it did not have to be Hitler' to produce recovery.

Yet Nazism made very powerful claims to have inserted its ideology into everything, including the economy. At the beginning of 1935, the *Völkischer Beobachter* boasted: 'all these capitalist institutions have received a new foundation. The system is an instrument in the hands of the politicians. Where capitalism still believes itself untouched, it has already been harnessed to politics' (Barkai, 1977, p. 109). How do we reconcile radical claims of this kind with other observations on how little had changed? In 1939, C. W. Guillebaud concluded:

It would not appear that, in adopting this policy, the Germans were governed by considerations based on economic theory and analysis, but rather by the necessities of the situation in which Germany found herself in 1933 . . . there is no evidence to show that the original policy was influenced at all by abstract theories. In so far as there could be said to have been an economic theorist of early National Socialism, Herr Gottfried Feder, who belonged to the extreme left-wing of the Party and subsequently fell into disfavour and obscurity, would seem to have the best claim to the title. Dr Schacht has been the financial genius of the new economic system, but the agricultural and industrial controls have mainly been worked out empirically by the civil servants and administrators, with some regard to war-time methods, e.g. those developed in England in 1917–18. (Guillebaud, 1939, pp. 215–16)

Nazi economics may initially be described as the extension of something rather non-ideological: a reaction to the Depression in the context of a controlled trade economy. As a consequence of the world economic crisis, Germany was isolated from the problems she had encountered when she had, in the 1920s, attempted to integrate herself into the world economy. After 1935/6, this gave way to a rearmament economy in which the room for political influence was much greater. Under the Four Year Plan, the scope for state direction of investment increased, and Germany became a state-planned economy.

Governments in depression have less room for manoeuvre, and less space for the intrusion of political ideology, than governments which are wrestling with recovery and economic success, when more options become available. At the beginning of the Nazi dictatorship, the scope for the application of ideology in economics was severely limited. It may be that the 'primacy of politics' (Mason, 1966) can only be established in favourable economic circumstances. On the other hand, a movement as intensely ideological as National Socialism could not bear to admit the extent of the limitations it faced, and so dressed up conservative policies in more populist and more lurid propaganda guises.

Historians have wondered how to assess the workings of economic policy in the Third Reich. In a remarkable passage, Peter Hayes (1987) presents a graphic and vivid analogy:

It is perhaps accurate to say that, to German industry, the emergent economic system was still capitalism, but only in the same sense that for a professional gambler poker remains poker, even when the house shuffles, deals, determines the ante and the wild cards, and can change them at will, even when there is a ceiling on winnings, which may be spent only as the casino permits and for the most part only on the premises.

Yet by 1933 this was already a familiar scene. Weimar's economy had already been highly politicised. Furthermore, the politicisation of the economy – and the association of successful politics with economic triumph – represents one of the reasons for the Nazi response, and for the insistence with which it pushed its propaganda image.

At the London Conference (July 1931) which recommended a voluntary freezing of credits to Germany in the wake of the financial crash, the prominent German banker Carl Melchior spoke to the State Secretary in the Finance Ministry, Hans Schäffer in the tranquil setting of St James's Park:

What I have just experienced means the end of a way of life, certainly for Germany, perhaps also for other people. Today we have renounced the rules on which rest economic relations between peoples. That means that in the future common values are no longer in force. These disturbances will extend to other areas and I fear that those who experience this will see things of which today none has any idea. Even the actors who will be called to play in this drama today still know nothing of it.[18]

What more perspicacious interpretation of 1931 could have been made?

The German economy as it emerged out of the economic crisis and out of the breakdown of 1931 was susceptible to a great deal of political and bureaucratic pressure. The Nazis did not – it hardly needs to be pointed out – inherit a well-run market economy and then proceed to turn it into a state-dominated command system. Instead they added layers of regulation and reglementation onto an already extensively regulated and reglemented system.

The contrast between Nazi economics and Weimar control during the 1920s can be reduced to two major breaks in continuity. The two structural changes that moulded the shape of the 'Nazi economic recovery' (which was in fact already under way from 1932) are first, the control of wages and the destruction of the labour movement, which removed the wage pressure experienced by the 1920s economy whenever output expanded; second, a dedication to cutting Germany off from the world economy through the instruments of frozen debts, trade regulation, and an over-valued exchange rate. Both of these 'innovations' can hardly be said to come from Nazi ideology; they had been elaborated as a bureaucratic/governmental response by the Brüning government in the second half of 1931. It was then that the rules of the capitalist game were fundamentally altered.

Notes

1 *Völkischer Beobachter*, 6 April 1932.
2 Bundesarchiv Koblenz (BAK), R2/13682, Proceedings of Bank-Enquête, session of 6 September 1933.
3 Bank of England (BoE), OV34/5, 6 October 1933 and 17 November 1933. G. H. Pinsent notes on interviews with Schacht.
4 BAK R2/13683, Dreyse on 24 November 1933, Kauffmann on 29 November 1933.
5 *Die deutsche Volkswirtschaft* 1933, p. 554.
6 BAK R2/21781 July 1939 memorandum 'Entwicklung der Ausgaben in

den Rechnungsjahren 1934–1939'.

7 BoE OV34/6, 11 March 1935 Overseas and Foreign Dept. Memorandum: 'The Export Problem'; Pinsent account of 22 July 1935 interview with Schacht.

8 There is a general issue here involving how statistical material on recovery should be presented. Some commentators claim that 'the significant variable is not whether 1935 investment and employment had reached 1929 levels; it is the increase over Depression levels'. (Maier, 1987, p. 99). If we are concerned with demonstrating ways in which policy contributed to structural economic change, a comparison of the economy at equivalent levels of employment is unavoidable. Any depression will show a large drop in producer goods (usually involving construction), and in the recovery phase there is a correspondingly larger percentage increase in such industries even if only to return to the status quo ante. Such figures illuminate neither the intention (if any) behind government policy, nor the impact on economic structure.

9 BAK R11/1365, 23 March 1932 RDI Handelspolitische Kommission, and 11 March 1932 RDI Memorandum.

10 BoE OV34/6, C. Rogers, 3 August 1934, 'Memorandum on a Visit to Berlin'.

11 Historical Archive of Gutehoffnungshütte 400101251/0b, 3 July 1932, Paul Reusch to Max Warburg.

12 Midland Bank archive, 30/207, 13 October 1933 W. F. Crick, 'Report on a Visit to Germany'.

13 BAK R58/1127, 5 March 1935 Düsseldorf Gestapo Report.

14 BoE OV34/5, 17 November 1933. Pinsent note on interview with Schacht OV34/7, 8 November 1935 Phipps report. W. E. Dodd Jr. and M. Dodd (eds) *Ambassador Dodd's Diary* (London, 1941), p. 185.

15 Institut für Zeitgeschichte ED172/72, 30 September 1936, Goebbels diary entry.

16 BAK R43II/541 Lohnerhebungen. For example: from the summer of 1935 to the summer of 1936, effective gross hourly wages for skilled metal workers rose from 95.6 to 98.3 Pfennig, but fell for pharmaceutical workers from 101.7 Pf to 100.5 Pf; effective hourly wages for the iron and steel industry fell from the winter of 1935 to the summer of 1936 from 92.0 Pf to 91.8 Pf.

17 BAK R43II/244, 2 February 1933 Wirtschaftspolitischer Ausschuss.

18 Hans Schäffer, 'Carl Melchior' (Manuscript).

References

Barkai, A., 1977, *Das Wirtschaftssystem des Nationalsozialismus: Der historische und ideologische Hintergrund 1933–1936*, Cologne.

Blaich, F., 1976, 'Die "Grundsätze nationalsozialistischer Steuerpolitik" und ihre Verwirklichung im Dritten Reich', in F. W. Henning (ed.), *Probleme der nationalsozialistischen Wirtschaftspolitik*, Berlin.

Borchardt, K., 1982, *Wachstum, Krisen, Handlungsspielräume der Wirtschaftspolitik: Studien zur Wirtschaftsgeschichte des 19. und 20.*

Jahrhunderts, Göttingen.

Borchardt, K., 1985, 'Das Gewicht der Inflationsangst in den wirtschafts-politischen Entscheidungsprozessen während der Weltwirtschaftskrise', in G. D. Feldman (ed.), *Die Nachwirkungen der Inflation auf die deutsche Geschichte*, Munich.

Born, K. E., 1967, *Die deutsche Bankenkrise: Finanzen und Politik*, Munich.

Domarus, M., 1965, *Hitler: Reden und Proklamationen 1932–1945: Kommentiert von einem deutschen Zeitgenossen*, Munich.

Grebler, L., 1937, 'Work-Creation Policy in Germany 1932–35', *International Labour Review*, 35: 329–51, 505–27.

Guillebaud, C. W., 1939, *The Economic Recovery of Germany*, Cambridge.

Hayes, P., 1987, *Industry and Ideology: IG Farben in the Nazi Era*, Cambridge.

James, H., 1985, *The Reichsbank and Public Finance in Germany 1924–1933*, Frankfurt.

James, H., 1986, *The German Slump: Politics and Economics 1924–1936*, Oxford.

Köhler, H., 1967, *Arbeitsdienst in Deutschland: Pläne und Verwirklich-ungsformen bis zur Einführung der Arbeitsdienstpflicht im Jahre 1935*, Berlin.

Kroll, G., 1958, *Von der Weltwirtschaftskrise zur Staatskonjunktur*, Berlin.

Lee, J. J., 1988, 'Policy and Performance in the German Economy 1925–1935: A Comment on the Borchardt Thesis', in M. Laffan (ed.), *The Burden of German History 1919–1945*, London.

Lewis, W. A., 1949, *Economic Survey 1919–1939*, London.

Ludwig, K.-H., 1974, *Technik und Ingenieure im Dritten Reich*, Düsseldorf.

Lurie, S., 1947, *Private Investment in a Controlled Economy: Germany 1933–1939*, New York.

Maier, C. S., 1987, 'The Economics of Fascism and Nazism', in C.S. Maier *In Search of Political Stability: Explorations on Historical Political Economy*, Cambridge.

Mason, T., 1966, 'Der Primat der Politik: Politik und Wirtschaft im Nationalsozialismus', *Das Argument* 8: 473–94.

Mason, T., 1977, *Sozialpolitik im Dritten Reich: Arbeiterklasse und Volksgemeinschaft*, Opladen.

Overy, R. J., 1975, 'Cars, Roads and Economic Recovery in Germany 1932–8', *Economic History Review* 28: 466–83.

Overy, R. J., 1982, *The Nazi Economic Recovery 1932–1938*, London.

Overy, R. J., 1985, 'Heavy Industry and the State in Nazi Germany: The Reichswerke Crisis', *European History Quarterly* 15: 313–40.

Overy, R. J., 1987, 'Unemployment in the Third Reich', *Business History* 29: 253–81.

Pohl, M., 1982, *Konzentration im deutschen Bankwesen 1848–1980*, Frankfurt.

Priester, H., 1936, *Das deutsche Wirtschaftswunder*, Amsterdam.

Rauschning, H., 1940, *Gespräche mit Hitler*, New York.

Riedel, M., 1973, *Eisen und Kohl für das Dritte Reich*, Göttingen.

Schiller, K., 1936, *Arbeitsbeschaffung und Finanzordnung in Deutschland*, Berlin.

Schmidt, G., 1981, *England in der Krise: Grundzüge und Grundlagen der britischen Appeasement-Politik*, Opladen.

Silverman, D. P., 1988, 'National Socialist Economics: The Wirtschaftswunder Reconsidered' in B. Eichengreen and T. Hatton (eds), *Interwar Unemployment in Historical Perspective*, The Hague.

Spenceley, G., 1979, 'R. J. Overy and the Motorisierung: A Comment' *Economic History Review*, 32: 100–106.

Statistisches Handbuch von Deutschland 1928–1946, Munich.

Turner, H. A. (ed.), 1978, *Hitler aus nächster Nähe: Aufzeichnungen eines Vertrauten 1929–1932*, Frankfurt.

Wagemann, E., 1935, *Konjunkturstatistisches Jahrbuch 1936*, Berlin.

Wendt, B.-J., 1971, *Economic Appeasement: Handel und Finanz in der britischen Deutschland-Politik 1933–1939*, Düsseldorf.

Witt, P.-C., 1982, 'Finanzpolitik als Verfassungs- und Gesellschaftspolitik. Ueberlegungen zur Finanzpolitik des Deutschen Reiches in den Jahren 1930 bis 1932', *Geschichte und Gesellschaft* 8: 386–414.

Wolffsohn, M., 1977, *Industrie und Handwerk im Konflikt mit staatlicher Wirtschaftspolitik? Studien zur Politik der Arbeitsbeschaffung in Deutschland 1930–1934*, Berlin.

5 Searching for recovery: unbalanced budgets, deflation and rearmament in France during the 1930s

L. D. Schwarz

By whatever criteria it is examined, the performance of the French economy during the 1930s was singularly unimpressive. From a dominant position in 1931, with one-quarter of the world's gold reserves, an apparently well-founded economic boom, a confident system of banking and credit and a relatively stable price level, the French economy declined and then stagnated, with production typically at around 80 to 85 per cent of the peak of 1929; gold progressively left the country and France came to depend economically, as well as militarily, on its alliance with Britain and the support of the United States. Even though the situation was not entirely bleak, and many signs of economic progress can be seen, especially in the field of industrial productivity, the failure was sufficiently impressive to haunt a generation of Frenchmen after the war, irrespective of party (Carré, Dubois and Malinvaud, 1972, pp. 287–90, 611–23).

As is well known, the policies of successive French governments towards the Depression appeared to alter sharply in 1936. Until then, conservative governments had sought, on the whole, to deflate and had set their faces against devaluation. After 1936, with governments more or less inclined to the left, there were successive devaluations and heavy spending on rearmament.

1930 to 1936: maintaining the conditions for recovery

French economic policy during the 1930s was, until recently, regarded as the height of folly. Alfred Sauvy, the doyen of this school, regularly described it as a combination of Gallic hubris and grotesque ignorance. The decade did not begin badly. Tardieu, Premier in 1930, inherited a budget surplus and planned to spend it in advance of the 1932 elections. It is doubtful whether he ever conceived such spending as anti-cyclical, but this nevertheless was the outcome. After this act of accidental wisdom, all is supposed to have been stupidity. The French did not devalue, so they were forced to deflate. The one advantage of a failure to devalue, cheaper import prices, was negated by the tariffs put on agricultural imports to protect farmers. The French, it was claimed, failed to understand the implications for their own economy of the British and American devaluations. Indeed, governments were not able to balance their budgets successfully; from a peak in the autumn of 1931 capital haemorrhaged from France. In 1935 Laval came to power and cut all the prices he could by 10 per cent. This was painful, but still insufficient to compensate for the higher level of French prices. With his deflationary policy blatantly failing, the way was left open for its reversal with the victory of the Popular Front in the 1936 elections.

More recent work has examined the context in which policy decisions took place, showing that while economic policy may have been wrong, it is at least comprehensible. So far as policy-making was concerned, neither hubris nor ignorance was much in evidence. It is necessary to counter the widespread view that the mistakes of French economic policy can be accounted for by an exceptional degree of ignorance of basic economics. Keynes was notoriously of this opinion: he informed the Macmillan Committee in 1930 that 'both in official and in academic circles in France it is hardly an exaggeration to say that economic science is non-existent' (Keynes, 1930, p. 154). This was the typical exaggeration of a Cambridge man. French knowledge of economics was not uncommonly poor by international standards, while the French parliament was probably no less ignorant than most other legislatures. The senior civil service and the Treasury were, by comparable standards, not unduly sclerotic.

It has become commonplace to denigrate French awareness of economics during this period. The subject was taught in law faculties where it was the poor relation. It was on the whole conservative and relatively inflexible, but such conservatism was not peculiar to France. In any case, it is by no means certain that a considerable acquaintance with Keynes's writings before the General Theory would have helped governments to have escaped the worst effects of the Depression. If the French suffered from conservative economists, their bankers – as conservative in matters of credit as their counterparts in Britain – had at least accepted the undervalued franc Poincaré. It was Moreau, as governor of the Bank of France, who advised Poincaré in 1926 that the rise in the value of the franc should be checked; it was Poincaré who had wished it to rise further (Moreau, 1954, p. 573).

As for the Treasury was concerned, it was staffed by *inspecteurs des finances*, the *crème de la crème* of the highly competitive and meritocratic French educational system. They were young: Wilfrid Baumgartner, at their head between 1933 and 1936 and his successor Jacques Rueff both had some thirty years of active life ahead of them. They were dynamic: many would have successful careers outside the civil service, and all had studied some economics. Given the very traditionalist *laissez-faire* economics that they studied, this may have been a drawback in the 1930s, but they did not all have closed minds. In the 1930s Rueff deservedly earned the reputation of being a monetary conservative, but he had advised the Governor of the Bank of France in 1926 that the rise in the value of the franc should be checked lest its further appreciation should cause unemployment and economic stagnation. In 1958, as eminent as he was conservative, he was advising de Gaulle on the highly successful devaluation of the franc carried out in that year (Rueff, 1959). Baumgartner progressed to being Governor of the Bank of France between 1949 and 1960, which suggests some capacity for redemption. Another inspector translated Keynes' General Theory within a year of its publication in England, circulating the sheets around the Treasury as he translated it, while Emmanuel Mönick, financial attaché to the French Embassy in London from 1934, was pressing for devaluation from his arrival in London.

None of this, however, denies the existence of a high degree of innate conservatism. If Baumgartner developed to be a central banker with whom the post-war planners could (just) manage to live, Rueff did not. To a certain extent, the economic conservatism of the inspectorate can be attributed to a recruitment process that may have stressed adaptability rather than originality. This was not a feature peculiar to the French civil service. But, as will be shown later when discussing the problems of finance, the conservatism was also pragmatic. The French 'Treasury view' was not particularly 'French'.

In the world beyond that of the economists, the Treasury and the Bank of France, the degree of ignorance of the consequences of economic policy was by no means as extreme as has sometimes been assumed. The financial press and the politicians were perfectly aware that the devaluation of sterling and the dollar posed a serious problem (Margairez, 1977, pp. 72–3). The attachment of successive French governments to their currency was perfectly in keeping with ordinary European preferences, and was not a particularly French neurosis, at least not at first. Borchardt has shown that in Germany there was no pressure group worth the name willing to advocate a devaluation in 1931, and indeed, that it is not easy to see how the German economy would have benefited from such a devaluation. Given the tendency of German asset holders to panic, those who argued that the German government should above all seek to restore confidence had a very strong case (Borchardt, 1984). In France there was no pressure group of any importance that advocated devaluation before 1935, and very few advocated it openly before 1936. The Germans feared a repetition of their inflation of 1918–23; the French feared a repetition of 1924–6.

Any understanding of French policies during the 1930s must begin on 14 January 1924. On that day the franc, already worth only about a quarter of its pre-war value against the dollar, fell by 11 per cent against the dollar. The situation was remedied by a foreign loan, but the Radical victory in the election of 1924 set in train a panic that erupted in April 1925, with nine finance ministers in a single year, rentiers panicking and the government not knowing from one week to the next whether it would be able to replace the section of the public debt that was falling due. The exchange rate of the franc rose from 19 per dollar in April 1925 to 40 in July 1926. At this point a left-inclined National Assembly accepted the right-wing Poincaré as Premier, the speculation stopped very abruptly, and the franc was stabilised. In 1928 the stabilisation of 1926 was formalised at five times the level of 1913, a fifth of its gold value. This was widely understood to mean that four-fifths of France's wealth had been lost. It did not matter that GDP was 10 per cent higher than in 1913 or that industrial production was 28 per cent higher (Sauvy, 1972, iii, pp. 339–40). Gold cost five times as much. After this experience, the French had no intention of devaluing again. From 1931 to 1935 the refusal to consider devaluation was agreed by all parties. By 1935 many leading politicians and economists privately accepted its inevitability, but only one, Paul Reynaud, dared say so aloud. He was already advocating devaluation in 1934 and by putting himself in the position of Cassandra, he instantly lost all influence and credibility.

Perhaps it was to justify the psychological impossibility of conceiving another devaluation that the French produced a coherent theory of the Depression. Professing an attachment to the gold standard as vehement as that of the Bank of England in 1926, they insisted on the virtues of stability and discipline. France's immunity to the slump until 1931 – more apparent than real, but still widely believed to be the case – seemed to bear this out. The French claimed that because various nations had failed to operate the gold standard according to the rules, not deflating when they should have done, and because of the over-valuation of sterling, international prices had risen to heights far greater than were justified. Governments around the world had then attempted to sustain these prices with devices such as tariffs, marketing boards, or the stockpiling of surplus raw materials, all of which exacerbated this state of affairs. The inevitable result was the slump – 'l'heure de la pénitence, économique et financière' as Joseph Caillaux, head of the Senate's financial committee was fond of saying. Prices were now falling to realistic levels, which would at last permit healthy growth. From this perspective, all that the French had to do was to await the end of the slump, and while waiting, to ensure that the conditions for internal recovery were in place. This meant ensuring that the budget should be balanced (or at least appear to be balanced) thus maintaining public confidence and permitting lower interest rates and easier discounting. One then awaited an export boom, or for the return to capital to become sufficiently attractive to encourage fresh investment. It was not, French economists said righteously, their fault if other nations chose to experiment with currencies or with demand management (Mouré, 1991a, pp. 27–45; 1991b; Rist, 1934, p. 451).

The financial press regularly stressed that those nations that had not waited for the revival and had devalued would surely suffer a price–wage spiral that would leave them as badly positioned as previously, and probably worse, as there was no longer the discipline of the gold standard to prevent undue inflation. That such a discipline was necessary was something the French had learned between 1918 and 1926. They knew more about inflation than Keynes.

France's insistence on maintaining the value of its currency carried with it two crucial implications. In the first place, by precluding all experiments with the exchange rate, it put the onus on governments to deflate. Government policy would therefore have lowering the price level as its chief objective. The most straightforward means of reducing the domestic price level would have been to take advantage of lower import prices, a consequence of the over-valued franc. But no politician could resist the pressure to resort to the traditional French reaction to depression, namely the unveiling of a truly impressive armoury of protective measures, tariffs and import quotas. No political party that wished to achieve a share in power could ignore a constituency as large and vital as agriculture. Nor could they ignore the Radical Party, who held the balance of power in the Chamber. Radical in the pre-1914, Dreyfusard sense, they favoured the 'small man', artisan or peasant. The Radicals opposed any measures that might affect their constituency but supported conservative rather than left-wing governments because of their belief in the eternal laws of economic liberalism (except for tariffs) (Berstein, 1978). In addition, between 1924 and 1926 they had learned – it had been a painful lesson for them – to have the utmost respect for the powers of finance. Financially orthodox right-wing governments were therefore maintained in power, able to raise tariffs with little difficulty, but not permitted to deflate, at least not seriously.

The second implication of rejecting devaluation was that it required the budget to be balanced, a condition not difficult for the French to accept, given their earlier experience of the effects of alleged financial laxity between 1924 and 1926. If the franc was not to be devalued, if the capital market was not to be controlled and capital exports permitted to continue while there still remained sufficient funds for government and industry, it was imperative that the budget should be balanced. The problem was that governments could not achieve this. Budgets were in deficit from 1930, on a very rough estimate the deficit forming some 1 per cent of national income in 1930, 3 per cent in 1933, and about 4 per cent in 1935 (Mouré, 1991b, p. 132). Government fiscal policy was gently reflationary, even while monetary policy demanded the maintenance of an overvalued franc. Capital progressively left France, gold reserves and bank deposits declined, and it became increasingly difficult for governments to borrow money. The history of government finance between 1931 and 1936 could be summarised as the gradual realisation by the French elite that the budget could not be balanced even with the most serious efforts at deflation, that government revenues could not be balanced by borrowing on the money market, and that the only alternative to inflationary note issue by the Central Bank was devaluation.

This realisation took time to develop within government circles. It was not considered seriously in 1931. By 1932, when Herriot became Premier, the implications of the budget deficit were beginning to emerge. Herriot, the Radical Prime Minister of 1924/5, whose ability to achieve much had been successfully stymied by the *mur d'argent*, had learned his lesson and took immediate steps to reassure opinion by appointing the ultra-orthodox Germain-Martin as Minister of Finance. 'You have', wrote Gaston Jèze, one of the foremost theoreticians of orthodox finance, 'reassured the opinion of capitalists, and this is not to be neglected. It is a force that broke you six years ago, and which would break you again like glass' (quoted in Berstein, 1982, pp. 218–19). His Radical successors Paul-Boncour and Daladier, Sarraut and Chautemps, who alternated the premiership between themselves from December 1932 until February 1934 and who supported various right-wing coalitions until 1936, did not forget the lesson either. They lent support to a deflation they were unwilling to invoke themselves, progressively alienated grass-roots opinion in their party, and only seriously came to support reflation in 1936.

Nevertheless, in 1932 confidence was still sufficiently high for the Herriot government to undertake a successful major debt conversion (Mouré, 1991a, pp. 163–4). However, during the early months of 1933, the continuing budget deficit was proving increasingly alarming. The Paris banks had to be persuaded to subscribe to one-month treasury bills – normally this had been no problem – and in March a long-term loan gained only half the 10 billion francs authorised (Mouré, 1991a, pp. 166–7). By now the French governments were beginning to experience what successive German governments had experienced from 1928. In 1933 Daladier was telling Blum in the Chamber that 'academic debates about systems and doctrines . . . have great interest but we, the government, each week have to face the problem of bills falling due, we have to pay the employees of the nation' (Jackson, 1985, p. 214). The problem of 1924–6, that of funding the floating debt, was beginning to recur. It was imperative to maintain confidence.

The senior civil servant most responsible for advising the government on economic policy and more particularly on government finance was the director of the 'mouvement général du Fonds'. In 1933 he was Wilfrid Baumgartner, who advised the government:

The functioning of the Treasury depends uniquely on the maintenance of public credit, which depends in turn on a balanced budget. The sooner this is accomplished, the sooner we will be out of danger . . . a country like ours must understand that in order to safeguard its credit and its currency, it must commit itself without delay to a definitive rehabilitation of its finances.' (Mouré, 1991a, p. 168)

Hence the need to consolidate the floating debt and avoid the nightmare of 1924–6. But despite the French Treasury's many fruitless lectures on the importance of virtue, the floating debt could not all be consolidated. By 1934 the Treasury was finding it quite difficult to obtain its money and employed various expedients to make the situation better, expedients that would be repeated throughout the rest of the decade. These involved borrowing on anticipated revenues from governmental agencies such as the railways or the post office, creating special funds to entice the public, and resorting to the Bank of France. Most of the expedients involved not only the approval of the Chamber, who were reasonably accommodating in such matters, but also of the Senate, the guardian of French financial morals, who were not accommodating at all. In addition, until 1936, the gauntlet of the Bank of France usually had to be run: like all central banks, it saw its primary task as safeguarding the currency; when that was achieved it could help to produce a little economic stimulation. At the beginning of 1935 the Bank was asked to advance money to the Treasury; it did so very reluctantly and sparingly. During 1935 the problem became worse. Flandin, Premier since November 1934, dismissed the Governor of the Bank of France, but his successor was hardly more successful in influencing the regents (Jeanneney, 1976, pp. 507–40).

During the course of 1935 it was becoming clear to the Treasury that without devaluation the budget could not be balanced; if there was no prospect of the budget being balanced the domestic money market would not accept government paper. The very budget balancing that was so necessary to maintain confidence in the currency, however, was itself impossible unless the currency was devalued. It was also clear that if a devaluation was anticipated, the capital outflow would become a haemorrhage, as had happened during the 1920s. This was amply demonstrated in the wake of the devaluation of the Belgian franc in March 1935. It led to greater export of French capital, a consequent running down of French bank balances and additional difficulties for the government on the Paris money market.

With devaluation ruled out, Flandin had no choice but to deflate. At the beginning of April 1935 the Treasury warned him that the government would only be able to meet its payments in May and June if public confidence was maintained and expenditure kept down. In May the Treasury had to borrow from other government accounts and discount a post office loan to meet immediate payments (Mouré, 1991a, pp. 173–7). It was an excellent example of the vicious circle that the Treasury feared throughout the 1930s: budget deficits damaged confidence, which in turn led to gold losses, which in turn made it more difficult to renew treasury bonds. The inevitable result was higher interest rates and diminished revenues, which only made the slump worse, thereby further aggravating the Treasury's difficulties.

If devaluation was unthinkable, the logical outcome was deflation *à l'outrance*. Since Flandin could not be trusted to do this, he was replaced in June 1935 by Laval, who promptly decreed a 10 per cent cut of all those prices that he could control, including interest on government bonds and state contracts. Over five hundred decree-laws were passed in a matter of months. But deflation had its limits. Apart from the overwhelming political need to sustain agricultural prices – no French government could ignore agriculture – there was now the burden of defence expenditure, forced upon Laval by Hitler. The supply of treasury bills rose from under

10 billion francs at the end of 1934 to 14 billion at the end of 1935 (Jackson, 1985, pp. 224–5; Jeanneney, 1976, p. 534). The regents of the Bank of France had evidently rediscovered a spirit of cooperation. So had the Senate. As Pierre Mendès-France said later, the Popular Front government of 1936, which came to power with the avowed policy of neither devaluation nor deflation, was bequeathed devaluation in its inheritance (Blum, 1965). 'I was more a receiver in bankruptcy than an executor of an estate' said Vincent Auriol, Blum's finance minister (Auriol, 1945, p. 36).

Laval was brought down early in 1936 by the Radicals who increasingly doubted his democratic credentials. But his economic policy had not succeeded. There was some evidence of an economic upswing, barely noticed at the time; his attempts to balance the budget had failed. The legal limits for the floating debt were reached by the end of 1935. Baumgartner, the senior civil servant in the Treasury, presented his successor with four options. He could draw on semi-public agencies such as the *caisse des dépôts* and the *caisse d'amortissement* funds, but this had already been done to excess, and Baumgartner felt that these funds should be reserved for real emergencies. The second option, that of advances from the Bank of France, would alarm public opinion. Alternatively, the government could appeal to the public and issue bonds in small denominations, but these might be subscribed by money drawn from other deposits, such as defence bonds. The success of such a measure depended upon the extent that hoards were invested in treasury bills, and this was not considered very likely. That left a fourth possibility, foreign loans (Mouré, 1991a, pp. 183–4). During the course of February 1936 the French Treasury borrowed £40 million at 3 per cent from London. This was exhausted as soon as it arrived, so the Treasury fell back on railway loans and pressured the banks to renew their subscriptions to treasury bills. On 18 March, Baumgartner warned that the only remaining source of finance for an indefinite period was the Bank of France and that this would be inflationary (Mouré, 1991a, p. 185). However, the German reoccupation of Rhineland on 7 March 1936 had stimulated the Chamber's mind wonderfully, and on 20 March it raised the ceiling on treasury bills from 15 billion to 22.8 billion francs, to be spent on arms. The members were quite clear that this was inflationary. Orthodox finance would have insisted on security for such an increased ceiling; there was none (Frankenstein, 1982, pp. 127, 350n).

1936 to 1939: reflation, rearmament and rentiers

The Popular Front coalition of 1936 had a carefully considered economic strategy. During the 1920s the various European social democrat parties had tended to lament the bad fortune that brought them to power before the final destruction of capitalism. As a consequence, they felt themselves obliged to manage the economy by what their civil servants told them were the rules of the capitalist system. By 1936 the French Socialist Party had moved beyond this. The fate of the Weimar Republic forced them to be flexible. In 1934 the leadership, Léon Blum at its head, had formally rejected the concept of capitalist planning, despite its widespread popularity in the Party and among the trade unions. The reasons were partly practical – power meant alliance with the Radicals who would never support planning – but also doctrinal. It was too much for the Party hierarchy to accept in principle, despite Blum's sympathy for it in practice. To admit that they were in business to save capitalism was more than a social democratic party could accept in 1934. To make matters worse, planning had suspicious fascist overtones (Jackson, 1985, p. 150).

However fascism not only continued in Germany, but appeared to be rising in France as well; it had to be countered by as wide a coalition as possible, from the Communists to the Radicals. The necessity of working out a common programme with the Communists (who were very accommodating) and the Radicals (who were not) was the principal factor behind social democratic thinking after 1934. The emerging programme of 'neither devaluation nor deflation' was of course pre-ordained – no left-wing coalition could admit to the first or accept the second – as was much else, especially the repeal of Laval's most deflationary decrees. Nationalisation of the Bank of France – 'rescuing the nation from the 200 families' who appointed the regents of the Bank – and the armaments industry was acceptable to the Radicals, who blamed the Bank for most of their problems in 1924/5 and were unimpressed by its support for Laval and insistence on deflation during the 1930s. The development by the Popular Front of a programme of reflation based on increased purchasing power may have been an inevitable consequence of their electoral base, but it was a serious attempt to break with the orthodoxy of deflation.

The programme was based on the not unreasonable assumption that there was a large margin of under-employed resources in the French economy. A reduction of the working week – the actual number of hours was not specified in the election manifesto – without a decrease in wages would increase demand. Other measures, especially those designed to help agricultural prices,

would have the same effects. In view of the under-employed resources in the economy, and the (supposedly) low importance of
labour as a cost of production, the reflation would not in itself be
particularly inflationary. It was to be combined with a large programme of public works (Jackson, 1988, pp. 299–302). Increased
economic activity would increase revenues, so the budget deficit
would not be a great problem; as for the unfortunate deficit that
should arise in the interval between this stimulation and the
subsequent economic revival, the Popular Front wished, in effect,
to 'privatise' the government's bond issue, by appealing to the small
saver rather than solely to the banks.

An obvious weakness in the programme was its failure to recog-
nise that because of labour immobility a shorter working week
would not necessarily reduce sectoral unemployment to any
appreciable extent. Neither were its authors fully aware of the
coexistence of unemployment in some sectors with a looming labour
shortage in others. Another weakness, less excusable, was under-
estimating the cost to industry of introducing the forty-hour week.
Measured by direct labour costs, it was believed that a 20 per cent
increase in the cost of labour would raise finished prices by 8 or 9
per cent; however this calculation ignored labour costs in producing
primary and intermediate goods, which would themselves raise
industry's costs by a further 12 to 15 per cent (Asselain, 1974,
p. 682).

All its plans notwithstanding the Popular Front, on coming to
power in 1936, found itself faced with a nationwide occupation of
factories and negotiated the Matignon agreement, which involved
considerable wage increases and paid holidays as well as a forty-
hour week. Somewhat against the wishes of ministers, the forty-
hour week was introduced rather rigorously during the course of
1937: it raised costs while revealing a labour shortage. The forty-
hour week was unanimously blamed by the right wing for the
failure of the economy to revive: it was attacked and defended in
Manichean terms, with all the passion that had been visited upon
the eight-hour day in Germany during the early 1920s. It was
impossible to view it dispassionately. French investors awaited its
abolition as a sign that the Popular Front had indeed ended.
Towards the end of 1938, with a more right-wing government in
power, the law was not formally repealed – even Vichy did not do
that – but it was rendered ineffective and investors returned their
money to France in abundance, almost as though the threat of war
and of inflationary rearmament did not exist.

Nevertheless, the forty-hour week was by no means the sole
cause of the failure of the Popular Front to revive the economy. A
combination of reflation and price increases without devaluation

did indeed prove sufficient to rule out recovery between June and September 1936. Production fell and unemployment rose. Devaluation moved from being inevitable to being urgent as gold left France. However, after the devaluation of October 1936 the French economy joined in the international upswing; the introduction of the forty-hour week in industry after industry during the autumn of 1936 and the spring of 1937 produced (with the exception of coal) a barely perceptible slowing down in the rate of growth, at least at first. But the full effects of the law soon became apparent. Its rigid imposition had not prevented an upswing. Gross hourly productivity in 1937 has been calculated at 22 per cent higher than 1935; 95 per cent of work capacity was by then being utilised (Asselain, 1974, pp. 695, 697–9; Rossiter, 1987, pp. 663–84). However, the forty-hour law may have prevented the upswing from continuing into 1937. Twice during the course of that year, during spring and autumn, it appears to have been the limitation of working hours that caused industrial production to hit a ceiling some 15 to 20 per cent below that of the peak of 1929/30 and to be unable to progress through that ceiling (Asselain, 1974). The effects of the forty-hour week in 1938 are more debatable. Asselain does not believe that these were very noticeable, primarily because the year began in any case with an economic downturn and ended with government decrees that abolished the law in all but name. Villa's recent econometric analysis of the 1930s complements Asselain's approach by suggesting that the fundamental problem of the upswing of 1936/7 was not so much the reduction in the hours of work as the increase in the age of fixed capital. Taking into account the introduction of paid holidays, there was an overall decrease of 13 per cent in the number of hours worked; 10 per cent of this was compensated for by a growth in employment and 90 per cent by productivity gains. The loss in productive capacity by shortening the hours of labour was therefore one-tenth of 13 per cent, or 1.3 per cent.

To many historians, it is obvious that the economic policies of the Popular Front were a failure. There was no lasting economic upswing, no lasting increase in living standards. On the other hand, the devaluation of the franc provoked an economic upswing and full employment; its policies also included a substantial increase in rearmament as well as a reduction in the working week and paid holidays. If its economic policies failed, the conservative administrations that preceded the Popular Front had failed much more. Thanks to Villa's work, historians are no longer constrained to ask crude questions on whether the Popular Front's economic policies 'succeeded' or 'failed'. Macro-economic policy between 1936 and 1938 was, he maintains, responsible for real wages increasing more than they would have done without such policies. The same applies to GDP, and in 1936 and 1937, to consumption. Popular Front policies can even be said to have increased company investment in 1936, although not in 1937 or 1938. Villa also demonstrates that a more important and less known aspect of Popular Front economics – or more precisely, of the Matignon agreement – was that the reduction of capacity in 1937 and 1938 led to a fall in exports and in consumption, as well as a rise in prices (Villa, 1991).

The Popular Front government fell in June 1937 not on the issue of economic revival, but specifically on the question of finance. The rules of the financial game had changed with the nationalisation of the Bank of France and the devaluation of the franc in 1936. But they had not changed sufficiently to solve the problems of a left-wing government, and it was finance that brought Blum down in 1936, no less than it had brought down Herriot in 1925. It was the lack of finance that forced the Popular Front government to announce a 'pause' in the furtherance of its radical policies in February 1937; it was a similar lack of finance that led Blum to ask the Senate for additional powers in June 1937, and to resign when they refused. Finally, it was the availability of finance that made possible the quantum leap in arms production during the year before World War II. But it was the same demand for rearmament that had produced the financial crisis that led to Blum's resignation.

As Blum continually said, when he was in power he went to considerable lengths to stay within the letter as well as the spirit of the Popular Front's manifesto. Exchange control was in fact in the manifesto, but only as a formality. Neither the Radicals nor the Senate would ever have accepted it, while Blum had no wish to alienate Britain and the United States. He presumably hoped that devaluation – by adjusting the franc to a more realistic level – would be sufficient to lead to a large-scale repatriation of capital; an optimistic assumption in any case, and, as will be discussed, more than optimistic when faced with the costs of rearmament.

The urgent question between 1936 and 1939 was not what should be done to help France recover from the Depression, but the extent to which the liberal financial system was compatible with rearmament. This was a version of the popular debating issue of the 1930s, namely the extent to which democratic governments could produce recovery from the Depression. In 1937 rearmament and the liberal financial system appeared mutually incompatible: the Popular Front government fell, and under its successor the pace of rearmament was slowed down. In January 1938 funds for rearmament were increased, over the objections of the Treasury, and in March Blum formed his second government. Nobody had any illusions about its durability, least of all Blum, and it only lasted for a month. It was, however, significant, first because during that month it laid the plans for increased rearmament that governed French arms production until the outbreak of the war, and second, because of the powers that Blum requested from the Senate. Unlike 1936, Blum was now accepting the inevitability of war. To him this implied that unless labour were to bear most of the costs of rearmament there would need to be much stricter control over the financial markets. He proposed a large increase in personal taxation as well as taxation of surplus profits for those firms working for the national defence, but he also proposed something very similar to the Mefo Bills in Nazi Germany, by which Schacht had financed the early stages of rearmament. State contractors, especially defence contractors, would draw bills, thereby creating resources, since such bills could be discounted. Banks could use them as security for lending, if they wished. This was direct credit creation and as such would not be popular with the Senate (Hitler had no Senate with which to concern himself). For this policy to work, it was necessary to 'close the circuit', in order to stop the additional credit from leaking abroad, meaning the 'centralisation of exchanges by the Bank of France', or exchange control, although this could not be openly admitted (Frankenstein, 1982, pp. 183–6; Drummond, 1979, pp. 30–31; Jackson, 1988, pp. 185–6).

Blum's government fell in April, his unorthodoxy rejected by the Senate; the new government wished to continue rearmament and did not wish to have exchange controls; it was prepared – as were the Chamber and Senate – to continue drawing on the central bank. But the corollary of its refusal to embrace exchange control was to do its utmost to draw French capital back to France, not only for the sake of economic confidence and growth, but also to reduce inflationary pressures on the Bank of France. And the way to achieve this was less a strict balancing of the budget – which, after all, was not happening in England either – but an attack on the symbol of working-class power and influence. In Germany in 1929 and in Britain in 1931 socialist governments had fallen when confronted with the choice of either cutting the dole or cutting state expenditure drastically. In France in 1938 the equivalent symbol of sacrifice was the forty-hour week. Although not formally abolished, legislation enforcing the forty-hour week was promptly rendered ineffective. The conditions for profitable accumulation were thereby assumed by French rentiers to have returned, and gold flowed back to France in abundance. The French liberal financial system revealed that it could cope with rearmament and deficit finance, or at least it could do so by the later 1930s, when fund-holders seem to have become more resigned to unbalanced government budgets; they did not need a Hitler to give them confidence, but they did need a new Poincaré, and persuaded themselves in 1938 that they had found him in Daladier. This was an insight they had failed to have during Daladier's previous tenure of power in 1934. Controls were not strictly necessary for recovery, but they were necessary for recovery to be combined with social peace.

Rhetoric and reality

Until more research has been done on the French economy during the 1930s, historians will not be in a position to analyse the impact of government policies with any degree of precision. The purpose of this chapter has been to suggest some of the major constraints on French policy-makers. Devaluation was inconceivable until unavoidable. Thereafter rearmament had to be financed somehow; the confidence of those who held capital required to finance the resulting deficit remained low and the regime was not in a position to force them to repatriate their capital. French governments of the earlier 1930s had more freedom of action than, say, the government of Brüning had enjoyed, but this freedom became progressively circumscribed. The rhetoric, however, remained unchallenged.

It is clear that the historian of French economic policy during the 1930s needs to be particularly careful to distinguish rhetoric from reality. The difference between the two was glaring, even by the standards of the Third Republic. Not only is there the conventional distinction between what was desired and what was achieved – a problem inevitable with the analysis of all economic policy – but in the case of France during the 1930s the gap between what governments claimed (and may honestly have believed) they were doing and what they actually did was particularly striking. Right-wing governments, in power until 1936, insisted that they were deflating in order to balance the government's current account budget, but the budget deficit remained stubbornly large and government spending remained persistently high. The other purpose of deflation was to lower prices as an alternative to devaluation, culminating in the attempt by Laval in 1935 simultaneously to lower some prices by decree, increase others (especially agricultural prices) by tariffs and other regulations, and systematically increase the budget deficit by rearmament. The left had a different rhetoric, electing a government that, despite its sincerest intentions to the contrary, did more for guns than for butter and found it difficult to admit, even to itself, that rearmament inevitably involved taking resources away from its own supporters. The public, or at least the propertied public, were no more consistent: the ubiquitous small and large savers of France, who had behaved in a manner of textbook rationality by withdrawing their savings from France increasingly from 1934, returned them by 1938/9 on a rather large scale when a right-wing government was engaging in deficit financing in a manner not seen since the reconstruction of the war-damaged areas after 1918. Whether the Third Republic was suffering from terminal sclerosis or not, there can have been few decades in the history of France after the Revolution when such a medley of economic policies had been tried out, intentionally or not.

But throughout all the changes, there remained the inescapable problem of finance. In 1941 Jean Zay, a former Radical minister wrote in his prison diary:

From 1932 to 1940 . . . one subject was 'taboo': monetary and financial liberalism . . . You could cover the head of state and his ministers with dirt . . . Bravo! Fair enough . . . but you were forbidden to criticize the mystique of the balanced budget, under pain of being considered a traitor. (quoted in Shennan, 1989, p. 260)

This was true until 1936; it became progressively less true thereafter. However, it would not be too great an exaggeration to say that, with the exception of a few months of the early Popular Front government in 1936, the most urgent concern of successive French governments was not economic revival but how to find their money for the next few months. It occupied them to the point of obsession, but with reason.

That economic problems should present themselves to policy-makers as financial problems was a common inter-war experience. But in countries that had undergone a high degree of inflation after the war, the financial perspective was particularly pressing. The classic country in this respect was Germany, where confidence in the currency was lacking for well over a decade from 1923, and inflation was equated not with a gentle rise in prices but with a collapse of the currency. France was not Germany, but French fears of financial chaos were acute. The constraint thus imposed on policy was overwhelming. Problems with agriculture or with tariffs could usually be avoided. Tariffs could always be adjusted, while aid could always be offered to agriculture. The consequences, in French eyes, of an unbalanced budget could not be escaped so readily.

Nowhere were the constraints on policy felt more than within the ranks of the Radical Party, the party that held the balance of power in the Chamber throughout the 1930s, providing most of the prime ministers. Any doubts that the Radicals may have had about the wisdom of orthodox finance had been quelled in the storms of 1924–6. Their belief in the eternal verities of orthodox finance was overwhelming. They were torn between their objection to the conservatives' supposedly anti-democratic tendencies and the 'unsound' economic policies of the socialists. It was a contradiction that haunted the Radicals for the entire inter-war period. Like the mythical French rentier, their heart was on the left but their pockets were on the right; the Radicals had occasional flirtations with the left, but they usually ended up safely on the right.

It followed that the only period when politicians in power were willing to experiment with unorthodoxy was during the brief period when the Radicals were veering towards the left, which in the 1930s meant the Popular Front. But the Popular Front was overwhelmed, not by the Matignon agreements and the forty-hour week, as historians used to claim until recently, but more by the problems of financing rearmament. This drove them inexorably in the direction of 'sound' finance, as defined by those with money to lend or to repatriate to France. The Radicals may have been right to have opposed exchange control in 1938: after all, such had been the capital exports of the preceding years that the need to repatriate such funds was particularly urgent. The Radicals' support for the overvalued franc of 1931–6, their failure to support the degree of deflation needed to support the franc and their continuous flirtations with the Socialists were symbolic of the dilemma of French liberalism in the 1930s: how best to sustain the apparently eternal verities of the world before 1914 when faced with the urgent need to adapt to the consequences of a prolonged world depression.

References

Asselain, J.-C, 1974, 'Une Erreur de Politique Économique: La loi des Quarante Heures de 1936', *Revue Economique*, 31: 672–705.

Auriol, V., 1945, *Hier . . . Demain* I, Paris, Charlot.

Berstein, S., 1978, 'Les Conceptions du Parti Radicalism en Matière de Politique Économique Extérieure', *Relations Internationales*, 13: 71–89.

Berstein, S., 1982, *Histoire du Parti Radical ii. Crise du Radicalisme, 1926–1939*, Paris, Presses de la Fondation Nationale des Sciences Politiques.

Blum, L., 1965, *Actes du Colloque: Léon Blum, Chef de Gouvernement 1936–1937*, Paris, Armand Colin.

Borchardt, K., 1984, 'Could and Should Germany have Followed Great Britain in Leaving the Gold Standard?', *Journal of European Economic History* 13: 471–497.

Carré, J.-J., Dubois, P., Malinvaud, E., 1972, *La Croissance Française*, Paris, Seuil.

Drummond, Ian M., 1979, *London, Washington, and the Management of the Franc, 1936–1939*, Princeton Studies in International Finance, 45, Princeton.

Frankenstein, R., 1982, *Le Prix du Réarmement Français (1935–1939)*, Paris, Publications de la Sorbonne.

Jackson, J., 1985, *The Politics of Depression in France, 1932–1936*, Cambridge, Cambridge University Press.

Jackson, J., 1988, *The Popular Front in France: Defending Democracy, 1934–1938*, Cambridge, Cambridge University Press.

Jeanneney, J.-M., 1936, 'L'oeuvre Scientifique de Quelques Économistes Étrangers. viii. John Maynard Keynes.' *Revue d'Économie Politique* 50 (2): 358–92.

Jeanneney, J.-N., 1976, *François de Wendel en République. L'Argent et le Pouvoir, 1914–1940*, Paris, Seuil.

Keynes, J. M., 1930, *Collected Writings*, vol. 20 D. Moggridge (ed.) 1981, London, Macmillan, Cambridge University Press.

Margairez, M., 1977, 'La Droite Française Face à la Crise: Incompétence ou Choix Politique', *Cahiers d'Histoire de l'Institut Maurice Thorez*, 20–1: 69–88

Moreau, E., 1954, *Souvenirs d'un Gouverneur de la Banque de France*, Paris.

Mouré, K., 1991a, *Managing the franc Poincaré. Economic Understanding and Political Constraint in French Monetary Policy, 1928–1936*, Cambridge, Cambridge University Press.

Mouré, K., 1991b, 'La Perception de la Crise par les Pouvoirs Politiques', *Le Mouvement Social*, 154: 131–56.

Rist, C., 1934, Review of H. Truchy, *Traité d'économie politique* (1934) in *Revue d'Économie Politique*, 48: 451.

Rossiter, A., 1987, 'Popular front economic policy and the Matignon negotiations', *Historical Journal*, 30: 663–84.

Rueff, J., 1959, 'Sur un Point d'Histoire: le Niveau de la Stabilisation Poincaré', *Revue d'Economie Politique*, 69.

Sauvy, A. (ed.), 1972, *Histoire Économique de la France entre les Deux Guerres*, iii, Paris, Fayard.

Shennan, A., 1989, *Rethinking France. Plans for Renewal, 1940–1946* Oxford, Oxford University Press.

Villa, P., 1991, 'Une Explication des Enchaînements Macroéconomiques sur l'Entre-Deux-Guerres', *Le Mouvement Social*, 154: 213–43.

6 Hoover, Roosevelt and American economic policy during the 1930s*

P. Fearon

The Depression which began in the United States in 1929 was totally unexpected in its severity. Between 1929 and 1933 money income in the US fell by 53 per cent. If account is taken of the sharp deflation, the decline in real income – 35 per cent – was less, but still great. Table 6.1 shows the movement of GNP both in real and money terms from the beginning of the Depression until the outbreak of World War II. Using constant prices, GNP fell to a low point in 1933 and then recovered to a cyclical peak in 1937 by which time pre-Depression levels had just been surpassed. The recession of 1937/8 put a temporary brake on the recovery which, influenced by war demands, advanced again steadily from 1939. If the substantial price falls of the Depression are acknowledged in GNP calculations, the impact of the collapse is seen to be more severe. Even in 1937, GNP measured in current prices was below 1929 levels and remained there until 1941 (Badger, 1989; Chandler, 1970; Fearon, 1987). The dramatic fall in wholesale prices of 38 per cent between 1929 and 1933 was seen by many contemporaries as a serious destabilising factor leading to rising real debt and increasing business uncertainty. However, in spite of attempts to inflate the economy, prices were still 14 per cent below 1929 levels in 1940.

The most serious socio-economic problem to emerge after 1929 was unemployment, the course of which is charted in Table 6.1. From around 1.5 million persons in 1929, the jobless reached a peak in 1933 of 12.8 million. Moreover, many of those classified as employed worked a considerably shortened week with a consequent reduction in pay. Others, especially after 1931, experienced sub-

* I would like to thank Professor A. J. Badger and Professor S. B. Saul for their comments on a draft of this paper.

Table 6.1 Key economic indicators 1928–41

| | | | | | Unemployed | |
	GNP 1929 ($ bn)	GNP Current ($ bn)	Total labour force (000s)	Total non-farm labour force employed (000s)	Civilian force (%)	Non-farm employees (%)
1928	98.5	98.7	47,367	34,626	4.2	6.9
1929	104.4	104.6	48,017	35,666	3.2	5.3
1930	95.1	91.2	48,783	33,843	8.9	14.2
1931	89.5	78.5	49,585	31,065	16.3	25.2
1932	76.4	58.6	50,348	27,918	24.1	36.3
1933	74.2	56.1	51,132	27,962	25.2	37.6
1934	80.8	65.5	51,910	30,320	22.0	32.6
1935	91.4	76.5	52,553	31,563	20.3	30.2
1936	100.9	83.1	53,319	33,899	17.0	25.4
1937	109.1	91.2	54,088	36,068	14.3	21.3
1938	103.2	85.4	54,857	34,302	19.1	27.9
1939	111.0	91.2	55,588	36,028	17.2	25.2
1940	121.0	100.5	56,180	37,980	14.6	21.3
1941	131.7	124.7	57,350	41,250	9.9	14.4

Sources: Dept of Commerce, 1975; Kendrick, 1961; Swanson and Williamson, 1972–3.

stantial wage cuts. The agricultural sector, dominated by family workers, was not plagued with unemployment; if the national figures are calculated to exclude the farm labour force, historically high figures are forced even higher. In spite of the New Deal, unemployment remained at unacceptable levels until World War II.

Unlike Britain, the United States had a large agricultural sector; indeed 25 per cent of the total population lived on farms. Furthermore, many Americans resided in villages or small towns which owed much of their prosperity, or lack of it, to the ability of farmers to purchase goods and services. The political power of the farm sector can be seen when it is realised that in 1930 46 per cent of the population was classified as rural, that is dwelling in settlements of less than 2,500 inhabitants. Table 6.2 qualifies some of the problems facing farmers during the Depression. Prices fell dramatically, but farm costs did not fall as steeply as farm revenue; the parity ratio clearly illustrates the farmers' plight. This ratio is a division of an index of farm prices by an index of farm costs, multiplied by 100. The higher the index – it rose to 120 in 1917 – the better for farmers. They watched in dismay as it fell from 92 in 1929 to 58 in 1932, and looked to the New Deal to achieve normality, by which they meant 100.

American recovery policy can best be analysed by dividing our period into two: 1929–33 and 1933–41. Such a division is not meant to imply that there was nothing in common between the policies of the Hoover and the Roosevelt administrations. Both Presidents supported managed capitalism and both looked for inspiration to World War I when agencies which harnessed the talents of business and government had proved effective during a crisis. It is to the problems facing Herbert Hoover that we turn first.

1929–33: Hoover's Depression

The pattern of economic descent after 1929 was uneven, a factor which added to the difficulties of policy-makers. There were three periods of recovery during these dark years which, unfortunately, could not be maintained. First, automobiles and steel led a brief revival in early 1930; second, a more pronounced expansion based on textiles, shoes and tyres came in the first half of 1931; and finally a sustained recovery seemed to be a real possibility during the summer and autumn of 1932, only to evaporate by the end of the year (Mitchell and Burns, 1936). Periodically, Hoover was deluded into thinking that the worst was over and that policy measures recently taken were sufficient to pull the economy from its trough.

Even today there is no unanimity as to the origins and, more importantly, explanations of the severity of the Depression. The lack of a universally accepted theory some sixty years after the event helps to explain why contemporaries, who were forced to act in a highly charged atmosphere with grossly imperfect data, found policy-making so frustrating. A common theoretical division is between monetarists and non-monetarists or Keynesians (Brunner, 1981; Fearon, 1987, pp. 149–61). The theoretical framework to which monetarists adhere is that changes in the rate of monetary growth explain economic fluctuations. The principal source of instability in the economy between 1929 and 1933, according to Friedman and Schwartz (1963, pp. 229–419), was the monetary policy pursued by the Federal Reserve. It was not the capitalist system which was disaster prone; the destabilisation came about because of the inordinate power wielded unwisely by a few men.

Monetarists concentrate on the actions of America's central bank, the Federal Reserve System (the Fed) in search of an explanation for 1929–33. The Fed consisted of twelve regional reserve banks and a Federal Reserve Board with offices in Washington DC.

Table 6.2 US agriculture in depression

	1928	1929	1930	1931	1932	1933	1934	1935	1936	1937	1938	1939	1940	1941
Total farm population (million)	30.5	30.6	30.5	30.8	31.4	32.4	32.3	32.2	31.7	31.3	31.0	30.8	30.5	30.1
Net income of farm operators from farming (average per farm)	924	945	651	506	304	379	431	775	639	905	668	685	706	1031
Index of average value of farm real estate per acre (1967 = 100)	32	32	31	28	24	19	20	21	22	23	23	23	21	21
Index of total farm output (1967 = 100)	–	53	52	56	54	50	43	52	47	58	57	58	60	62
Parity ratio (1910–14 = 100)	91	92	83	67	58	64	75	88	92	93	78	77	81	93

Source: Dept of Commerce, 1975.

Control over the system was shared by the directors of individual banks and by the Reserve Board. The system was held to be politically independent; the Board members were difficult to remove from office, and although appointed by the president were not answerable to him. As the directors of the reserve banks were chosen from both banking and non-banking backgrounds, dominance by large commercial banks was avoided. In other words the Fed was a complicated compromise between those who felt that a central bank would give the financial system much needed stability and those who were apprehensive of the power such a body might wield.

From 1922 until 1927, the Fed entered a short but seemingly golden age. For much of the 1920s the New York Reserve Bank exercised great power. New York was a sophisticated banking centre with strong international links; it also had as its governor Benjamin Strong, a man of formidable personality. It was under his influence that the sales and purchases of government securities by the federal reserve banks were coordinated and used as a new policy tool, open market operations (Chandler, 1950, pp. 76–80; Friedman and Schwartz, 1963, pp. 251–4). The Fed came to realise that buying and selling securities brought about changes in credit. For example, if the Fed sold government securities this reduced bank reserves and, as a result, banks were forced into debt to the Federal Reserve. If this policy was reversed (i.e. the Fed buying securities) credit would become liberal and business expansion was encouraged. In 1923 the Federal Open Market Investment Committee was established by the Board in the belief that if the quantity and quality of credit was controlled, fluctuations in economic activity could be moderated. The Fed reached the conclusion that it could, by the use of open market operations and the discount rate, manage money so that business activity would be stabilised (Chandler, 1950, pp. 423–35).

During the 1923/4 recession the Fed bought securities and lowered discount rates and the economy recovered. From late 1924 through to 1926 securities were sold in an attempt to restrain an expanding economy. In 1927, during another recession, the use of open market operations was followed quickly by economic revival. Monetary interventions had another advantage: they made it easier for countries such as Britain and France to adopt the gold standard since lower interest rates discouraged gold inflows to the US. In spite of substantial gold movements into and out of the US, this was a period of price stability for which the Federal Reserve was given credit; fluctuations in seasonal interest rate movements seem also to have been eliminated (Friedman and Schwartz, 1963, pp. 292–8). It seemed that the track record of the Reserve as a stabilising force was good, but during 1928 the Fed became increasingly concerned about the growth of speculative pressure, especially on the New York stock market, and embarked upon a restrictive monetary policy. The discount rate at the New York Bank rose from 3.5 per cent in January 1928 to 4 per cent in February and 5 per cent in July. However, higher interest rates and open market operations had no effect on Wall Street; indeed speculation fever increased until the crash of October 1929.

The Fed exhorted member banks not to lend for speculative purposes, but was in no position to force banks to follow its advice even if it had been possible to distinguish between legitimate credit needs and speculative borrowing. It is probable that speculation could have been ended by tighter money and even higher interest rates, but the Board sensibly hesitated to embark upon a policy which it felt could bring about a serious business collapse. Moreover, the banking system was not the main source of the increase in lending to brokers. Major corporations, foreign banks and individuals found the market an irresistibly attractive venue for idle funds, especially at higher interest rates. Once Wall Street crashed the Fed reduced interest rates and began to buy a limited quantity of securities. Although there was a revival which lasted until mid-1930, the economy was set on a downward course for which the Federal Reserve has been blamed.

Friedman and Schwartz's account of events between 1929 and 1933 is clear. The key factor is that the stock of money in the economy fell by a dramatic one-third between these years. As a result aggregate demand and real output collapsed. The restrictive policies used by the Fed in 1928 and 1929 helped to check expansion by raising interest rates and by slowing the rate of growth of the money supply. From this point the economy was hit by a number of shocks, the first of which was the Wall Street crash, the remainder being episodes of banking panic. The first banking panic was evident in 1930, but more serious were those of March 1931, late 1931, and the winter of 1932/3. These crises brought a halt to periodic recoveries, but, most important, the bank failures and the determination of the public to convert deposits into cash brought about the decline of the money stock which was the reason for the Depression's severity. The Federal Reserve could have prevented monetary decline by pursuing vigorous open market operations. Instead, during times when the banking system was under great strain a perverse tight money policy was introduced which directly led to deepening depression. It was, therefore, intervention by the Fed which transformed a recession into a deep depression. Friedman and Schwartz insist that the Fed pursued the correct monetary policies during 1924 and 1927. Faced with economic decline they used open market operations to liberalise credit and the economy expanded. If the Fed had provided additional reserve funds to the banking sector after 1930, which it could easily have done, bank failures would not have been so great and the decline in the stock of money would have been arrested. The failure of the Fed to respond properly, according to Friedman and Schwartz, is explained by the death of Benjamin Strong in 1928. He had been the guiding hand in 1924 and 1927 but his successor had neither the vision nor the authority to embark upon the politics which Strong would have pursued had he lived (Friedman and Schwartz, 1963, pp. 412–14, 692–3).

Although monetary decline took place continuously between 1929 and 1933, it was most marked after the middle of 1931. In September 1931 Britain left the gold standard and speculators turned their attention from sterling to the US dollar. The Fed, fearful that the United States might be forced off gold, responded to a gold outflow by sharply raising the discount rate. This action was taken in spite of the fact that America had gained gold over the previous eighteen months and was precisely the opposite of the liberal discounting policies which the beleaguered banking system required. Similarly, when speculation mounted against the dollar in the interval between Hoover's defeat and Roosevelt's inauguration, the response of the Fed was to protect the dollar. By now the banking system was too weak to withstand the additional strain imposed by the central bank. In February 1933 the Governor of Michigan proclaimed a bank holiday in that state; by the end of the month another twenty-nine governors had introduced restrictions on the sums which depositors could withdraw. On the day of Roosevelt's inaugural address the banking system did not function normally in any state.

The Fed has been harshly treated by critics who see a reversal in monetary policy before and after 1928. Wicker, however, demonstrates clearly that much of the praise lavished on the Reserve for its seemingly successful stabilisation policies was misplaced. Moreover, far from departing from previous practice after 1928, Fed policy was consistent and understandable. Open market operations in 1924, and in 1927, were conducted primarily not to help domestic economic recovery but because of international monetary considerations. Strong was an ardent supporter of the gold standard and the action taken by the Fed, especially in 1927, discouraged a gold influx to the US and helped to ease the position in London. Because the gold standard was not in jeopardy in 1930, the Fed saw no reason for open market operations; when it was, in 1931, swift action was taken. This was damaging to the domestic banking system, but consistent with policy moves during the 1920s.

The expansionary policies of 1924 and 1927 were therefore fortuitous; positive action taken to deal with external monetary matters happily coincided with domestic needs. Nor is there clear evidence that Strong, had he lived, would have advocated aggressive open market purchases. Even if he had there is scant evidence to support the proposition that his argumentative powers would have held sway (Chandler, 1971, p. 89; Wicker, 1965; 1966, pp. 77 *et seq*). Too much has been made of monetary policy during a few years of the 1920s and the position of Strong as the saviour of the money supply after 1929 has little foundation (Toma, 1979).

During the first half of 1932 the Federal Reserve did undertake a vigorous open market operations policy, but one which was terminated before sustained recovery got under way. The most likely explanation for the timing of this programme was the passage of the Glass–Steagall Act in early 1932 which freed additional gold for export by allowing government securities to be used as backing for Federal Reserve notes. Unfortunately, open market purchases lowered the yields on short-term government securities upon which banks now depended for income. In addition, some banks still felt themselves to be desperately short of gold. These circumstances combined to raise protests by the banking community and the open market purchase programme came to an end (Epstein and Ferguson, 1984).

Internal conflict within the unwieldy Federal Reserve system, the poor quality of economic intelligence, the lack of a widely accepted theory to explain the Depression, the fact that not all banks were members of the system, and the attention paid to international events account for the Fed's frequently unhelpful stance. Hoover was bitterly critical of the Fed, even though he had been able to appoint his own candidate, Eugene R. Meyer, as Governor of the Board in 1930. He found the Fed weak, indecisive and unimaginative (Kettl, 1986, pp. 36–42); many later critics agreed. The issue, however, is not so much how an expansionary monetary policy could have helped, but whether it is reasonable to assume that such a policy would have been readily advocated by the Reserve Board.

Many monetarists believe that if a vigorous open market policy had begun in early 1930 the recession would not have developed into a depression. Not all investigators, however, see the slump as solely the product of monetary forces, and certainly not before the autumn of 1931 (Fearon, 1987; Gordon and Wilcox, 1981; Temin, 1976). Construction and consumer durables, which had kept the economy buoyant during the recessions of 1924 and 1927, had reached the end of their long phase of expansion. Bernstein sees the severity of the Depression as the result of the unfortunate coincidence of a cyclical downturn with a secular shift from a manufacturing to a consumer economy (Bernstein, 1987, 1989). International factors, too, played a part and certainly any analysis of economic weakness during the 1920s would need to emphasise the increasingly unfavourable distribution of income (Holt, 1977) and the decline in the real wealth of stock holders once Wall Street fell from the dizzy heights reached in 1929 (Mishkin, 1978). Some monetarists also stress the impact of the Hawley Smoot tariff, especially as the US retained the fixed exchange rate rules of the gold standard (Meltzer, 1981; Saint-Etienne, 1984, pp. 13–15, 28–35). This is not an exhaustive list of non-monetarist factors which may have caused or contributed to the crisis, but it casts serious doubt upon a solely monetary explanation (Brunner, 1981; Fearon, 1987; Kindleberger, 1979, pp. 11–14).

It is not possible to show exactly what would have happened if the Fed had pursued a vigorously expansionary monetary policy after 1929 any more than it is possible to demonstrate what Benjamin Strong would have done had he lived to 1933. An expansionary policy certainly would have modified the downturn and helped the recovery, but it is not unreasonable to claim that the Fed's policy lapses were quite understandable, and that its actions over the period 1922 to 1933 were more consistent than many critics are prepared to concede.

If we turn to non-monetary policy, one striking feature is the tremendous activity of Herbert Hoover who had previously coordinated the Harding administration's anti-depression strategy during 1920/21. In an attempt to keep demand buoyant in 1930, Hoover appealed to business to maintain wage rates until cost of living falls made this impracticable; he advocated industrial peace; he encouraged governors and mayors to expand public works; he had numerous meetings with bankers and businessmen in an attempt to boost confidence; and he tightened immigration rules in a vain attempt to create more jobs for Americans. Hoover believed in an activist government stimulating voluntary activities to combat the deflationary spiral. He was not a *laissez-faire* capitalist but one who had been clearly identified, during the 1920s, with the emergence of modern economic management (Arnold, 1970; Hawley, 1979; Metcalf, 1975; Reagan, 1988a, 1988b).

The president had always been in favour of protective tariffs and his refusal to veto the Hawley Smoot tariff in 1930, in spite of vehement opposition from many economists, has been singled out as a significant contributory factor in the Depression. Once it was on the statute books US import duties were raised to record levels; retaliation soon followed. Hoover, however, had considered the tariff a domestic issue and discounted the effects of retaliation

(Pastor, 1980, pp. 77–84, 186–8). Although it has been argued that the increase in protection given by Hawley Smoot has been exaggerated (Lake, 1988, pp. 193–6), there can be no doubt that it encouraged an upward spiral in trade restrictions. American trade would have fallen sharply without a tariff increase, but this was an act of short-sighted insularity which had destabilising international ramifications.

By the middle of 1931 Hoover's strategy, despite the occasional sign of recovery, had failed. States, municipalities and counties found that their tax base, heavily dependent upon property taxes, had been significantly eroded. Far from undertaking more public works, states were struggling to balance their budgets. Increasingly, influential members of the battered business community looked to the security of planning as a means of restoring prosperity. Hoover did not support initiatives such as those proposed by Gerard Swope who advocated the compulsory consolidation of all firms with more than fifty employees into trade associations in order that prices, output and employment could be stabilised. Hoover was out of sympathy with corporate planners, and yet his own recovery programme had proved ineffective. A new plan of action was clearly called for.

By late 1931, in the wake of Britain's departure from the gold standard and a growing crisis in the domestic banking system, Hoover was faced with an unprecedented crisis. He was emphatic that the US should stay on gold and vigorously argued against those who advocated devaluation or radical monetary experiments to raise prices. His first priority was to preserve the financial sector and to maintain the convertibility of the dollar into gold at the prevailing exchange rate (Barber, 1988, pp. 126 *et seq.*). So frightening were international debt suspensions, bank failures and the strain on other financial intermediaries that an attempt at stabilisation was a sensible action. As the Fed seemed incapable of preserving the banking system, at Hoover's prompting a number of banks agreed to form the National Credit Corporation which would lend money to distressed banks. The task, however, was beyond its powers. In January 1932 the Reconstruction Finance Corporation, also designed to assist ailing banks, was established but could not prevent the eventual disintegration of the commercial banking system. Hoover supported the Glass–Steagall Act, and also signed into law the Home Loan Bank bill which established twelve regional Home Loan Banks whose purpose was to assist institutions involved in the mortgage business. Positive attempts were therefore made to tackle the crisis, but these newly established agencies either moved too cautiously, or were created too late to abate the decline.

Hoover lacked the political skill needed to control Congress and therefore responded in an obstructionist manner to many of its political initiatives which he viewed contemptuously as political point-scoring or reckless extravagance. When additional expenditures on relief or on public works were proposed Hoover, where possible, used his veto. He did not, however, oppose the Emergency Relief and Construction Act of 1932 which provided loans to states to finance self-liquidating public works if a need for funds could be demonstrated. This constituted a departure from Hoover's traditional view that relief was a local matter (Romasco, 1965, pp. 211–24, 226–7).

The President was driven by the mistaken belief that America had imported the Depression. He blamed the debt structure which had built up during the war and post-war years, and the failure of European countries to manage their economies with prudence, thus ensuring that their debts would be discharged. In 1931 he had unilaterally proposed a moratorium on inter-governmental (but not private) debt for a twelve month period: for a year no reparations or war debts would be paid. This action, however, came too late, and it was naïve to believe that after such a short period repayment could resume. Within a few months Germany had introduced exchange control, and within a year the repayment of reparations and war debts was at an end.

America's large agricultural sector was smitten by low prices and a rise in real debt. The collapse in farm fortunes (see Table 6.2) led to the organisation of the Cotton Stabilization Corporation and the Grain Stabilization Corporation which began to buy crops in order to support prices. Unfortunately the price falls were so steep and so protracted that this costly exercise was terminated in the middle of 1931, from which point the federal government had nothing to offer farmers who became deeply resentful of their misery. Gradually agricultural pressure groups came to accept that the farm problem could not be solved unless surpluses were curtailed. The public, and business, came to believe that a general recovery was not possible until the purchasing power of those on the land was substantially raised (Finegold, 1982). A radical rethink of farm policy, of which Hoover seemed incapable, was needed (Fausold, 1977, p. 51); by 1932 the farm vote was lost.

Many economists today would argue that, given the circumstances of 1929–33, the most effective route to economic revival would have been a counter-cyclical policy designed to increase aggregate demand by tax cuts, by increased government spending, or by some combination of the two. The most volatile economic variable during these years was investment which fell from $16.2 billion in 1929 to $1.4 billion in 1933. Hoover initially attached great importance to the role which public works could play in stimulating recovery. Indeed, spending by the federal government on public works rose from $201 million in 1929 to $507 million in 1931. The President had hoped that the main source of funding would come from the states and local government, not from Washington. Unfortunately state and local tax revenues were so rapidly reduced that funds for public works became increasingly scarce.

The key problem was the relatively small size of government. In 1929 federal expenditure was only 2.5 per cent of GNP, while state and local expenditure was 7.5 per cent of GNP. Stimulation from expenditure had to come from the federal government whose tax base and capacity for running budget deficits placed it in a more powerful position than smaller units. In fact total federal spending did rise during these years from $3.3 billion to $4.6 billion, but an increase of only $1.3 billion could not possibly offset the decline of $14.8 billion in investment. A colossal expansion in government expenditure leading to budget deficits of unique proportions was needed. Such action was not only politically impossible, there was no widely accepted economic theory which could be used to justify it.

A number of economists had broken away from the stranglehold of orthodoxy. They urged Hoover to run large and continuous budget deficits, arguing that only generous federal spending without increases in taxes could bring about a recovery in the economy (Davis, 1968). Hoover did not subscribe to that view; in late 1931 tax rates were raised very sharply, a move which was strongly deflationary. The reason for the tax increase is not that Hoover took the concept of budget balance literally. He was intelligent enough to realise that creative accounting could give some leeway in expenditure and that he could also justify current deficits by promising to run surpluses at a later date. The key to the 1931 tax raise was that Hoover was most anxious to keep the US on the gold standard and felt that speculators would respond favourably to attempts to eradicate the deficit. Moreover, he believed that a higher deficit financed by government borrowing would create competition for funds with banks and business which would force up interest rates, penalising the private sector (Stein, 1960, pp. 31–8). This explains why, in 1932, Hoover was only interested in self-liquidating public works projects: that is those schemes which would eventually pay for themselves.

Hoover was an interventionist President, a man of great energy, high intelligence and strong character who was embroiled in an economic crisis for which, given the economic theories of the day, there was no apparent solution. One way out of the Depression – in retrospect – was through massive budget deficits, but a substantial body of informed opinion advocated balanced budgets. Indeed, during the 1932 election campaign Roosevelt attacked the excessive spending and persistent intervention of his opponent. The public would not have embraced a programme of huge state-spending. In 1932 the electorate chose a new President, but Roosevelt had not won the White House by advocating a package of radical economic ideas.

The Roosevelt presidency

During the election campaign Roosevelt failed to present a detailed plan for recovery. He portrayed himself as a fiscally cautious budget-balancer and supporter of the gold standard who saw some merit in an unspecified type of economic planning. His aim was election victory, and policy options which might be considered controversial were fudged; thus, when Roosevelt was presented with two opposing views on the tariff issue and was asked to select one, his response was to instruct an advisor to weave both together in a single policy statement (Burns, 1956, p. 44; Leuchtenberg, 1963, p. 37). A period of frantic activity was therefore necessary between the election triumph and the assumption of power to produce those policies which would become the early New Deal.

With the benefit of hindsight we can see that the situation in 1933 called for a massive increase in government spending to boost aggregate demand. This was a macro-economic problem which required vigorous and expansionary macro-economic measures. However, the magnitude of the deficit required was enormous in the context of the 1930s. The business community, Congress, indeed the public at large, would have regarded a massive programme of government spending as seriously destabilising, unleashing, as they felt it would, the threat of runaway inflation and the rapid erosion of investor confidence. It is hardly surprising that the new President did not look to deficit finance to expand purchasing power or to reflate the economy; he did not believe that America could spend its way out of the Depression. Once that strategy had been discarded the prospect of sustained recovery was bleak, though the reasons for his action are understandable. All decision-makers were assailed with widely differing theories concerning the nature of the Depression (Chandler, 1971, pp. 129–46; Spulber, 1989, pp. 5–17). Confusion abounded but it was clear that the problem could not wait until the economy had naturally shaken off the crisis.

As a policy innovator Roosevelt had a number of advantages in

1933. Both the House and the Senate had commanding Democrat majorities; the new President, moreover, had a vast store of public good will. Roosevelt had no formal knowledge of economics and no rigid economic philosophy; he saw events in political terms. He was in favour of the profit motive but felt that some restrictions on business were necessary in order to control its destabilising effects; such controls would be modest. Even though the famous inaugural address had called for 'action and action now', what emerged was a refinement of policies already in existence or the adoption, with some urgency, of ideas which had previously been subject to lengthy debate.

The New Dealers looked back to World War I, not only for inspiration but also to provide a model for the regulatory agencies they sought to establish (Leuchtenberg, 1964, pp. 132 *et seq.*) Although these voluntarist agencies had existed to control an economy functioning at full employment and output, it was felt that they had been so successful that their recreation was preferred to a totally fresh start. We should note that the structure of the federal government did mitigate against radical policies. As Skocpol and Finegold have argued (1982, pp. 260–61), governments that have, or can create, their own highly qualified administrative infrastructures are in a much better position to intervene directly in the economy than those who must rely heavily on external advice or expertise. Washington was synonymous with small government; there was no large and expert bureaucracy which could be used to implement new programmes. Moreover, the federal government lacked both the experience and the institutions which could readily be used to activate an employment policy. Central government had experience of regulation and little else. It would have been possible to create the necessary framework for a consolidation of central government economic power, but not immediately (Weir, 1988, pp. 162–4). This would have required a massive reorganisation at a time when public and congressional demand was for more immediate action.

By 1933 the advocates of orderly planning, who had been gaining converts as the Depression worsened, were listened to with respect. The public yearned for a return to stability which, they believed, traditional capitalism could not achieve. A contemporary study of the farm problem reflected a view not confined to rural America: '[T]he competitive system is breaking down . . . The comfortable theory of the identity of mass prosperity with the unrestricted pursuit of private gain no longer serves' (Mead and Ostrolenk, 1933, p. 1). Many decision-makers considered that unfettered competition had brought ruin and that now was the time to regulate a force which in the past had been associated with increasing prosperity by the public. Thus the root of the economic crisis was believed to be structural and planning seemed to be the logical way to deal with it.

The route to recovery chosen by Roosevelt concentrated upon the domestic economy. He ignored those who suggested that his priorities should be to solve the issue of war debts, to stay on the gold standard and to do all in his power to ensure that sterling returned to it. The President also used native American ideas in his quest for recovery; an overseas influence is absent. Thus it was World War I, the cooperative associationalism of the 1920s and Hoover's informal attempts at economic intervention which were his guides, though Roosevelt was always more willing to use explicit federal authority than his predecessor had been (Hawley, 1975, pp. 57–8). What emerged, however, was a political rather than a manifestly economic programme. Indeed, the New Deal must be judged as an exercise in politics with the President acting as a broker between various interest groups, rather than one where economic issues were of primary importance.

It is difficult to analyse the New Deal because it contained so many differing programmes. Always pragmatic, Roosevelt's ideas shifted radically between 1933 and 1941, reflecting changes in the advisors closest to him. Although there is continuity in the agricultural policy adopted by New Dealers, their industrial strategy underwent a radical review. Nor can it be claimed that either monetary or fiscal policy were used systematically as tools to regenerate the economy. Shifts of emphasis stemming from the lack of a carefully crafted economic strategy constituted a serious impediment to full recovery. It will be argued, however, that the most formidable barrier against the restoration of full employment and output was the absence, until the very end of the decade, of an economic theory which explained the Depression.

Planning and the New Deal

Planning, it was believed, could solve the problems of overproduction in both industry and agriculture by creating a balance between supply and demand. In addition, destructive competition between businesses could be moderated and the destabilising effects of individualism curbed. During a 'fireside chat' in June 1934 Roosevelt claimed that the aims of the New Deal were 'relief, recovery and reform'. There was, of course, considerable overlap between these three categories, but by far the most important was recovery. Only with a revival of the economy could relief needs be reduced. The New Dealers did, however, attach particular importance to agriculture in the search for recovery. They believed that the nation as a whole would not return to prosperity unless the farm sector led the way; a revival in farm purchasing power was therefore essential (Romasco, 1988, pp. 157–9). The widespread support for this view made the implementation of policies to raise prices acceptable even to business interests which had opposed this in the past.

The two principal recovery weapons of the early New Deal were, first, the Agricultural Adjustment Act (AAA 1933) and, second, the National Industrial Recovery Act (NIRA 1933). The farmers and their organisations had been courted by Roosevelt during the 1932 election but no details had emerged regarding legislation to help them. Farmers had become politicised during the 1920s and through their associations – the National Farmers' Union, the National Grange and the American Farm Bureau Federation – had mounted several campaigns to raise farm income. Farm interests were successful in persuading Congress, on a number of occasions, to pass a bill embodying the McNary–Haugen plan. This called for the creation of an agency which would remove farm surpluses from the domestic market at a high price and dump them overseas. However, President Coolidge vetoed the bill each time it came to him. Among the sternest critics of McNary–Haugenism was big business, which feared that cheap food would enable their overseas competitors to reduce wages and thus gain a price advantage.

What was different, indeed radical, about the New Deal legislation was that it proposed production controls for farmers who had always believed that their task was to grow as much food and fibre as possible. Production restrictions had been mooted during the worst years of the Depression – Senator Huey Long had proposed an agreement between cotton-producing states not to plant in 1932 – but it proved impossible to persuade all growers to cooperate (Snyder, 1984). Agricultural economists, however, produced several variants of a domestic allotment plan which proposed payment for farmers who agreed not to plant certain crops. By 1933 farm leaders were persuaded that some form of control on output was essential if farm prices and incomes were to be raised (Finegold, 1982; Perkins, 1969, pp. 36–48; Romasco, 1988, pp. 157–61).

Department of Agriculture experts played a vital role in convincing the leaders of farm organisations to accept production controls. Their backing was essential if the majority of commercial farmers were to support the scheme. Not all farmers belonged to farm organisations, whose membership was dominated by larger commercial operators rather than tenants or share croppers. It was these operators who were able to move into positions of power and influence in the local committees which administered the AAA

(Saloutos, 1982, pp. 261–3). It was their needs which were always to the fore when experts at the Department of Agriculture considered farm problems.

The aim of the AAA 1933 was to restore 'parity' by paying farmers to reduce the acreage on which they planted. The scheme, essentially an emergency measure, was initially voluntary though some element of compulsion was later introduced. Those who agreed to take part were paid cash for working an allotted acreage. Only farmers producing crops which were considered 'basic' and in surplus could be included in the scheme. At the outset such crops included wheat, cotton, field corn and tobacco, but the list was lengthened later. Payment to those participating was financed by a controversial new tax on food processors. In an effort to reduce surpluses immediately, part of the cotton crop of 1933 was ploughed under and a hog slaughter programme introduced.

In January 1936 the Supreme Court declared the AAA unconstitutional; Congress quickly replaced it with the Soil Conservation and Domestic Allotment Act. The aim was still to raise farm prices to parity through acreage reduction, but due account was now taken of the serious environmental problems caused by drought. Farmers who grew soil-depleting crops which included corn and tobacco were encouraged to shift to soil-conserving crops, for example grasses. Funding for benefits, however, had to come from general taxation as the Supreme Court had struck down the tax on food processors. In 1937, after favourable weather, problems of overproduction resurfaced and new legislation, AAA 1938, retained acreage allotment and introduced marketing quotas. It aimed, however, for a balanced agricultural surplus capable of being stored. In poor years part of the surplus could therefore be released without destabilising prices.

The acreage allotment schemes were just part of the agriculture package. The Commodity Credit Corporation (CCC), established in 1933, enabled farmers who participated in the acreage allotment scheme to obtain cash loans by offering their crop as collateral. If the price of the crop was higher than expected the farmer could repay the loan; if lower, the farmer could refuse to pay and forfeit his crop to the CCC. In addition, the Farm Credit Act (1933) and the Emergency Farm Mortgage Act (1933) helped farmers refinance mortgages at a time when farm debts were a serious problem.

The architects of the farm programme sought to raise farm income by a combination of initiatives. Acreage reduction would lead to higher prices; allotment payments and CCC loans would provide a valuable addition to farm coffers. Banking reform and general reflation, moreover, would ease the burden of debt. The rise in farm spending was supposed to generate sustained recovery throughout the rest of the economy. New Deal intervention in agriculture had other aims too – for example, rehabilitation and relief – but our concern is with the effect of this complex legislation upon the restoration of full employment and output.

Farm income, as measured by the parity ratio (see Table 6.1) rose from a low of 58 in 1932 to 93 in 1937 before falling to 77 in 1939. Farmers, therefore, did not achieve the target of 100 which they desired. If the parity ratio is recalculated to include the value of government payments, the figure of 97 was reached by 1937. The net income of farm operators from farming also rose, though pre-Depression levels were not reached even by 1937. Nor did the farm sector escape the ravages of the 1937/8 recession.

Thirty million farm dwellers, widely scattered across the country, many of whom were members of organisations which lobbied vigorously for their cause, constituted a powerful political group. Members of Congress had to listen to their voices. It is not surprising, therefore, that the administration chose 100 per cent parity as its aim. This did not necessarily make it a totally defensible strategy. The parity ratio was calculated on the base years 1910 to 1914. The restoration of pre-World War I price relationships was not a particularly sound strategy for the 1930s, when the structure of the economy and economic conditions were very different. Moreover, other government policies made 100 per cent parity very difficult to achieve. Other attempts to raise the price level generally, and particularly those which inflated manufacturing costs, continually increased the cost of goods which the farmer purchased. The rise in farm prices necessary to achieve the desired goal would, in all probability, have been destabilising for the rest of the economy. If so, agriculture itself would not have been unscathed as the movement of indices after 1937 demonstrates. Any attempt to raise farm prices steeply would also have affected the disposable income of non-farm people. The poor in particular would have been badly affected, but so would manufacturers who depended upon domestically grown raw materials. Indeed, such a programme would not have received widespread public support.

It is possible to identify other instances where New Deal agricultural policies were of dubious advantage to recovery. A planned reduction in output, if accomplished, would have meant less business and fewer jobs for the railroads, the principal transporter of bulky commodities. The processing tax was passed on to consumers in the form of higher prices and was therefore regressive since the poor spent a relatively high proportion of their income on food and clothing. Even the reduced value of the dollar could not revitalise export markets lost to high-priced American farm products.

The attempts to reduce output by acreage controls were, in fact, a failure. Total farm output (Table 6.2) was higher after 1937 than in any year between 1929 and 1933. The American farmer became more efficient and achieved ever greater output from a reduced acreage. The years 1934 and 1936 witness a significant drop in output; both were times of serious drought. Nature was far more successful in curbing farm output than were New Deal policies. Without the drought farm prices would not have risen so far.

New Dealers misjudged the situation greatly in believing that the 32 million people living on farms, many of whom were poor croppers and tenants, could act as the engine of national economic expansion. Agricultural good fortune depended upon a revival of urban America with new jobs for the rural under-employed, not vice versa. Farm policies were of some help to the economy since those on the land were consumers as well as producers, but they could not perform the role of recovery catalyst. The fact that agriculture was given such a prominent position in the recovery strategy during Roosevelt's presidency demonstrates a failure to see where the real problem lay (Benedict, 1953, pp. 311–15; Fearon, 1987, pp. 183–92; Nourse, Davis and Black, 1937, pp. 420–48; Romasco, 1988, pp. 184–5). The problems facing farm policy-makers, however, were formidable and should not be minimised. Something had to be done to help farmers and done quickly. What emerged can be criticised but alternative policies such as guaranteeing the farmers' costs of production or raising the consumption of low income groups were open to the same objections as the production control–price support programme. With New Deal help the surplus rural population survived until wartime expansion provided vital urban jobs (Badger, 1989, pp. 163–9).

Although the principal thrust of economic revival was to be provided by agriculture, industry was also ripe for consideration. Many business groups advocated a relaxation of the anti-trust laws which, they claimed, encouraged destructive competition. They called for a new spirit of cooperation and law which would curb unfair trading practices. Organised labour supported attempts by Congressmen to shorten the working week and to introduce a minimum wage, arguing that this was the only way to increase demand and create more jobs quickly.

It would have been surprising if New Dealers had introduced an industrial policy without recognising the popularity of planning. There were, however, sharp differences between the more radical national planners and those who advocated the regulation of different business groups. Many business planners merely sought to introduce a wider application of scientific management which had been popular during the 1920s, a decade which had also seen trade associations attempt to outlaw unfair trade practices (Chandler, 1970, pp. 224–5; Himmelberg, 1976). Most industrialists favoured a form of self-regulation under federal leadership. Roosevelt, of course, had to take into account countervailing views such as those of labour, the farmers and others who were deeply suspicious of monopoly power.

The legislation which provided the industrial counterpart to the AAA was the result of a compromise between several conflicting groups. New Dealers proposed a more formal link between business and government than had been possible under Hoover, but one which still owed much to past practice (Hawley, 1975, p. 57). By giving a boost to both business and wages it was hoped that the result would be extra sales and higher profits which would in turn enable the wages to be paid. Regulation was necessary to prevent unscrupulous operators obtaining an unfair competitive advantage by paying low wages.

The National Industrial Recovery Act (NIRA 1933) had two parts. The first created the National Recovery Administration (NRA) which attempted to plan prices, output and employment by encouraging committees representing management, the public and labour to draw up codes of fair competition for each industry. As no one wanted to prevent all forms of competition the concept of 'fair' competition was introduced. Labour was given minimum wages, maximum hours and the right to bargain collectively, a package which was described as 'fair'. By March 1935, 546 basic codes and 185 supplementary codes covered approximately 95 per cent of the industrial work force.

Disenchantment soon set in. Business, which had initially embraced the NIRA in the atmosphere of crisis prevailing in March 1933, became hostile to the recognition that had been given to organised labour. Small businesses felt particularly aggrieved as they were compelled to pay union rates but were prevented from engaging in effective price competition (Collins, 1981, pp. 31–3). The industries which had suffered most in the Depression still favoured output restriction and price maintenance, but those who saw the opportunity for growth wanted to free themselves from the shackles of regulation (Bernstein, 1987, pp. 200–203).

The NIRA was struck down by the Supreme Court in May 1935. Even without this legal obstacle it is doubtful if this experiment would have survived given the movement of the economy. A vigorous boom had greeted Roosevelt's accession to power, but economic decline struck during the summer of 1933. It was not until the autumn of the following year that the economy began the sustained rise which was terminated in mid-1937. Compared to the rapid recovery which followed 1920/21 this was disappointing, as was the failure of manufacturing employment to grow. The problem was that the NRA was not, nor could it be, a plan for recovery, even though that word occurs in the title (Romasco, 1988, pp. 189–90). Rather than stimulating industry, the NRA encouraged the proliferation of a large number of monopolistic agreements. In drawing up the codes big business, being better organised, triumphed not only over the small operator, but also over trade unions and consumers. Complex regulations, however, turned business into a bureaucratic nightmare where self-interest prevailed (Bellush, 1975; Weinstein, 1986).

The inflationary effects of the NRA codes had the unfortunate result of offsetting the expansionary effects of an increase in the money supply (Weinstein, 1980). The imposition of minimum wages, moreover, heralded an era of relatively high wage rates. Macro-economists have been puzzled by the remarkable rise in real hourly wage rates which began in 1933 and which was sustained, in spite of heavy unemployment, after the demise of the NRA. Any explanation must take account of the public support for higher wages which were regarded as a prerequisite to increased purchasing power. After all, wage cutting between 1929 and 1933 had failed to assist falling output and had contributed to declining morale (Baily, 1983). Wright suggests that New Dealers may have been attempting to create a labour market in which low-wage jobs would be eliminated. Women and children would no longer need to work since the wage of the head of a household would be sufficient to support a family. Though a laudable long-term aim, it is probable that high wages held back recovery and made it more difficult for blacks in particular to obtain low pay employment (Wright, 1987, pp. 337–40). The rise in real wages benefited those with jobs but not those who needed them.

The NRA was not an experiment in planning. If key sectors in the economy could have been identified and a national plan agreed, then tangible benefits may have followed. But the federal government had no expertise in this area, had few trained staff, and would likely have received only limited support for such an option. The action of 1933 was a product of frustration: something had to be done. None of the panaceas of the time, whether they lay in the realm of business planning or the imposition of a more competitive system, could provide the solution (Hawley, 1966, pp. 130–46).

The second part of the NIRA was the Public Works Administration (PWA 1933). The aim of the PWA was to reduce unemployment and to restore purchasing power through the construction of useful public works. This agency was in operation until the outbreak of World War II, and did indeed build a variety of dams, bridges, public utilities and even a small quantity of low-cost housing. The problem with the PWA was that it moved too slowly and spent too cautiously to provide the immediate boost which the economy needed.

To sum up, industrial strategy took heed of a number of differing theories designed to solve a structural problem, and tried to satisfy them. There was an unfortunate fixation with the view, also evident in agriculture, that if only prices and wages were to rise, recovery must follow. In fact, neither pre- nor post-1935 policies have much to commend them, reflecting as they do the confusion in which policy-makers found themselves. To some extent, government vacillation merely reflected the ambiguity of the American people. They wanted the benefits of big business, though they were deeply suspicious of giant corporations. They had a strong romantic attachment to the small producer able to supply the consumer durables they wanted. New Deal policies reflected the electorate's conflicting emotions (Hawley, 1966, pp. 472–6).

Monetary policy

Roosevelt was determined to raise prices to the levels which had prevailed before the Depression began. Savage deflation had depressed business expectations, and had proved ruinous for many debtors. In order to restore purchasing power New Dealers agreed that some inflation was necessary; indeed, many Congressmen representing rural interests were strong inflationists. Drawing on the tradition of the Populists, they believed that an increase in the money supply, with the addition of bimetallism, could solve virtually all depression ills. Senator Thomas of Oklahoma sponsored a monetary amendment to the AAA (1933) bill which, when it became law, gave the President enormous discretion over the monetary system which included the authority to issue $3 billion in greenbacks, to establish bimetallism and reduce the weight of the gold dollar by up to 50 per cent. Opposing the inflationists was a sound money group which favoured a balanced budget and the maintenance of the gold standard. They were fearful of inflation reaching the dramatic heights endured by central Europe during the early 1920s. To reduce these anxieties, supporters of price increases often described themselves as reflationists rather than inflationists. Roosevelt was prepared to undertake unorthodox monetary experiments in order to achieve what he believed was an essential correction to Depression prices.

The grounds for domestic monetary experiment were prepared when Roosevelt announced to the World Economic Conference that he was unwilling to support a joint declaration on monetary policy.

To do so, he believed, would restrict his freedom of action in the domestic sphere which was his priority. Even before the conference it had become illegal for Americans to own gold, and gold exports and foreign exchange transactions were controlled. To the horror of traditionalists the US left the gold standard in April 1933 and the dollar was devalued (Anderson, 1979, pp. 314–18). Roosevelt believed that he was creating the freedom necessary for inflationary policies which were inconsistent with the fixed exchange rates of the gold standard.

The President fell under the influence of Professor George Warren who claimed that all New Deal programmes would be irrelevant if his plan to reduce the gold content of the dollar were implemented. The result would be not only a general price increase, but also a proportionally greater rise in commodity prices thus redressing the imbalance in price falls. The price level could only be raised, argued Warren, by an increase in the price of gold: as domestic price levels would rise by about the same amount as this increase, recovery would follow rapidly (Blum, 1959, pp. 61–77). From October 1933 the Reconstruction Finance Corporation began to purchase gold at high prices and as the dollar price of gold increased the gold value of the dollar fell. In January 1934 the Gold Reserve Act fixed the price of gold at \$35 an ounce and the gold content of the new dollar at 41 per cent of the old. A similar programme was undertaken to raise silver prices (Chandler, 1971, pp. 272–95). If successful these schemes had the attraction of quick results without sustained state or bureaucratic intervention.

The bullion purchase policy was a failure and the response of farm prices to it was especially disappointing. Devaluation had an inflationary effect, but as US exports were only 3.2 per cent of national income in the late 1930s it was a moderate one. Devaluation, however, did assist exports, the prices of which were being inflated but in a decade during which foreign trade contracted the impact of a marginal improvement in export performance was very slight.

The most important and long-lasting legacy of the Roosevelt presidency in the monetary sphere came in the reform of banking and other financial institutions. The banking system was resuscitated by the Emergency Banking Act of March 1933 and the Glass–Steagall Act, passed three months later. The early reform of the banking system was, however, a result of Senate initiatives and cannot be described as forming part of the New Deal. Restoration of stability owed most to the introduction of deposit insurance, to which Roosevelt was initially opposed, as a temporary measure in the Glass–Steagall Act. Deposit insurance was the only way to prevent crises in the unit banking system which most Americans wished to retain. (Golembe, 1960, pp. 218–22; White, 1981). The establishment of the Federal Deposit Insurance Corporation (FDIC) heralded a new era of stability in commercial banking. The Banking Acts of 1933 and 1935 strengthened the Federal Reserve, especially the Reserve Board which from 1935 had mandatory authority to change member bank reserves, to set the rediscount rate and to regulate loans in securities. Other important reform measures included the Federal Savings and Loan Insurance Corporation which performed much the same function as FDIC for these institutions, the Home Owners Loan Corporation which refinanced those in mortgage difficulties, and the Securities Exchange Commission which attempted to recapture public confidence in Wall Street.

Reform apart, monetary policy lacked authority. Friedman and Schwartz characterise Fed policy during the New Deal era as almost entirely passive since the Fed made virtually no attempt to alter the quantity of high powered money by the use of open market operations. Moreover, the discount rate was kept consistently high relative to market rates. The system was inert except when it dealt with the issue of excess reserves in the banking system, the implications of which will be analysed later. Friedman and Schwartz suggest three reasons for this passivity with which most observers would agree. First, the disasters of 1929 to 1933 which undermined Fed confidence; second, the shift in power base from New York to the Board in Washington DC; and finally, the acceptance by decision-makers that monetary policy was of much less significance than fiscal measures (Friedman and Schwartz, 1963, pp. 511, 532–4). Indeed Marriner Eccles, Chairman of the Board of Governors, attached far more importance to deficit financing than he did to monetary policy.

During the decade from 1929 the real money supply rose by 48 per cent, the result not of vigorous open market operations but of a massive influx of gold. The American banking system was considered a safe haven for gold by investors who had become increasingly alarmed by political extremism. A faster rate of monetary expansion would have had a more positive inflationary effect than the gold purchase programme and, between 1935 and 1940, would have reduced interest rates (Gordon, 1981, pp. 128–9). Such a policy, however, was not tried.

One result of the gold influx was an increase in bank reserves which reached far higher levels than was necessary as a backing for deposits. The Fed believed that the reserves could serve as the basis for a destabilising credit expansion such as had occurred in 1928 and 1929. To counter this possibility action was taken to raise reserve requirements in August 1936. At the same time the

Treasury prevented banks from adding to their reserves by sterilising increases in the gold stock. The reaction of the banks was to re-establish their previous excess position which led to a contraction in the growth money stock (Friedman and Schwartz, 1963, pp. 520–32, 538–41). Coinciding with fiscal retrenchment this tight money policy ushered in a stock market crash and the severe recession of 1937/8. From the spring of 1938 the money supply rose rapidly, but the performance of the economy lacked vigour until war demand exerted an influence in the middle of 1940.

New Deal monetary policy was weak and ineffectual. The President was given a wide range of options designed to raise the price level which he chose not to use. Indeed, the fact that prices in 1940 were still below 1929 levels demonstrates timidity in an area where New Dealers anticipated great recovery possibilities. The fear of uncontrolled inflation, in spite of the high degree of under-utilised capacity, was strong enough to moderate policies. Few saw recovery emanating from an aggressive open market policy, and, therefore, when the gold and silver purchase programmes were discarded monetary policy could do little more than ensure that the deficit would be financed cheaply. It was, however, unfortunate that the change in reserve requirements introduced by the Fed in 1936 had such serious implications for the economy.

Fiscal policy

The key economic issue for the Depression years was how the low levels of output and employment could be raised quickly. Keynes maintained that unemployment was largely involuntary, the cure for which was not to be found in substantial wage reductions but in the raising of aggregate demand, itself a function of consumption and investment. Contrary to the received wisdom which praised saving, Keynes argued that the more parsimonious households and businesses were, the lower would be the level of aggregate demand and the higher the level of unemployment. Aggregate demand was a function of consumption and investment, but whereas consumption was in fact relatively stable, investment was highly volatile. Full employment was only possible if the amount of real savings was offset fully by expenditure on private investment, net foreign investment, or a budget deficit. American foreign investment was at exceptionally low levels during the 1930s and, as Table 6.3 shows, private investment never recovered from the shock it received during the worst years of the Depression. For recovery the New Dealers needed to stimulate private investment and to run budget deficits.

Table 6.3   Gross private domestic investment 1929–41 ($ billion)

Year	Gross private new construction	Producers' durable equipment	Total gross private domestic investment
1929	8.9	5.6	16.2
1933	1.5	1.5	1.4
1934	1.9	2.2	3.3
1935	2.4	2.9	6.4
1936	3.3	4.0	8.5
1937	4.4	4.7	11.8
1938	3.9	3.5	6.5
1939	4.9	4.0	9.3
1940	5.7	5.3	13.1
1941	6.9	6.6	17.9

Source: Swanson and Williamson, 1972–3.

Even in 1937 private domestic investment was considerably below pre-depression levels, and the effect of the 1937/8 recession on this variable is especially striking (see Table 6.3). Construction was particularly weak. An engine of growth during the 1920s, this sector, which proved such a vital force to the economies of Britain and Sweden, was not even able to achieve half its 1929 level during the 1930s. The performance of producer durables, which include office and transport equipment and industrial machinery was better, but not wholly satisfactory.

Why was the level of private investment so disappointing? All New Deal critics, which by the late 1930s included most of the business community, blamed Roosevelt's policies. The deficit, increasing taxes, pro-union legislation, minimum wages and the anti-business rhetoric of the New Deal were held responsible for reducing profits and undermining business confidence (Anderson, 1979, pp. 475–82; Roose, 1954, pp. 45–7). Rates of interest were relatively low during the 1930s, but, despite a seeming abundance of capital, business was reluctant to borrow. The shattering blows which both manufacturing and commerce had received between 1929 and 1933 certainly introduced a new caution. In addition, the very high rates of investment during the 1920s may have led to a temporary exhaustion of investment opportunities.

Though business complained bitterly about much of the New Deal, especially the welfare, labour and post-1935 tax policies, it would be simplistic to assume that if Roosevelt had abandoned his cherished plans investment would have risen sharply. Moreover, such a change of direction would have had severe political repercussions. There can be little doubt, however, that the vacillations of the New Deal cannot have helped create the stable atmosphere in which business liked to operate. The business community was, however, more coherent in its attack on the New Deal than in proposing policies which would vanquish the Depression. Little emerged from chambers of commerce which can be regarded as an opportunity missed.

During the 1920s the construction industry and consumer durables, especially automobiles, had been a powerful force in the economy. While the construction industry remained depressed during the 1930s, automobile output had, by 1937, just equalled its 1929 level. Unfortunately the recession which began in that year cut sales by half. Some industries did grow rapidly: up to 1937, refrigerators, rayon, glass, tin cans, canned fruit and vegetables, washing machines and radios are the most prominent examples. Aggregate physical output in manufacturing was about the same in 1937 as it had been in 1929. It is clear, however, that the manufacturing sector could not have been the source of the rapid increase in jobs required in the 1930s. Employment in manufacturing, after all, had not grown during the 1920s, a time of very favourable circumstances. An expansion of employment in the service sector which would have had a significant effect on unemployment was dependent upon a massive government expenditure programme. Table 6.1, which shows not only the extent of unemployment but also the swelling labour force, illustrates the problem facing New Dealers.

Darby has argued that the unemployment figures used in Table 6.1 exaggerate the true position since all those who had found places on federal emergency relief projects are classified as unemployed. He maintains that such people had voluntarily ceased to search for jobs and should, therefore, not be classified as unemployed. Subtracting them from the total reduces the 1937 figure from 14.3 to 9.1 per cent. According to this view, but for the 1937/8 recession, unemployment would have reached its natural rate, which Darby puts at 5 per cent, within a short period (Darby, 1976).

It is, however, unlikely that a high proportion of those on relief work would have obtained private employment. The federal government attempted to provide work relief for all able-bodied unemployed through the Works Progress Administration, but no more than one-third of those eligible could be given places. The series from which Darby extracts relief workers actually understates the extent of unemployment as it excludes the 10 per cent of the labour force in part-time employment. If the base for calculating unemployment was as a percentage of non-farm employees (see Table 6.1), the level would be much higher (De Long and Summers, 1988, pp. 441–3; Gordon, 1976; Kesselman and Savin, 1978). However, long-term unemployment was a serious problem during the 1930s leading, as it did, to a loss of skill and a change of attitude in those affected. A faster rate of employment growth would have been especially beneficial as it would have significantly reduced the numbers of long-term unemployed (Margo, 1988).

Table 6.4 Federal government finance ($ billion)

	Receipts	Outlays	Surplus or deficit (−)
1929	3.8	2.9	0.9
1933	2.1	4.7	−2.6
1934	3.1	6.5	−3.4
1935	3.8	6.3	−2.5
1936	4.2	7.6	−3.4
1937	5.6	8.4	−2.8
1938	7.0	7.2	−0.2
1939	6.6	9.4	−2.8
1940	6.9	9.6	−2.7
1941	9.2	14.0	−4.8
1945	50.2	95.2	−45.0

Source: Dept of Commerce, 1975.

To explain the failure of the economy to create more jobs we must examine New Deal fiscal policy. Table 6.4 shows that federal spending rose steadily between 1933 and 1940 but so did federal receipts. Roosevelt failed to balance receipts and expenditures, though in 1938 the deficit was practically eliminated. Unfortunately, spending was not directed towards recovery: it was the need to finance New Deal programmes that was the determining factor. There was no attempt to run a planned budget deficit in order to raise aggregate demand. Instead of being cut, taxes were raised in an attempt to reduce the deficit. Moreover, although one of the aims of fiscal policy was a more equitable distribution of income, tax increases were often regressive. Taxes were raised for political and ideological purposes, not as a vehicle for economic recovery. No one thought of stimulating the economy through tax-cutting because of the fear that the deficit would increase (Sweezy, 1972). As the relief problem stubbornly remained, more expenditure and hence more tax revenue was required.

The New Deal was not a Keynesian strategy. Roosevelt disliked deficits and his Treasury Secretary, Henry Morgenthau, unfortunately, was even more orthodox. One of the few top officials who argued consistently for deficit finance was Marriner Eccles who was, from 1934, Governor of the Federal Reserve Board. Eccles had intuitively become a Keynesian before the publication of the General Theory. Those who advanced the case for additional spending, however, had no intellectual backing for their arguments until Keynes's seminal work had been absorbed by an influential group of American economists. They were finally able to influence the President as he reeled from the shock of the 1937/8 recession.

We have already seen that tight money played a role in the 'Roosevelt Depression'; a contractionary fiscal stance was also of great significance. After the 1936 election Roosevelt made a determined attempt to balance the budget: expenditure was cut, and taxes were raised. The result was a self-inflicted disaster which not only held back recovery for several years but also aided the enemies of the New Deal. What was Roosevelt to do? Conflicting advice included the view that the government should revert to NRA style planning, that the budget should be balanced, that those parts of the New Deal which most distressed business should be discarded, and that he should continue with a neo-Brandeisian assault on the private concentration of economic power. Finally, a group to which the President increasingly listened advocated more spending: a bigger deficit (Stein, 1969, pp. 101–23).

A number of young economists who had absorbed Keynes's ideas were able to present a coherent case for a bigger deficit. It is most likely, however, that Roosevelt accepted this as a political argument rather than an economic one. By 1938 the various New Deal agencies had built up a great political constituency: to disband them would have been unpopular with the very people on whom Roosevelt relied for support. In the spring of 1938 spending increased, though in a more cautious manner than the Keynesians would have liked.

Although New Deal spending was not designed as a vehicle for recovery, it did aid economic expansion. The crude deficit, however, is not a good guide to the expansionary effect of fiscal policy. Using the full employment deficit, E. Cary Brown calculated that federal fiscal policy under Hoover in 1931 was more expansionary than it was in 1933, 1937, 1938 and 1939. However, during the 1930s states and local units ran budget surpluses which countered the expansionary effect of federal expenditure. If all elements of fiscal policy were taken together, 1931 emerged as the most expansionary year of the 1930s (Brown, 1956). Further research by Peppers showed that fiscal policy in 1933, 1937, 1938 and 1939 was no more expansionary than in 1929 (Peppers, 1973). The deficits which caused Roosevelt such anguish were not big enough to bring about recovery. It was not until World War II that the nation was prepared for levels of government expenditure which guaranteed full employment. The pity of the New Deal was that neither fiscal nor monetary policies were tried as a recovery device.

Conclusion

Both Hoover and Roosevelt wanted to bolster and preserve capitalism as, indeed, did Keynes. Hoover's presidency was submerged by the greatest depression which America had experienced, and there is no evidence that had Roosevelt been at the White House during those difficult years he would have produced a formula for more than marginally lessening its impact. Roosevelt would, however, have been more politically adept than his predecessor, and far more willing to experiment. Indeed the curiosity of the New Deal is that so much political benefit was derived from policies which, with the benefit of hindsight, can be criticised as ambiguous and counter-productive.

Much good did come from the New Deal. For agriculture there was a new concern with the environment, the spread of electricity, cash payments for desperate farmers and credit stabilisation. The reform of the banking system and the attempt to provide a minimum standard of living for all Americans were praiseworthy ventures. Full employment, however, remained an elusive goal. Although government programmes involved spending sums of money which were large by the standards of the day, they were not great enough to generate rapid recovery. Vigorous macro-economic measures implemented from 1933 would have positively affected output and employment (De Long and Summers, 1988). As this was not evident until World War II, we cannot blame Roosevelt for failing to implement those policies. Although an understandable economic disappointment, the New Deal was a successful political balancing act.

References

Anderson, B. M., 1979, *Economics and the Public Welfare. A Financial Economic History of the United States, 1914–1946*, 2nd edn, Indianapolis, Liberty Press.

Arnold, P. E., 1970, 'Herbert Hoover and the Continuity of American Public Policy', *American Public Policy*, 20: 523–44.

Badger, A. J., 1989, *The New Deal. The Depression Years 1933–1940*, London, Macmillan.

Baily, M. N., 1983, 'The Labor Market in the 1930s', in James Tobin (ed.), *Macroeconomics, Prices and Quantities. Essays in Memory of Arthur M. Okun*, Oxford, Basil Blackwell.

Barber, W. J., 1988, *From New Era to New Deal: Herbert Hoover, the Economists, and American Economic Policy, 1921–33*, Cambridge, Cambridge University Press.

Bellush, B., 1975, *The Failure of the NRA*, New York, W. W. Norton.

Benedict, M. R., 1953, *Farm Policies of the United States*, New York, Twentieth Century Fund.

Bernstein, M. A., 1987, *The Great Depression. Delayed Recovery and Economic Change in America, 1929–1939*, Cambridge, Cambridge University Press.

Bernstein, M. A., 1989, 'Why the Great Depression was Great: Towards a New Understanding of the Interwar Economic Crisis in the United States', in S. Fraser and G. Gerstle, *The Rise and Fall of the New Deal Order, 1930–1980*, Princeton, Princeton University Press.

Blum, J. M., 1959, *From the Morgenthau Diaries. Years of Crisis, 1928–1938*, Boston, Houghton Mifflin Co.

Brown, E. C., 1956, 'Fiscal Policies in the Thirties: a Reappraisal', *American Economic Review*, 46: 857–79.

Burns, J., 1956, *Roosevelt: The Lion and The Fox 1882–1940*, New York, Harcourt, Brace and World Inc.

Brunner, K. (ed.), 1981, *The Great Depression Revisited*, The Hague, Martinus Nijhoff.

Chandler, L. V., 1950, *Benjamin Strong: Central Banker*, Washington, DC, Brookings Institute.

Chandler, L. V., 1970, *America's Greatest Depression, 1929–1941*, London, Harper & Row.

Chandler, L. V., 1971, *American Monetary Policy 1928–1941*, New York, Harper & Row.

Collins, R. M., 1981, *The Business Response to Keynes, 1929–1964*, New York, Columbia University Press.

Darby, M. R., 1976, 'Three-and-a-Half Million US Employees Have Been Mislaid: Or an Explanation of Unemployment, 1934–1941', *Journal of Political Economy*, 84: 1–16.

Davis, J. R., 1968, 'Chicago Economists, Deficit Budgets and the Early 1930s', *American Economic Review*, 58: 476–82.

De Long, J. B. and Summers, L. H., 1988, 'How Does Macroeconomic Policy Affect Output?', *Brookings Papers on Economic History*, 2: 433–74.

Department of Commerce, 1975, *Historical Statistics of US, Colonial Times to 1970*, Washington DC, Dept of Commerce.

Epstein, G. and Ferguson, I., 1984, 'Monetary Policy, Loan Liquidation and Industrial Conflict: The Federal Reserve and Open Market Operation of 1932', *Journal of Economic History*, 44: 957–83.

Fausold, M. C., 1977, 'President Hoover's Farm Policies, 1929–33', *Agricultural History*, 51: 362–77.

Fearon, P., 1987, *War, Prosperity and Depression. The U.S. Economy 1917–45*, Deddington, Philip Allan.

Finegold, K., 1982, 'From Agrarianism to Adjustment. The Political Origins of New Deal Agricultural Policy', *Politics and Society*, II: 1–27.

Friedman, M. and Schwartz, A. J., 1963, *A Monetary History of the United*

States, 1867–1960, New York, National Bureau of Economic Research.

Golembe, C. H., 1960, 'The Deposit Insurance Legislation of 1933. An Examination of its Antecedents and Purposes', *Political Science Quarterly*, 75: 218–22.

Gordon, R. J., 1976, 'Recent Developments in the Theory of Inflation and Unemployment', *Journal of Monetary Economics*, 2: 185–216.

Gordon, R. J., 1981, *Macroeconomics*, 2nd edn, Boston, Little Brown.

Gordon, R. J. and Wilcox, J. A., 1981, 'Monetarist Interpretations of the Great Depression: An Evaluation and Critique', in K. Brunner (ed.), *The Great Depression Revisited*, The Hague, Martinus Nijhoff.

Hawley, E. W., 1966, *The New Deal and the Problems of Monopoly*, Princeton, Princeton University Press.

Hawley, E. W., 1975, 'The New Deal and Business', in J. Braeman et al., *The New Deal. The National Level*, Columbus, Ohio University Press.

Hawley, E. W., 1979, *The Great War and the Search for a Modern Order. A History of the American People and Their Institutions, 1917–1933*, New York, St Martins Press.

Himmelberg, R. F., 1976, *The Origins of the National Recovery Administration: Business Government and the Trade Association Issue 1921–33*, Boston, Fordham University Press.

Holt, C. F., 1977, 'Who Benefitted from the Prosperity of the Twenties?', *Explorations in Economic History*, 14(3): 277–89.

Ioma, M., 1979, 'The Policy Effectiveness of Open Market Operations in the 1920s', *Explorations in Economic History*, 26(1): 99–116.

Kendrick, J., 1961, *Productivity Trends in the US*, Princeton, Princeton University Press.

Kesselman, J. R. and Savin, N. E., 1978, 'Three and a Half Million Workers Were Never Lost', *Economic Inquiry*, 16: 205–25.

Kettl, D. F., 1986, *Leadership and the Fed*, London, Yale University Press.

Kindleberger, C. P., 1979, 'The International Causes and Consequences of the Great Crash', *Journal of Portfolio Management*, 6: 11–14.

Lake, R. A., 1988, *Power, Protection and Free Trade. International Sources of U.S. Commercial Strategy, 1887–1939*, Ithaca and London, Cornell University Press.

Leuchtenberg, W. E., 1963, *Franklin D. Roosevelt and the New Deal*, New York, Harper & Row.

Leuchtenberg, W. E., 1964, 'The New Deal and the Analogue of War', in J. Braeman et al. (eds), *Change and Continuity in Twentieth Century America*, Columbus, Ohio University Press.

Margo, R., 1988, 'Interwar Unemployment in the United States: Evidence from the 1940 Census Sample', in B. Eichengreen and T. J. Hatton (eds), *Interwar Unemployment in Historical Perspective*, Dordrecht/Boston/London, Kluwer Academic Publishers.

Mead, E. S. and Ostrolenk, B., 1933, *Voluntary Allotment. Planned Production in American Agriculture*, Philadelphia, University of Pennsylvania Press.

Meltzer, A. H., 1981, 'Comments on "Monetarist Interpretations of the Great Depression"', in K. Brunner (ed.), *The Great Depression Revisited*, The Hague, Martinus Nijhoff.

Metcalf, E. B., 1975, 'Secretary Hoover and the Emergence of Economic Management', *Business History Review*, 49: 61–6.

Mishkin, F., 1978, 'The Household Balance Sheet in the Great Depression', *Journal of Economic History*, 38: 918–37.

Mitchell, W. C. and Burns, A. F., 1936, 'Production During the American Business Cycle of 1927–1933', *NBER Bulletin 61*, New York, 7–20.

Nourse, E. G., Davis, J. S., and Black, J. D., 1937, *Three Years of Agricultural Adjustment Administration*, Washington DC, The Brookings Institute.

Pastor, R. A., 1980, *Congress and the Politics of U.S. Foreign Economic Policy 1929–1976*, Berkeley, University of California Press.

Peppers, L., 1973, 'Full Employment Surplus Analyses and Structural Change: the 1930s', *Explorations in Economic History*, 10: 197–210.

Perkins, V. L., 1969, *Crisis in Agriculture. The Agricultural Adjustment Administration and the New Deal, 1933*, Berkeley and Los Angeles, University of California Press.

Reagan, P. D., 1988a, 'From Depression to Depression: Hooverian National Planning, 1921–1933', *Mid-American*, 702: 35–60.

Reagan, P. D., 1988b, 'Creating the Organizational Nexus for New Deal Planning', in J. E. Brown and P. D. Reagan (eds), *Voluntarism, Planning and the State. The American Planning Experience 1914–1946*, London, Greenwood Press.

Romasco, A. U., 1965, *The Poverty of Abundance. Hoover, the Nation, the Depression*, Oxford, Oxford University Press.

Romasco, A. U., 1988, *The Politics of Recovery*, Oxford, Oxford University Press.

Roose, K. D., 1954, *The Economics of Recession and Revival*, New Haven, Yale University Press.

Saloutos, T., 1982, *The American Farmer and the New Deal*, Ames, Iowa State University Press.

Saint-Etienne, C., 1984, *The Great Depression 1929–1938. Lessons for the 1980s*, Stanford, Hoover Institution Press.

Skocpol, T. and Finegold, K., 1982, 'State Capacity and Economic Organisations in the Early New Deal', *Political Science Quarterly*, 97: 255–78.

Snyder, R. E., 1984, *Cotton Crisis*, Chapel Hill, University of North Carolina Press.

Spulber, N., 1989, *Managing the American Economy from Roosevelt to Reagan*, Bloomington, Indiana University Press.

Stein, H., 1969, *The Fiscal Revolution in America*, Chicago, University of Chicago Press.

Swanson, J.A. and Williamson, J.H., 1972–3, 'Estimates of National Product and Income for the United States Economy, 1919–1941, *Explorations in Economic History*, 10: 53–73.

Sweezy, A., 1972, 'The Keynesians and Government Policy 1933–39', *American Economic Review Papers and Proceedings*, 62: 116–24.

Temin, P., 1976, *Did Monetary Forces Cause the Great Depression?* New York, W. W. Norton.

Toma, M., 1979, 'The Policy Effectiveness of Open Market Operations in

the 1920s', *Explorations in Economic History*, 26: 99–116.
Weinstein, M. M., 1980, *Recovery and Redistribution under the* NIRA, North Holland Publishing Company.
Weinstein, M. M., 1986, 'Industrial Planning and Economic Policy Making: Lessons from the 1930s', in J. S. Cohen (ed.), *International Monetary Problems and Supply Side Economics*, London, Macmillan.
Weir, M., 1988, 'The Federal Government and Unemployment: The Frustration of Policy Innovation from New Deal to Great Society', in M. Weir, A. S. Orloff and T. Skocpol (eds), *The Politics of Social Policy in the United States*, Princeton, Princeton University Press.
White, E. N., 1981, 'State Sponsored Insurance of Bank Deposits in the United States, 1907–1929', *Journal of Economic History*, 41: 537–57.
Wicker, E. R., 1965, 'Federal Reserve Monetary Policy, 1922–33. A Reinterpretation', *The Journal of Political Economy*, 73: 325–43.
Wicker, E. R., 1966, *Federal Reserve Monetary Policy 1917–1933*, New York, Random House.
Wright, G., 1987, 'Labor History and Labor Economics', in A. J. Field (ed.), *The Future of Economic History*, Boston, Kluwer-Nijhoff Publishing.

7 Policy responses to the crisis: Australasia in the 1930s

A. M. Endres and K. E. Jackson

This study analyses policy responses to the Depression in the 1930s in two quite distinct economies, New Zealand and Australia, and from differing perspectives. In the case of New Zealand our primary concern is with unemployment policy in the context of shifting policy priorities during the 1930s. Creative public works experiments were substantially modified in New Zealand when mass unemployment became persistent from 1931. Indeed unemployment policy itself was gradually re-ranked as a subordinate social, rather than strictly economic, response to the Depression as policy turned increasingly to the fostering of an export-led recovery via budgetary stringency, tariff reductions, real wage and price reductions and an exchange rate depreciation. A similar reliance upon an export-led recovery is found in Australia in the 1930s. Improvements in international competitiveness were sought via reductions in wages and the imposition of budgetary restraint. Externally Australia encouraged import replacement industries in a 'beggar-thy-neighbour' world through tariffs rather than extensive use of exchange rate policies. Direct relief measures on the other hand were driven more by social than by economic considerations and if economic policy was less draconian than it might have been this was only because of the fear of the social and political reactions that might thereby have been incurred. We turn first to the policy responses in each country before contrasting the salient features of their experiences over the decade.

New Zealand

Our purpose here is to shed light on the official ranking and role of unemployment policy *vis-à-vis* other economic policy responses in the Depression and early recovery period in New Zealand. In inter-war Britain deep commitment to a doctrine of minimum government interference counted against adoption of a planned, 'radical' interventionist unemployment policy (Garside, 1990). New Zealand's long tradition prior to the 1930s of government economic management and decades of *ad hoc* social interference, which produced a remarkable exfoliation of interventionist institutions, is well documented.[1] Indeed, a doctrine of maximum government experimentation – where experiments could pragmatically be designed to counter a perceived problem – was prevalent in New Zealand well before the 1930s. Unlike the British (or Australian) case therefore, we would expect *a priori* that the foundations had been laid in New Zealand for an enlightened and activist unemployment policy in response to the economic crisis of the 1930s.

The reality proved very different. Although deficit finance was used creatively in the late 1920s to reduce the jobless total, unemployment policy after 1930 was rendered a caretaker role, pending an agricultural, export-led economic recovery. Budgetary orthodoxy became more entrenched after 1930, viewed as a necessary concomitant of the resuscitation of the agricultural sector.

Policy responses in the early 1930s

During the late 1920s government authorities in New Zealand had taken countervailing, discretionary action to increase public works expenditure on behalf of the unemployed despite a rising budget deficit. Officials were not necessarily mindful of the macroeconomic effects of this additional spending. None the less, the significant share that public works spending took of the government's internal deficit (75 per cent in 1927/8) proved of direct benefit to the unemployed. The onset of depression, however, brought a less tolerant official attitude to emergency public relief works financed by central and local government even though they had made a substantial contribution to reducing unemployment before 1930. Such measures were increasingly regarded as too extravagant, poorly organised, lacking in public accountability and offering only temporary employment rather than long-term solutions to unemployment. At the same time, an Unemployment Fund was established in 1930, financed initially by contributions from workers and the government but solely from a regressive tax levy on wages, salaries and other income from 1932, to provide special unemployment relief schemes (rather than normal public works schemes) on a more deliberate and accountable scale. Revenue and expenditure of the Fund in the 1930s are detailed in Table 7.1.[2]

When unemployment peaked in 1933, unemployment relief amounted to nearly 15 per cent of government spending (see Table 7.1). This did not, however, mean that unemployment policy was becoming a supremely important aspect of government activity in the economy. Government subsidies to the Fund were abandoned in 1932 to assist in balancing the budget (Economic Committee 1932, summary section, pp. 4–5), after which unemployment relief policy became completely self-financing. There were no bold initiatives using deficit finance as there had been in the late 1920s. The Unemployment Fund on the whole operated within a 'balanced budget' mode. The minister in charge of unemployment policy stated proudly and confidently in 1932 that despite the fact of mass unemployment the Fund would have a surplus of £1 million by March 1933. He averred that it

is questionable if in any part of the world financial arrangements of the Government for handling the unemployment problem are as sound as in New Zealand. The whole of this money, amounting to 3.5 and 4 million [pounds] is being raised by taxation . . . The payments given to relief workers continue to be paid in return for work done. Most of this work is useful . . . without adding to the national debt. (Hamilton, quoted in New Zealand Political Correspondent, 1932, p. 240)

This is to say that in *some* years, even with unemployment at historically high levels, more was raised from the unemployment tax than was spent from the Fund. At the end of the 1934/5 financial year the Fund had a credit balance of £1.3 million while the unemployment rate was approximately 8 per cent of the workforce (Sutch, 1941, p. 136). For the Depression and recovery period as a whole however, Table 7.1 demonstrates that revenue from unemployment tax roughly equalled expenditure from the Fund.

The unemployment problem in the 1930s was regarded not so much as an economic issue or as a pre-eminent element in national economic policy, but as a pressing social problem that had more to do with poverty and its 'relief'. There was no presumption that unemployment could be removed by greater policy activism in the broader macro-economic sense. The prevailing *Zeitgeist* in New Zealand was one of almost 'primitive morality requiring that adverse conditions be conquered by sacrifice and hardship' (Condliffe, 1959, p. 51). In 1932, J. M. Keynes had suggested to Horace Belshaw, a leading New Zealand economist, that an Empire reconstruction loan might be raised to promote extensive public investment, but to no avail (Endres, 1990b).

Public works expenditure as such contracted in the early 1930s, halving in 1931/2 (see Table 7.2). This was due in large measure to reduced borrowing following the philosophy of the balanced budget.

Table 7.1 Revenue and expenditure of the Unemployment Fund 1930–38 (£ million)

Years (March)	Revenue from unemployment tax	Percentage of total government revenue	Expenditure from unemployment fund	Percentage of total government expenditure
1930/31	0.28	1.48	0.3	–
1931/2	2.34*	10.5	3.37*	12.4
1932/3	4.10	20.8	3.79	14.3
1933/4	4.41	20.4	4.24	14.9
1934/5	4.56	17.2	3.91	13.8
1935/6	3.92	15.4	4.88	15.9
1936/7	4.22	13.5	4.41	12.6
1937/8	5.10	13.9	4.34	10.9
Total	28.93		29.24	

Sources: Canterbury Chamber of Commerce, 1936, No. 141; 1937, No. 154; Riches, 1933, p. 35; Unemployment Board, 1932, p. 9.

Note: * Includes a £1.12 million supplement from the Consolidated Fund, i.e. general tax revenue.

Table 7.2 Public works expenditure 1930–35 (£ million)

	Financial years ending March 31					
	1930	1931	1932	1933	1934	1935
Railways	2981	3015	952	161	132	126
Roads	2158	2233	1465	538	552	689
Telegraph extension	594	420	250	100	144	136
Development of water power*	504	1188	1242	589	570	556
Public buildings	772	924	455	91	149	287
Land and river improvement[†]	262	234	117	107	153	188
Land settlement	–	–	–	119	352	348
Total	7271	8014	4481	1705	2052	2330

Source: Condliffe, 1959, p. 40.

Notes: * Including maintenance
[†] Settlement of unemployed workers and (from 1933/4) native land settlement

Retrenchment of normal public works activity accentuated the unemployment problem; relief work as such was rendered increasingly unattractive, demeaning and unproductive in economic terms (Campbell, 1932, pp. 102–3; Neale, 1932, p. 132). By 1933, unemployment policy had assumed a social policy role; relieving poverty became its sole *raison d'etre* as the Depression took hold.

Policy priorities during the Depression

Although mass unemployment was clearly one of the more visible effects of the Depression, unemployment in the 1930s played a caretaker role pending successful operation of other strictly economic policies which centred on increasing production of primary sector staples. The design and untimely implementation of other economic policies, however, had unintended, or at least undesired, consequences in so far as they exacerbated the unemployment problem and retarded economic recovery. We turn initially to policy initiatives aimed at influencing the balance of external receipts and payments.

The Depression in New Zealand from mid-1931 was not primarily the outcome of a balance of payments problem. Only in the years ending March 1930 and 1931 were the net overseas assets of the banking system drawn down. According to Hawke (1985, p. 134):

Current account items other than the balance of trade, notably payments made abroad for public debt interest and private interest and dividends, hardly declined, and certainly did not fall like import payments, but the joint movement was enough to cover the decline in exports and still leave a surplus in the overseas accounts.

Agricultural export volumes grew during the Depression while export values declined by almost 11 per cent between 1930 and 1933 before recovering and surpassing the 1930 performance by value in 1934 (Hawke, 1985, p. 128). Contemporary debate over the priorities of economic policy concentrated on government management of the exchange rate as a strategic instrument combining both favourable income and substitution effects. Real income effects related to redistributing, by exchange rate devaluation, the income losses of the Depression to obtain greater 'equality of sacrifice' between various sectors of the economy without which losses would have fallen disproportionately upon the export sector. Nominal income effects of a managed exchange rate devaluation implied avoidance of more drastic reductions in nominal incomes by using an extreme deflationist solution. A deflationist policy package would have necessitated, *inter alia*, an exchange rate approximating sterling parity and further falls in the domestic wage and price level relative to export prices as a first step in promoting a farm-based, export-led recovery over a longer time horizon. While the market may not have dictated an exchange rate depreciation in 1932 – as British economists Niemeyer and Gregory maintained – the government's Economic Committee argued in February 1932 in favour of substantial devaluation on the grounds of its favourable real and nominal income effects (Economic Committee, 1932).[3]

The substitution effects of devaluation, critically drawn out in Fisher (1932), were not expressly of concern to economists who constituted the Economic Committee. The Committee was interested solely in short-period responses and its report assumed negligible increases in per capita productivity (Economic Committee, 1932, p. 16). Export-led growth through expansion of export volumes via exchange rate devaluation was, however, a possible long period consequence of their exchange rate recommendation. Resources, on the margin, presumably would move into the agricultural sector as the benefits of devaluation were realised. As Fisher (1932) argued, reliance on a government initiated export-led recovery was apparently desired by the Economic Committee barring exclusive dependence on higher productivity in agriculture or some hoped-for exogenous increase in agricultural commodity prices. Fisher's view was reinforced by the Economic Committee's suggestion of export subsidies as an alternative to devaluation (Endres, 1988).

The government did not act to implement the Economic Committee's suggestion of exchange rate devaluation until early 1933 when the New Zealand pound was altered from NZ £110 = stg. £100 to NZ £125 = stg.£100. The diary of the Minister of Finance, Downie Stewart, leaves no doubt that the farmers and not the unemployed were the prime, immediate concern of the government when the decision to devalue was taken (Dale, 1981, p. 166). The Treasury Secretary Park and Minister of Finance Stewart opposed devaluation on balanced (internal) budget grounds, arguing that a lower-valued currency would increase the foreign debt interest burden and reduce customs receipts as the demand for imports contracted. Given its balanced budget mentality, Treasury concern about devaluation leading to a narrowing of the tax base was warranted only in the absence of alternative revenue-raising measures such as a sales tax which was introduced at a rate of 10 per cent in 1932 (as recommended by the Economic Committee). The revenue-augmenting effects of devaluation from rising exporters' incomes, including the multiplier effects on other incomes, were ignored by a Treasury still locked in the manacles of pre-Keynesian economic theory.

The Economic Committee in February 1932 recommended gradual movement toward a balanced budget for the 1934/5 fiscal year while calling for active government policy to promote recovery in agriculture. 'New Zealand trod the more puritanical path towards early budget equilibrium' throughout 1932, continuing both to reduce public works spending (Table 7.2), and to finance unemployment relief out of special taxation in the interests of reviving confidence in the private sector (Belshaw, 1936, pp. 52–3). Initially in May 1931 the government imposed 10 per cent reductions in both nominal interest rates and wages. This gave more assistance to farmers than to (mostly urban) wage and salary earners. However, real wages had increased by 0.5 per cent between 1929 and late 1931. Thus, in insisting that the 10 to 15 per cent loss of real national income up to the end of 1931 'be spread throughout the community if sound economic conditions are to be restored', the Economic Committee (1932, p. 28) called for a further crude, all-round 10 per cent money wage reduction. The government acceded to this request forgetting, conveniently, the existing impact of the unemployment tax on workers' disposable income. Subsequent currency devaluation also impacted disproportionately on workers' living costs in 1933, but no compensatory money wage adjustments were forthcoming (Endres, 1990a). From 1933 policy-makers became less obsessed with the goal of an immediate balanced budget and further significant relief was brought to the farm sector by devaluation. This boosted the farmers' share of national income and, combined with a somewhat fortuitous increase in agricultural commodity prices, especially for wool, gave impetus to a slow economic recovery which began late in 1933.

The income effects of devaluation were lessened considerably, however, by the government's agreement with local banks to buy back surplus foreign exchange in order to cover uncertainty associated with the possibility that the exchange rate may be revalued at some future date. Essentially this indemnity agreement, formalised in the Banks Indemnity Act (1933), enabled the banks to sell surplus sterling to the government in return for treasury bills which bore a high interest rate and effectively set an egregiously high floor to domestic interest rates at 5 per cent or slightly above (Hawke, 1985, p.156; 1987, p. 120). According to Hawke (1988, p. 131), 'real interest rates were high, both in international terms and relative to historical trends. The low levels of investment especially in housing, are therefore readily understandable'. Economic recovery was therefore severely, although unintentionally, retarded in 1933 and 1934. Immobilised cash assets of some £23 million were accumulated in London which could have been used to expand credit within New Zealand. Relief was not forthcoming until the Reserve Bank of New Zealand was established late in 1934; the existing exchange rate was lent greater credibility by central bank support and sanction, and the Reserve Bank moved to legitimate more active use of idle London funds by incorporating them in its inaugural cash reserves (Hawke, 1973, p. 40). New Zealand therefore emerged from the Depression in a strong (external) financial position.

While unemployment policy was ranked well below policies for a balanced budget and revival of agricultural production through interest rate and exchange rate manipulation, commercial policy in the 1930s figured even less significantly. New Zealand had little domestic manufacturing to protect during the Depression. Factory production, mostly for the local market, employed approximately 15 per cent of the work-force in 1933 and constituted nearly 24 per cent of the value of production.[5] Domestic manufacturing was not fostered actively and directly as a matter of policy. The 1933 devaluation might have given some stimulus to import substitution although that was not intended as a principal policy consideration. Although the record is sketchy, it appears that private confidence was at such a low ebb that increases in the relative profitability of home production following the statutory 10 per cent reduction of money wages and 20 per cent reduction of interest rates in 1932 and 25 per cent depreciation of the currency in 1933, were not in general responded to very quickly by private industry (Hawke, 1987, pp. 120–21).

According to Drummond (1972, p. 222) the Dominions 'did not understand that their own industrial protectionism helped to impoverish their primary producers'. This generalisation, upon closer examination, cannot legitimately be applied to New Zealand in the 1930s. While the historical record presents a rather complicated picture (Hawke, 1987, pp. 111–13), it appears that the 1930s saw reductions rather than increases in the level of protection provided by tariffs. Moreover, tariffs at the beginning of the 1930s in New Zealand were moderate by international standards, with rates above 60 per cent only for alcohol and tobacco products (Bertram, 1988, pp. 2, 26). It was the rural bias in contemporary thought and political economy in New Zealand in the 1920s and 1930s which prevented any substantial surge in higher protective duties, except in the special cases of protection for arable farming (wheat, tobacco) and forestry (Bertram, 1988, pp. 9, 11). On a value basis over 85 per cent of imports used directly in farming entered New Zealand duty free while another 10 per cent were subject to duties varying between 10 and 15 per cent *ad valorem*. In addition, other revenue-raising measures such as the 1932 sales tax exempted farm implements and other farm inputs (Rodwell, 1936).

Economists' trade policy prescriptions emphasised the relatively small character of the local market for manufactures, and explored ways of reducing tariffs below their already moderate pre-Depression levels (Copland, 1932a, p. 88; Fisher, 1932, p. 77). The 1933 Tariff Commission, which included among its members Barney Murphy, a leading conservative economist with free trade convictions, generously interpreted New Zealand's obligations under the Ottawa Agreement, 'so much so that of the 103 changes made in the early liberal British tariff, 100 items consisted of reductions or the abolition of duties' (Sutch, 1936, pp. 131–2). In general, therefore, the tariff was reduced in the midst of the Depression. Deliberations over tariff policy were often constrained and directed by a bilateralist trade policy strategy, particularly arrangements to obtain primary product access to the British market (Bertram, 1988, pp. 16–17).

Commercial policy was neither coordinated with the unemployment policy nor with the special package of measures designed by the Economic Committee (1932) to balance the budget and revive agriculture. Revenue-raising to assist in balancing the budget and/or to ensure continuing and stable farm product access to the British market were pre-eminent in decisions to adjust tariffs in New Zealand during the Depression of the 1930s. Additional protection of selected manufacturing establishments to diversify the production base and to expand the range of factory employment opportunities did not figure as a prime policy *desideratum*. By 1938, in Wood's assessment, the protective tariff was still 'exceedingly moderate; so much so that New Zealand had little to offer in the way of further reductions in duties in bartering for concessions in overseas markets for New Zealand farm produce' (Wood, 1938, p. 64).

It would be unfair to claim that the New Zealand government did not wish to act to reduce unemployment in the Depression. Given constraints imposed by an evaporation of loanable sterling funds for development purposes and a prevailing pre-Keynesian mode of economic thought and policy advice, the government attempted to respond indirectly to unemployment. Government manipulation and regulation of the sterling exchange rate and interest rates in order to encourage greater output and employment, initially in agriculture and associated services, assisted, rather belatedly, in recovery. An uncompromising deflationist policy stance was therefore avoided in the process. Doubtless the government acted too slowly and cautiously even in respect of exchange rate devaluation. Recovery in employment was also hampered by an ill-conceived policy to indemnify banks from exchange rate risks. In addition, commercial policy was too conservative in that it was not geared towards developing a broader industrial base capable of expanding labour absorption to a greater degree than was ever likely from policies aimed at nurturing the agricultural sector.

Australia

Economic problems in the 1930s

At the start of the 1930s Australia was perceived to be at a critical stage in its economic development. The immediate extent of the problem was reflected in the statistics of national product and unemployment. Annual average rates of decline in real gross domestic product per capita of approximately 1.8 per cent were experienced in the late 1920s (Pope, 1987, p. 35). After having fallen only slightly between the beginning of 1929 and the end of 1930, GDP at constant prices exhibited a precipitate decline during 1931 (Valentine, 1987, p. 65). Real GDP fell by 9 per cent between 1929 and the trough of 1932 (Gregory, Ho, McDermott and Hagan, 1988, p. 401). Although this compares very favourably with, say, the USA, which recorded a 29 per cent decline in real GDP during the same period, if we compare unemployment in 1929 with the peak unemployment of 1933, it increases by 22 per cent in the USA and 9 per cent in Australia. The difference of 13 percentage points is approximately two-thirds of the 20 percentage points difference in the output loss between the two countries, reflecting a relatively worse unemployment record in Australia than might be expected from the output loss (Gregory, Ho, McDermott and Hagan, 1988, p. 405).

The economic problems Australia faced in the 1930s had external as well as internal origins. Evidence points towards the emergence of a chronic balance of payments constraint as early as the 1920s. A persistent deficit on current account was only balanced by capital inflows. The critical situation of the early 1930s resulted from a continuation of this international constraint combined with a failure to restructure the domestic economy in a way likely to maintain, let alone improve, Australian export competitiveness.

It is easy in hindsight to point to the folly of actions such as that of extending the area under wheat cultivation against the dictates of market trends, but it must have been less obvious to the individuals involved at the time. Farmers were given encouragement by the central government on the strength of the inflow of funds from Britain (Boehm, 1971, p. 76). Later events suggest that reliance upon a relatively restricted range of primary products for a high proportion of export receipts laid the economy open to extremes of volatility and merely compounded the situation. By the early 1930s wool, wheat, meat and butter accounted together for nearly two-thirds of all export receipts (Boehm, 1971, p. 68). At this time there was a sharp fall in the prices received for all these products so that the existing balance of payments problem was exacerbated. In addition there was a cessation of the inflow of overseas funds. Borrowing to cover the shortfall in the overseas trade account was then difficult, if not impossible.

The foreign borrowing previously undertaken for public investment in rural and urban areas had contributed to the balance of payments problem. Interest and dividend payments sent abroad had risen by some 50 per cent during the 1920s and as a proportion of export receipts they had increased from less than one-sixth to something in excess of one-quarter of the total outpayments (Schedvin, 1970, p. 73). This growing burden upon export income quickly became critical as that export income shrank. Funds available for purchasing imports, after the existing level of debt had been serviced, were severely curtailed.

The domestic consequences of these developments cannot be estimated exactly. The available unemployment figures are less than complete or consistent in their coverage, but they do at least provide some indication of the extent and nature of the problem, particularly in the urban areas and the manufacturing sector. The full extent of rural unemployment is very difficult to ascertain. Some of the traditional statistics relate principally to the incidence of unemployment among members of particular trade unions. This gives them an industrial and urban bias which overstates the overall extent of unemployment (Jonson and Stevens, 1983, p. 1). More recent estimates utilise the 1933 population census, the 1939 National Register and trade union data, adjusted to conform to official benchmarks, but still do not resolve all statistical problems. None the less, the level of unemployment rises considerably during the early 1930s whatever series is used[6] peaking to at least 20 per cent in 1932 (Gregory, Ho, McDermott and Hagan, 1988, p. 405).

Policy advice

Advice on what to do about the prevailing situation was far from lacking. At the federal level a principal actor in the drama was L. F. Giblin, who occupied the Ritchie Chair of Economics at the University of Melbourne from 1929. According to Cain, 'Giblin, confidante of politicians who mattered . . . was regularly sought out for advice during 1930–3, when the depression was at its most severe'. Giblin's original attitude was very straightforward. Government intervention in any recovery ought to be limited, if not totally absent, in favour of relying upon the private sector (Cain, 1983, p. 194). The orthodox policy response to which this kind of evidence gave rise was soon tempered, however, by the political and social climate in which it was forced to operate. But Giblin was not alone in opposing any radical attack on the Depression. The Premiers' Plan of 1931 proposed an increase in tax on income and sales together with a 20 per cent cut in most items of government expenditure from their 1929/30 level. Apart from R. F. Irvine, there was little apparent support among economists for more radical alternatives such as the repudiation of debt, propounded by Lang in New South Wales (Mendelsohn, 1979, p. 104). Whereas Theodore, the Labour Treasurer, advocated an expansionist approach with, implicitly, central bank credit being used to finance the budget deficit (Schedvin, 1970, pp. 226–7), the Premiers' Plan relied upon a reduction in the budget deficit for internal balance and, in the longer run, export recovery to achieve external balance. Little, if any, real attention appears to have been paid to domestic expansionary alternatives. Most of the debate from 1931 onwards, when it did occur, was focused upon the practical possibilities of operating a domestic deflationary response. There were increasing signs of division between those who strongly favoured deflation and those who were fearful of the political, economic and social consequences of such action.

The general tenor of economic advice proffered to government, however, was deflationary in tone. Where it did focus on costs and the need to reduce them, it tended to concentrate almost exclusively upon wage rates, for the most part neglecting repudiation of foreign debt and the possibilities for economic expansion that a reduction in real interest rates might have produced (Schedvin, 1970, p. 254). Judging by the recent findings of Newell and Symons (1988, p. 87) this was a far from trivial oversight. They attribute a significant part of the increase in unemployment to the effect of abnormally high real interest rates. Politicians of the 1930s, however, viewed the interest rate problem largely in terms of the debt position of the rural sector rather than as an issue of general macro-economics.

The decision to move towards a balanced budget internally while awaiting an external, export-induced recovery meant that the burden of adjustment in the 1930s would be borne by wage-earners and the unemployed. Expansion of domestic demand was not an option. Market forces largely determined policy decisions in relation to the exchange rate, balance of payments and interest rates (Schedvin,

1970, p. 350). Wage rates were expected to accommodate economic shocks, with rising unemployment viewed as the inevitable outcome of any failure of prices to adjust.

This emphasis upon internal deflation, though tempered somewhat by fears of social and political backlash, was particularly unfortunate given the inadequacies of policies to cope with rising unemployment. The relief system in force at the start of 1930 could not hope to cope with a problem on the scale with which it was about to be confronted, nor was it ever intended that it should. Direct federal expenditure on unemployment relief during the Depression was almost totally lacking (Mendelsohn, 1979, pp. 382–5), although central government did allocate funds to the states for relief purposes (Snooks, 1988, p. 316). The fundamental responsibility was reckoned to be a local one. Only Queensland with its contributory insurance scheme seemed to have made any significant move away from a system which was essentially dominated by the old Poor Law approach. At the start of the Depression the administrative structure for dealing with relief provision was a disjointed collection of charitable groups, religious organisations, local government bodies, social clubs and increasingly, albeit unwillingly, state governments.

The scale of the demands for relief quickly exceeded the capacity of the traditional sources. In addition, traditional responses to unemployment such as tramping were actively discouraged by the insistence of local authorities that outsiders should not receive relief in any shape or form.

Old Poor Law attitudes were never far below the surface. Something akin to the concept of the distinction between the deserving and undeserving poor is clearly discernible in the 1932 Victorian Act to revise relief administration, where part of its intent was to avoid mixing together the 'dissolute' and the 'decent' (Mendelsohn, 1979, p. 103). Rations, relief works and dole payments were all tried in varying degrees, with continual attempts to insist upon a work test before relief was granted. Much of the work involved in such 'workfare' schemes was rural-related and not always economically motivated, being more in the nature of a deterrent to seeking relief. The policy mix of local and charitable response was clearly inadequate to cope with a problem of the magnitude of the 1930s.

Judged by the results of recent work on the worldwide experience at the time, Australia failed to come to grips with the underlying causes of depression, neglecting especially the impact of an external price shock on real wages and interest rates (Newell and Symons, 1988, p. 73). Policy shortcomings are clearer in hindsight. An earlier reduction in the exchange rate could have lessened the impact of the price shock. Attempts to address the external balance problem were concentrated too heavily upon tariff protection which was itself undermined by the maintenance of a high exchange rate.

When devaluation was effected in December 1932 it had the appearance of a final and somewhat grudging acceptance of a market solution. Price changes were resorted to because quantitative measures had failed. The contribution of devaluation to the recovery of 1932/3 was significant to the extent that it gave a general protective boost to domestic development, working in concert with, rather than against, tariffs, subsidies and other more specific protective devices. But, separating out devaluation's specific value as a policy instrument is a difficult task. Valentine's simulations suggest that its principal contribution derived from its assistance in easing the balance of payments constraint (Valentine, 1988, p. 171).

Australia's willingness to adopt a judicial approach to wage determination also enabled wage deflation to bite with particular effect. Wage reductions were seen as one of the means of checking the increase in unemployment. The Commonwealth Court argued in January 1931 that because national income and spending had declined, wages of one-fifth of the labour force would need to be reduced by 10 per cent if industry was to remain competitive (Anderson, 1931, pp. 117–20). Proto-Keynesian ideas were hardly in evidence in the early 1930s; there were lone voices arguing against wage reductions as a way of increasing employment, but not many (Kuhn, 1988, p. 56). Australian nominal wages fell by around 20 per cent in the early 1930s; a faster rate of decline than was experienced in most other industrialised nations (Gregory, Ho, McDermott and Hagan, 1988, p. 401). Real wages remained relatively static for those fortunate enough to remain in employment.

The thrust of policy initiatives in the wake of depression were directed therefore towards deflation, particularly of wage levels. Unemployment relief policy was afforded a very low priority, with states obliged to take on much of the central government's contribution to relief. Some efforts were made to secure industrial expansion through the rise of direct controls and tariff barriers to effect import replacement but the principal aim remained one of seeking short-term results while awaiting an upturn in export demand to ensure complete recovery, whatever the price in terms of social justice.

Both Australia and New Zealand, therefore, opted for modified internal deflation in response to depression while awaiting a revival of exports to bring about full recovery. Unemployment relief through direct government expenditure was limited in each case, although New Zealand imposed special tax provisions on wages and salaries on those in employment to provide funds for the unemployed. This had the effect, however, of reducing any observable rise in real income for those remaining in jobs. Nominal wage levels were attacked in both countries as reaction set in to any deliberate expansion of demand either by fiscal or wage-fixing mechanisms. The tone of policy throughout the Depression years was contractionary, tempered only by the fear of creating social and political upheaval.

Notes

1 See Condliffe, 1930; Le Rossignol and Stewart, 1910; and Reeves, 1902.
2 Detailed descriptions of various relief schemes administered by the UB may be found in *New Zealand Official Yearbook*, 1937, pp. 705–17; Riches, 1933, pp. 28–36; Robertson, 1982; pp. 26–34; and Williams, 1933.
3 For the ensuing debate between New Zealand and British economists see Belshaw et al., 1932; Copland, 1932b, pp. 376–9; and Gregory, 1932. Gregory urged that New Zealand should wait for clearer trends in sterling prices (of New Zealand staple exports) because he expected that they would rise of their own accord, rather than risk 'the psychological and other difficulties of government interference with the exchange rate' (Gregory, 1932, p. 656).
4 From 1930 to 1935 the share of customs receipts in government revenue fell from 50 per cent to almost 30 per cent (Canterbury Chamber of Commerce, 1936, No. 141, p. 3).
5 Calculated from data from the Canterbury Chamber of Commerce (1936, No. 135, p. 2) and MacRae and Sinclair (1976, pp. 38, 40). Estimates of the value of factory production are available in Economic Committee, 1932, p. 48.
6 For a comprehensive discussion of the current problems in using such data see C. Forster, 1985, pp. 1–11.

References

Anderson, G., 1931, 'The Commonwealth Conciliation and Arbitration Act, 1930', *Economic Record*, VII: 82–99.
Boehm, E. A., 1971, *20th Century Economic Development in Australia*, Camberwell, Longman.
Belshaw, H., 1936, *Recovery Measures in New Zealand: A Comparison with the New Deal in the United States*, Wellington, New Zealand Institute of Pacific Relations.
Belshaw, H. et al., 1928, 'Unemployment in New Zealand, in National

Industrial Conference', *Report of Proceedings*, Wellington, Government Printer, 57–71.

Belshaw, H. et al., 1932, 'Professor Gregory's Views on Exchange', *Belshaw Papers*, 34D.

Belshaw, J. P., 1933, 'Post-War Unemployment and Unemployment Relief in New Zealand', *Economic Record*, 9: 58–75.

Belshaw, J. P., 1934, 'The Crisis in New Zealand, 1930–1934', Research Dissertation, University of Auckland.

Bertram, G., 1988, 'Barney Murphy and New Zealand Tariff Policy Between the Wars', Victoria University of Wellington Working Papers in Economic History, 88/1.

Cain, N., 1983, 'Recovery Policy in Australia 1930–3: Certain Native Wisdom', *Australian Economic History Review*, XXIII (1): 193–218.

Campbell, R. M., 1932, 'Unemployment Relief in New Zealand', *Economic Record*, 8: 103–5.

Canterbury Chamber of Commerce, 1925–39, *Economic Bulletins*, Department of Economics, Canterbury University College, Christchurch.

Condliffe, J. B., 1930, *New Zealand in the Making*, London, George Allen & Unwin.

Condliffe, J. B., 1931, 'The Effect of Falling Prices on Labour Conditions in New Zealand', *International Labour Review*, 23: 476–505.

Condliffe, J. B., 1959, *The Welfare State in New Zealand*, London, George Allen & Unwin.

Copland, D., 1932a, 'The New Zealand Economic Problem – A Comment', *Economic Record*, 8: 88–91.

Copland, D., 1932b, 'New Zealand's Economic Difficulties and Expert Opinion', *Economic Journal*, 42: 371–9.

Dale, S., 1981, 'Gentleman of Politics: A Life of William Downie Stewart, 1878–1949', MA Thesis, University of Otago, Dunedin.

Drummond, I. M., 1972, 'The British Empire Economies in the Great Depression', in H. Van Der Wee (ed.), *The Great Depression Revisited*, The Hague, Nijhoff.

Economic Committee, 1932, Report, *Appendices to the Journals of the House of Representatives*, B3, Wellington, Government Printer.

Endres, A. M., 1988, 'Structural Economic Thought in New Zealand: The Inter-War Contribution of A. G. B. Fisher', *New Zealand Economic Papers*, 22: 35–50.

Endres, A. M., 1990a, 'The Economics of Wages and Wages Policy in the Depression and Recovery Period', *New Zealand Journal of Industrial Relations*, 15: 1–18.

Endres, A. M., 1990b, 'The Development of Economists' Policy Advice in New Zealand, 1930–34', *Australian Economic History Review*, 30: 64–78.

Fisher, A. G. B., 1932, 'The New Zealand Economic Problem: A Review', *Economic Record*, 8: 74–87.

Fisher, A. G. B., 1933, 'New Zealand in the Depression', *Roundtable*, 23: 697–716.

Forster, C., 1985, 'Unemployment and the Australian Economic Recovery of the 1930s', *A.N.U. Working Papers in Economic History*, No. 45.

Garside, W. R., 1990, *British Unemployment, 1919–1939: A Study in Public Policy*, Cambridge, Cambridge University Press.

Gregory, T. E., 1932, 'New Zealand's Economic Difficulties and Expert Opinion: A Comment', *Economic Journal*, 42: 649–56.

Gregory, R. G., Ho, V., McDermott, L. and Hagan, J., 1988, 'The Australian and US Labour Markets in the 1930s', in B. Eichengreen and T. J. Hatton (eds), *Interwar Unemployment in International Perspective*, Dordrecht, Kluwer Academic Publishers.

Gruen, F. H., 1983, 'The Prices and Incomes Accord: Employment and Unemployment', *A.N.U. Centre for Economic Policy Research Discussion Paper*, No. 75.

Hawke, G. R., 1973, *Between Governments and Banks*, Wellington, Government.

Hawke, G. R., 1984, 'New Zealand in the 1930s and 1970s with some Australian Comparisons', *Victoria University of Wellington Working Papers in Economic History*, 84/4.

Hawke, G. R., 1985, *The Making of New Zealand: An Economic History*, Cambridge, Cambridge University Press.

Hawke, G. R., 1987, 'Australian and New Zealand Economic Development from About 1890 to 1940', in K. Sinclair (ed.), *Tasman Relations: New Zealand and Australia 1788–1988*, Auckland, Auckland University Press.

Hawke, G. R., 1988, 'Depression and Recovery in New Zealand', in R. Gregory and N. G. Butlin (eds), *Recovery From the Depression: Australia and the World Economy in the 1930s*, Cambridge, Cambridge University Press.

Holt, L. W., 1933, 'The New Zealand Budgetary Problem', *Economic Record*, 9: 115–121.

Jonson, P. D. and Stevens, G. R., 1983, 'The 1930s and the 1980s: Some Facts', *Reserve Bank of Australia Research Discussion Paper*, 8303.

Keynes, J. M., 1982, *Collected Writings*, Vol. 12, London, Macmillan.

Kuhn, R., 1988, 'Labor Movement Economic Thought in the 1930s: Underconsumptionism and Keynesian Economics', *Australian Economic History Review*, XXVIII: 53–74.

Lawn, G., 1931, 'Unemployment Relief in New Zealand', *Economic Record*, 7: 304–7.

Le Rossignol, J. and Stewart, W. D., 1910, *State Socialism in New Zealand*, London, Macmillan.

MacRae, J. and Sinclair, K., 1976, 'Unemployment in New Zealand During the Depression of the Late 1920s and Early 1930s', *Australian Economic History Review*, 16: 25–44.

Mendelsohn, R., 1979, *The Condition of the People: Social Welfare in Australia 1900–1975*, Sydney, George Allen & Unwin.

National Industrial Conference, 1928, *Proceedings*, Wellington, Government Printer.

Neale, E. R., 1932, 'The Crisis in New Zealand', *Economic Record*, 8: 115–32.

New Zealand Official Year Book, 1937.

New Zealand Political Correspondent, 1932, New Zealand Domestic Problems, *Roundtable*, 23: 227–44.

Newell, A. and Symons, J. S. V., 1988, 'The Macroeconomics of the Interwar Years: International Comparisons', in B. Eichengreen and T. J. Hatton (eds), *Interwar Unemployment in International Perspective*, Dordrecht, Kluwer Academic Publishers.

Paisley, A. D., 1930, 'Employment in New Zealand: New Legislative Measures', *Economic Record*, 6: 288–91.

Pope, D., 1987, 'Population and Australian Economic Development 1900–1930', in R. Maddock and I. W. Mclean (eds), *The Australian Economy in the Long Run*, Cambridge, Cambridge University Press.

Reeves, W. P., 1902, *State Experiments in Australia and New Zealand*, London, Macmillan.

Riches, E. J., 1933, 'Unemployment Relief Measures in New Zealand', *International Labour Review*, 29: 21–42.

Robertson, R. T., 1982, 'Government Responses to Unemployment in New Zealand, 1929–35', *New Zealand Journal of History*, 16: 21–38.

Rodwell, H. R., 1936, 'Taxation, Grants and Subsidies in Relation to Farming', in H. Belshaw et al. (eds), *Agricultural Organisation in New Zealand*, Melbourne, Melbourne University Press.

Schedvin, C. B., 1970, *Australia and the Great Depression*, Sydney, Sydney University Press.

Snooks, G. D., 1988, 'Government Unemployment Relief in the 1930s: Aid or Hindrance to Recovery', in R. G. Gregory and N. G. Butlin (eds), *Recovery from the Depression: Australia and the World Economy in the 1930s*, Cambridge, Cambridge University Press.

Sutch, W. B., 1936, *Recent Economic Changes in New Zealand*, New Zealand Institute of Pacific Relations, Whitcombe and Tombs.

Sutch, W. B., 1941, *Poverty and Progress in New Zealand*, Wellington, Modern Books.

Unemployment Board, 1932, Report, *Appendices to the Journals of the House of Representatives*, H-11, Wellington, Government Printer.

Valentine, T. J., 1987, 'The Depression of the 1930s', in R. Maddock and I. W. Mclean (eds), *The Australian Economy in the Long Run*, Cambridge, Cambridge University Press.

Valentine, T. J., 1988, 'The Battle of the Plans: A Macro-Econometric Model of the Inter-War Economy', in R. G. Gregory and N. G. Butlin (eds), *Recovery from the Depression: Australia and the World Economy in the 1930s*, Cambridge, Cambridge University Press.

Williams, D. O., 1933, 'Small Holdings for Unemployed in New Zealand', *Economic Record*, 9: 76–81.

Wood, G. E. F., 1938, 'Economic Philosophy and Structure', in Institute of International Affairs, *Contemporary New Zealand*, Auckland, Whitcombe and Tombs.

8 Depression and recovery: the Eastern European experience

Derek H. Aldcroft

Throughout the inter-war years the new and reconstituted states of Eastern Europe (Czechoslovakia, Hungary, Poland, Yugoslavia, Romania and Bulgaria) faced a constant struggle for survival, politically as well as economically. Weak states, barely fit for nationhood, internally rent by nationality conflicts and divided one against the other, they became pawns in the renewed struggle among the major powers for the hegemony of Europe. (Momtchiloff, 1944, p. 84; Newman, 1968, pp. 11–13, 27, 201; Ranki, 1983, pp. 33–4). Apart from Czechoslovakia, which inherited an economic structure more closely resembling that of the West,[1] all the states in the region remained heavily dependent on agriculture for a living. Between one-half and three-quarters of the occupied population was engaged in agriculture which generated up to one-half or more of total income (Dovring, 1960; Polonsky, 1975, p. 164; Royal Institute of International Affairs, 1940, p. 86). More to the point, despite varying degrees of land reform in the post-war period agriculture was extremely backward by any standard, with yields a fraction of those in Western countries (Moore, 1945, pp. 35, 51; Warriner, 1939, p. 9). The result was low incomes, limited domestic purchasing power, and the absence of agrarian accumulation, all of which inhibited structural diversification towards industry (Teichova, 1989, pp. 903–4). Rapid population growth exacerbated the pressure on the land leading to widespread under-employment and surplus labour (Moore, 1945, pp. 63, 71).

The backward state of Eastern Europe can be seen from a glance at Table 8.1, which shows some of the salient economic features of the countries in this region. The Balkan countries were, in every respect, the poorest nations, while Czechoslovakia stands out as being much closer to the West than any of the other countries. Poland and Hungary occupy an intermediate position. What is

Table 8.1   Economic characteristics of Eastern Europe in the inter-war years

	1	2	3	4	5	6	7	8
Bulgaria	84	1.34	36.5	96.1	70.9	68	300	110
Czechoslovakia	37	0.71	4.1	28.0	30.9	176	450	200
Hungary	53	0.76	9.3	71.3	40.4	112	340	150
Poland	65	1.44	24.6	76.6	40.4	104	400	130
Romania	79	1.27	42.0	99.1	73.9	70–75	290	80
Yugoslavia	79	1.45	48.0	91.9	69.7	81	300	100
Great Britain	6	0.49						
France	36		5.5			236	580	280
Germany	26					337	790	290
United States			4.3			521	1730	580

Key:
1 Percentage of active population engaged in primary sector, circa 1930.
2 Annual growth rate of population during inter-war years (per cent).
3 Illiteracy percentage of those aged 10 and over in 1929.
4 Primary products and semi-manufactures as a percentage of total exports, 1929–38.
5 Finished goods as a percentage of total imports, 1929–38.
6 Net national income per head of population in current (1938) US dollars.
7 Value of net output per worker in industry and handicrafts in current (1938) US dollars (Czechoslovakia 1937, United States 1936).
8 Value of net output per worker in agriculture in current (1938) US dollars.

Sources: Deldlycke, Gelders and Limbor, 1968; Kaser and Radice, 1985, pp. 358–9, 532; Polonsky, 1975, pp. 172, 178.

especially noticeable, with one or two exceptions, is the high proportion of the population engaged in agriculture, the rapid rate of population growth, and the skewed structure of foreign trade. Such characteristics epitomised the 'gigantic backlog of backwardness', to use Spulber's phrase (Spulber, 1966, p. 75), that faced Eastern European nations in this period, and which required a major structural transformation of their economies at a time when world events conspired to overwhelm them. Wartime hostilities and the aftermath had left a legacy of problems – destitution, reconstruction, territorial changes, inflation, currency instability, ethnic and social tensions – which took many years to solve (Aldcroft, 1988, p. 595). The new and reconstituted states which emerged as a result of the post-war peace settlement were scarcely designed to facilitate economic progress since they destroyed many of the former pre-war economic relationships. Consequently economic performance was chequered in the first half of the 1920s since most of these countries were grappling with the tasks of territorial and ethnic assimilation as well as a host of other problems in the wake of post-war reconstruction. It was not until the latter half of the decade that a measure of stability and progress was achieved but this was based on insecure foundations as the ensuing Great Depression demonstrated all too well.

Prosperity in the latter half of the 1920s – and ultimately the means of breaking the structural bottleneck in the longer term – was very much dependent on three factors: (1) a favourable market environment for agrarian products; (2) trade expansion; and (3) capital imports. Each in turn was also a source of weakness. First, agriculture, despite its inefficiency, was the main foreign exchange earner with dependence on a narrow range of crops. Market conditions, however, became increasingly less favourable in the later 1920s as Western countries sought to protect their home markets and as prices weakened, especially in cereals where stocks were piling up rapidly (Royal Institute of International Affairs, 1937, p. 287). Second, the loss of the large internal market of the Austro-Hungarian Empire meant that the new states were more trade-dependent than previously, and therefore more trade-sensitive and vulnerable to the vagaries of the international business cycle. Third, because of low domestic accumulation, increasing reliance was placed on capital imports. Foreign capital may have made a positive contribution to development but it also had its drawbacks (Lethbridge, 1985, p. 557; Nötel, 1986, p. 287). Inflows of capital were less than self-liquidating primarily because of the unproductive use to which much foreign capital was put (Political and Economic Planning, 1945, p. 110). The consequence was that servicing the foreign debt absorbed a steadily increasing proportion of export earnings. By the end of the decade most Eastern European countries had incurred unmanageable debt levels and were forced to continue borrowing in order to service past loans (Aldcroft, 1991, p. 53). In 1928 outpayments on account of capital services were 40 per cent of net capital inflows in the case of Hungary and 28 per cent for Poland, while, apart from Czechoslovakia, debt service payments constituted 25 per cent or more of the value of current export receipts (Aldcroft, 1977, p. 254; Political and Economic Planning, 1945, p. 110; United Nations, 1949b, p. 59).

Impact of the crisis

Arguably, therefore, Eastern Europe was already facing an untenable situation even before the start of the international slump of the 1930s (Bandera, 1964, p. 115; Lee, 1969, p. 141). The crisis itself shattered the region's fragile prosperity and eliminated any hope of its reintegration into the international economy. In aggregate terms east-central Europe, especially those countries closely associated with the German economy, suffered more severely from the

Great Depression than many Western countries (Maddison, 1973, pp. 20–21). The most important manifestations of that event as far as Eastern Europe was concerned were the massive fall in primary product prices, the collapse of international lending, and the shrinkage of international trade. Each of these had serious implications not only for the economies in general, but in particular for their balance of payments, budgets and debt burdens.

The price collapse had multiple implications. Agrarian prices, especially for cereals, fell by one-half or more, faster in fact than import prices of industrial products so that all countries except Czechoslovakia suffered a significant deterioration in their terms of trade. The decline was accentuated in the early stages as farmers attempted to compensate for the price decline by increasing output and raising the quantities exported. This policy met with only limited success, however, as external market conditions deteriorated rapidly after 1930 and export volumes declined. Thus, through a combination of price and quantity factors export receipts dropped sharply. In the case of Romania they fell by no less than 73 per cent and on average they had shrunk by 1932/3 to around 40 per cent of the 1929 level. This massive drop in export earnings entailed a serious loss of international purchasing power and a rising debt burden. Since international debts remained fixed the debt servicing power of exports fell by between one-half and two-thirds in the case of Hungary and the Balkan countries (Nötel, 1986, pp. 217–19). Only Czechoslovakia escaped the burden though her export earnings were affected as severely as anywhere because of the collapse of her former markets.

The price changes had equally momentous repercussions on the domestic front. Agrarian incomes declined by up to one-half in Poland and the Balkans, and by one-third in Hungary. The situation was aggravated by the unfavourable gap between agrarian and industrial prices. Whereas the former fell by 50 to 60 per cent, the price of goods purchased by the peasants rarely declined by more than 30 per cent (Seton-Watson, 1946, p. 82). At times the gap became so great that food producers had to give up nearly double the pre-war amount of grain and cattle to secure the same amount of manufactured articles (Hertz, 1947, p. 194). As incomes declined debt burdens increased as a proportion of income and by 1932 many peasants were on the verge of bankruptcy. In Yugoslavia, for example, more than a third of all rural households were heavily in debt – and many more were far too poor even to obtain credit – and the sum of their indebtedness was equal to 80 to 90 per cent of their total cash incomes (Rothschild, 1974, p. 271). The situation was even worse in Hungary where debt as a proportion of agrarian income rose from 78 to 133 per cent between 1928 and 1933 (Berend and Ranki, 1974a, p. 245). Together with a heavy burden of taxation the peasants' lot became intolerable: many sold their land simply to survive.

The diminished incomes of the farming community also had a serious fiscal impact. The main tax base of the government was eroded at a time when the demand for relief payments became greater. This forced governments to curtail expenditure wherever possible and therefore left little scope for the implementation of more expansive policies to combat the Depression. As Schönfeld (1975, pp. 197–8) notes, 'Der finanzielle Spielraum der Regierungen, die Depression durch öffentliche Aufträge und Subventionen zu bekämpfen, wurde immer geringer.'

It was the breakdown of the international financial mechanism in 1930/31 which finally undermined the solvency of Eastern Europe. Long-term foreign lending, already faltering in 1928/9, had virtually dried up by 1931, gold and foreign exchange reserves had drained away, and short-term credits were hastily withdrawn in the panic flight of capital in 1931 (United Nations, 1949b, p. 10). The cessation of foreign lending not only led to a curtailment of investment and activity but it also had a more immediate impact through the balance of payments. Most of the debtor countries had been dependent on capital imports in the later 1920s to close the gap in their external accounts. Thus of the total inflow of funds (both long and short) into Hungary, Poland, Bulgaria and Yugoslavia between 1924 and 1928, five-tenths went to cover an import surplus of goods and services, four-tenths to provide interest and dividends on foreign debt service, and one-tenth for the purchase of gold. In 1929 capital inflows barely covered interest and dividends and thereafter they dwindled to insignificant proportions. For the whole of the crisis period, 1929 to 1933, they covered less than one half of interest and dividends, which meant that the former import surplus on goods and services had to be converted into a positive balance (Nötel, 1974, pp. 84–5; 1984, pp. 182–3).

The collapse of export receipts, together with the cessation of capital inflows effectively rendered Eastern Europe insolvent. Nötel (1986, p. 227) sums up the situation as follows:

The financial crisis of mid-1931, superimposed upon the protracted export crisis in both commodities and manufactures, transformed the haunting spectre of the collapse of national currencies, within a few months or weeks, into an immediately threatening and practically unescapable reality for most east European countries. The sudden shift from continuing, even if irregular, capital imports to fast-spreading capital withdrawal and flight – with balance-of-payments position already weakened by the sharp and long-lasting fall in export receipts and the rising or at least maintained debt service – in all countries threatened to exhaust, or actually exhausted, the rapidly shrinking proceeds and reserves of foreign exchange.

It was little consolation that the industrial sector suffered less acutely from the crisis since for most countries in the region industry accounted for a small share of economic activity. Experience varied more widely than in the case of agriculture depending in part on the structure of individual economies. The light sector of manufacturing appears to have been the worst hit and it was this branch which predominated in the region as a whole (Zauberman, 1976, p. 598). Yet for the Balkan countries industrial over-production was scarcely a major problem given the insignificant weighting of the sector, and in any case reduced consumption was offset by increasing import protection. Thus, production declined only moderately in Romania thanks to a large increase in oil output, while Bulgaria actually managed to record a significant advance in manufacturing output between 1929 and 1932. Czechoslovakia was one of the worst to suffer in this respect because of her advanced industrial sector, while the mixed agrarian–industrial countries of Poland and Hungary were affected to a lesser extent. Nevertheless, except in the case of Czechoslovakia, it was the agrarian sector which determined the scale and severity of the crisis (Aldcroft, 1980, pp. 110–11).

The contours of policy action

There was no lack of policy response to meet the exigencies of the crisis of the 1930s, but it is difficult to detect any clearly defined and coordinated strategy designed to combat the Depression. In fact the majority of policy measures, at least in the early part of the 1930s, were *ad hoc* defensive ones, often inconsistent and contradictory, more likely to depress than to lift the level of economic activity. That the approach was orthodox and restrictive is not altogether surprising when one recalls the circumstances of the time. The problem initially was not so much one of recovery than one of sheer economic salvation. Drastic measures were therefore required to shore up tottering economies and these were soon forthcoming: they included severe deflationary policies together with a battery of restrictions typical of siege economies, and designed primarily to deal with the external account. Among these were temporary closure of banking institutions, rigorous exchange control, limitation on debt payments, and the imposition of tariffs, quotas and import restrictions. Moreover, given the speed and intensity of the crisis, the strong defensive measures taken by many of the major economic powers, and the limited theoretical guidance and practical experience on how to deal with a major economic crisis, it is difficult to conceive of a viable alternative open to the Eastern European economies. Desperate problems called forth desperate remedies. Only when conditions began to improve by the mid-1930s did they turn their attention to more constructive policies.

The policy response was not, however, quite so indeterminate as one might suspect from the more immediate reaction to the crisis. There were several more fundamental factors which helped to shape the course of policy over the medium term. One was the almost pathological fear present in most of the countries of the region of repeating the inflationary episode of the 1920s, which above all else was associated with currency depreciation and budgetary deficits. Hence the strong emphasis on financial rectitude, which meant balanced budgets and currency stabilisation at all costs (League of Nations, 1938, para. 8; 1944, p. 167).

Second, in keeping with this approach, and to maintain international confidence in the hope that foreign lending would be resumed, the debtor nations were reluctant initially to repudiate or default on their foreign debts. A corollary of this was an equal reluctance to depreciate their currencies since this would entail a rise in the nominal value of debts and service costs in domestic currency (Bandera, 1964, p. 119).

A third important factor shaping the course of policy was the growing force of nationalism. This had already been evident in the nostrification policy (the reduction or confiscation of alien property rights) of the 1920s which gathered force in the following decade (Pasvolsky, 1928, p. 75). It was associated with increasing state intervention and the ideology of autarky and self-determination which appeared to offer a more promising solution to the problems of the region than any attempt to regain re-entry into the international economy (Condliffe, 1941, p. 303). Liberal capitalism and bourgeois democracy had become discredited and this left the way open for right-wing autocratic governments to exploit nationalistic sentiments in both the economic and political spheres. Ultimately, as subsequent events were to demonstrate, this proved a high-cost exercise in both respects (Macartney and Palmer, 1962, pp. 285–8).

One final issue which became increasingly critical in the later 1930s was rearmament. Defence expenditure had always been a significant component in the budgets of these countries, but the increasing international tension in the later part of the period threw it into even greater prominence. Thus from the mid-1930s many of the sponsored or assisted industrial developments were geared in some way to the military needs of rearmament (Tomasevich, 1949, p. 179).

Within this framework of determining factors one can detect some subtle shift in policy direction during the course of the decade. Up to the mid-1930s policy tends to be highly orthodox and defensive, largely in an effort to avoid complete financial collapse and to provide relief for the most distressed sectors. Thereafter there is an element of relaxation both on the external and domestic fronts, aided by the recovery in international trade, the pressure of rearmament and the growing influence of Germany in the economies of the Danubian states. The change was reflected in some of the more ambitious policies to foster industrial development.

We now turn to a consideration of the relevance of various policy measures within the context of the following themes: (1) external protection; (2) macro-economic policy; (3) the relief of agriculture; and (4) state intervention and the promotion of industry. The final section provides an overall assessment.

In defence of external accounts

'By 1935 Europe had descended to a historical nadir in trade and commercial policy' (Friedman, 1978, p. 158). Almost every conceivable form of trade restriction, barring blockade, was then in use to a greater or lesser degree. Soon after the start of the crisis all European countries attempted to defend their external position and to improve their trade balances by utilising various methods of controls. Most of them – the main exceptions were France, Sweden and Czechoslovakia – managed to improve their trade balances but at considerably lower levels of trade and income (Friedman, 1974, p. 413). Thus, though commercial policy achieved its immediate purpose, it was at the expense of economic activity since countries were unable to offset the contractionary effects of much reduced trade levels.

Eastern Europe was no exception in this respect. Indeed, external policy was pursued more vigorously than in many other countries. Tariff levels were raised sharply between 1929 and 1931 to be followed by an extensive system of import controls (Condliffe, 1941, p. 103; Pollard, 1981, p. 302). In the latter half of 1931 Bulgaria, Yugoslavia, Hungary and Czechoslovakia introduced exchange control, followed by Romania in May 1932. Only Poland remained free of exchange control until April 1936 (League of Nations, 1933, pp. 222–3; 1937, p. 11; 1942, p. 70).

Strong action was even more important in Eastern Europe than elsewhere. Trade balances had on average been unfavourable before 1929 and they were soon hit badly by falling export values and adverse trade terms. Rapidly dwindling capital imports reduced the ability to finance import surpluses and so imports had to be reduced at all costs. Protection of domestic agriculture and industry also became an important consideration in a world awash with products. Initially, however, there were even more pressing motives for the introduction of exchange control. One of the main factors was to stem the capital outflow in the financial panic of 1931. A second reason seems to have been the states' desire to collect foreign exchange to cover foreign debt services. Initially it was hoped to maintain debt servicing in order to demonstrate financial soundness. Additionally, Eastern European countries were reluctant to relinquish their old currency parities, associating devaluation with inflation and mindful, as we have noted, of the implications for debt service costs (League of Nations, 1943, pp. 9–11; 1944, pp. 162–7).

During the course of the 1930s the burden of foreign debt was considerably eased by one means or another. Partial or complete suspension of servicing was declared by all countries between 1931 and 1933. Subsequently the burden was reduced through negotiation with creditors, both as to capital sums and repayment terms, while devaluation in the major creditor countries – the United States and Britain – afforded a substantial measure of relief. Overall, the total outstanding debt of the six countries fell from $3.8 to $2.0 billion between 1931 and 1937, and by the latter date servicing costs as a proportion of exports had fallen to less than 10 per cent compared with 25 per cent or more at the earlier date (Condliffe, 1941, pp. 243–4; Nötel, 1974, pp. 89–91).

Rigorous exchange control achieved some of its immediate objectives. It staunched the capital flow and reversed the deterioration in trade balances. The overall trade balance of the six countries was converted from a deficit of $32.5 million in 1929 to a surplus of $107.8 million in 1930 and $141.9 million in 1931 (Nötel, 1974, p. 87). But the costs involved were not inconsiderable. Harris (1936, p. 103) noted that exchange control countries tended to suffer a worse trade position than gold or paper currency countries. In the case of Hungary, Ellis (1941, p. 152) could find little net gain apart from the obstacles placed in the way of capital flight. Exchange control tended to raise domestic prices and to make exporting more difficult in so far as the control helped to maintain fictitious currency parities. This then led to a lower level of trade and income than under conditions where the currency is allowed to find its equilibrium level (Heuser, 1939, p. 230; League of Nations, 1938, p. 49). By 1934 Eastern European currencies were overvalued in relation to the pound and the dollar by up to 60 per cent (Nötel, 1986, p. 229). Furthermore, exchange control countries tended to trade more among themselves and less with free exchange countries and at higher prices than those ruling in the free market (League of Nations, 1938, p. 37).

Several countries eventually relaxed the controls to a certain extent to counter the adverse effects. At the end of 1934 Bulgaria modified its exchange control system with considerable benefits to its trade performance in the following year (League of Nations, 1938, p. 41). In time most countries, apart from Poland, introduced a measure of devaluation, either overt or concealed. The latter took the form of an export bonus or premium whereby exporters received a larger amount of domestic currency for their exports than under the official rate. The premia varied over time and from country to country, but usually ranged between 20 and 50 per cent (Lampe and Jackson, 1982, pp. 464–5; League of Nations, 1944, p. 171; Ranki, 1983, p. 90; Royal Institute of International Affairs, 1936, pp. 85–9). Even so their currencies continued to remain overvalued in relation to those of free market countries (League of Nations, 1938, p. 5).

One important development arising out of the closer affinity among exchange control countries was the spread of clearing agreements. By 1937 around 12 per cent of world trade and more than 50 per cent of the trade of Hungary, Bulgaria, Romania, Yugoslavia, Greece and Turkey passed through clearing, while in the case of Germany it was as high as 80 per cent (League of Nations, 1935, p. 15; 1942, pp. 70–72; 1944, pp. 182–3). Clearing agreements were one of the principal instruments for minimising the need for and maximising the acquisition of foreign exchange. They allowed the bilateral balancing of claims between exchange control countries thereby eliminating the need for foreign exchange.

The chief drawback was that they enabled Germany to exert an increasing influence on the economies of south-east Europe (Hungary and the Balkans) since Germany was one of the few countries prepared to accept agrarian products and other commodities at favourable prices. Though trade with the whole of Eastern Europe rarely accounted for more than around 10 per cent of Germany's total foreign trade, Germany managed to secure a very firm foothold in the trade of south-eastern Europe, especially following the *Anschluss* with Austria in 1938. The extent of the penetration in Hungary and the Balkans can be seen from the trade shares indicated in Table 8.2.

There is still controversy as to what benefits south-east Europe derived from the system. The conventional argument is that Germany exploited the region to gain access to food and raw materials on advantageous terms, and piled up large import surpluses, the Reichsmark balances from which could only be used to purchase

Table 8.2   Germany's share of Eastern Europe's trade (%)*

	Exports to Germany				Imports from Germany			
	1929	*1932*	*1937*	*1938*	*1929*	*1932*	*1937*	*1938*
Hungary	11.7	15.2	24.0	40.0	20.0	22.5	25.9	40.9
Romania	27.4	12.5	22.3	26.5	24.1	23.6	28.9	40.0
Yugoslavia	8.5	11.3	21.7	42.0	15.6	17.7	32.4	39.4
Bulgaria	29.9	26.0	43.1	59.0	22.2	25.9	54.8	52.0
Poland	34.2†	16.2	14.5	24.1	26.9†	20.1	14.5	23.0
Czechoslovakia	22.1†	19.6	13.7	20.1	24.9†	22.9	15.5	19.1

Sources: Hiden, 1977, p. 173; Kaiser, 1980, pp. 325–6.

Notes: * Figures for 1938 include Austria
          † Figures refer to 1928

German goods, thereby indirectly financing a German rearmament programme at the expense of weaker countries. Such balances also rendered the client countries highly vulnerable to political and economic pressure when market conditions deteriorated as they did in the later 1930s. In return Germany exported large quantities of unwanted goods such as aspirins and cuckoo clocks to requite the balances (Berend and Ranki, 1969, p. 183; 1974a, ch. 11). Einzig (1938, p. 26) quotes the case of Yugoslavia buying enough aspirins from Germany to last her a decade or more in order to reduce her balances with Germany.

On the credit side one has to bear in mind that these countries had few other secure outlets for many of their products and that they did receive more than ephemeral goods in return. They secured a large part of their machinery imports from Germany (Basch, 1944, p. 179) and detailed trade statistics certainly show a variety of producer goods, including arms supplies, being purchased from Germany (Momtchiloff, 1944, p. 56, Appendices 1–4). Though *The Economist* (1938b, pp. 262–7; 1939, pp. 537–8) had reservations about Germany's monopsonist power, the position was by no means an exploitive one. German purchases helped to raise export prices and incomes of the countries in question since normally they were made well above world prices (Bonnell, 1940, p. 131; Kaiser, 1980, p. 160), while Germany did not take advantage of her position to turn the terms of trade in her favour (Royal Institute of International Affairs, 1939, p. 119; see also Munting and Holderness, 1991, pp. 38–9). No doubt increasing dependence on the stronger economy delayed diversification and reintegration into the world economy as Basch (1944, p. 183) suggests, but this is perhaps a somewhat academic point given Germany's long-term plans for the region. On balance therefore, south-east Europe probably gained from its association with Germany. Rothschild (1974, p. 22) has little doubt on this score:

Contrary to frequent allegations at the time and since, Germany did not flood East Central Europe with cuckoo clocks, aspirin and thermometers in exchange for grains, minerals, and timber; rather she supplied capital goods for industry, encouraged the diversification of vulnerable one-crop agriculture, and supplied a steady market at reasonable prices.

So far as trade shares are concerned the main impact was in the sharp increase in intercourse between members of the Reichsmark bloc countries, which raised their share of intra-European trade largely as a result of increased trade between the dependent countries and Germany. On the other hand, Eastern Europe's share in world trade declined between 1928 and the later 1930s, mainly due to a contraction in the region's trade in primary products. By contrast a small gain was recorded in their share of world exports of manufactures, though as with the rest of Europe that share remained well below the level recorded in 1913 (Aldcroft, 1989, p. 32; Yates, 1959, pp. 32–3, 47–50).

Macro-economic stance

Even with the protection of their external accounts secured, there was very limited scope for imaginative fiscal and financial policies to counter the crisis. The financial position of Eastern Europe was far too weak to allow constructive government spending policies of a magnitude to produce worthwhile results, even assuming they had been disposed to contemplate such action in the first place (Royal Institute of International Affairs, 1936, p. 114). Public finance was in severe straits as revenue collapsed during the Depression. The yields from indirect taxes and dues fell by at least one-third, those from direct taxes by more than one-half (Schönfeld, 1975, pp. 197–8). Governments were therefore primarily concerned with the task of offsetting recession-induced budget deficits by expenditure cuts and increased taxation wherever possible, than in devising ways of stimulating activity and employment by fiscal means. The orthodox goals of currency stabilisation and budgetary equilibrium were regarded as top priorities in order to re-establish confidence at home and abroad (Spigler, 1986, p. 141).

Thus in the first half of the 1930s at least monetary and fiscal policy tended to take on a distinctly deflationary tone. Poland provided the most extreme manifestation in this respect as a consequence of her determination to maintain the value of the zloty without resorting to exchange controls. Stringent credit control was implemented by the commercial banks while total budgetary expenditure was reduced by about one-third in the four years 1930 to 1934 (Gorecki, 1935, p. 109; Taylor, 1952, p. 43). The approach very much mirrored that of contemporary France, where the authorities were similarly forced to adjust the whole cost and price structure downwards to accommodate the overvalued currency (Smith, 1936, pp. 168–78; Zweig, 1944, pp. 54–6). The deflationary policy undoubtedly helped to intensify and prolong the Depression in Poland and it was not until 1936 that a marked shift in direction occurred.

Hungary and the Balkan countries also followed the orthodox line with varying degrees of intensity. The belief in Hungary was that a rigid deflationary policy was necessary in order to secure foreign funds again, while the retrenchment policy adopted in Yugoslavia relied heavily on French advice (Polonsky, 1975, pp. 56–7; Royal Institute of International Affairs, 1936, p. 127). Only in the case of Czechoslovakia did government fiscal policy exert a small but positive impact to offset the decline in economic activity in the early 1930s (Pryor, 1979, pp. 236–7.)

Conventional budgetary practice did not of course prevent governments from taking measures such as public works and unemployment relief to ease the impact of the crisis, while at the same time trimming expenditure in other directions in an effort to balance their budgets. Moreover, towards the middle of the decade there were noticeable signs of relaxation. Yugoslavia was first off the mark in this respect in 1934/5 when cheaper money and reflationary government expenditure through public works loans signalled a decisive break with past orthodoxy (Royal Institute of International Affairs, 1936, p. 128). Soon after other countries, notably Hungary and Poland, relaxed their stance and announced major programmes of expenditure and investment. The slow improvement in economic conditions and state finances was partly responsible for this shift, but perhaps the major factor in the later 1930s was the ever-pressing needs of defence. Such requirements befitted the more interventionist and directive outlook of the autocratic regimes. As Hauner (1986, p. 50) notes:

The rising military expenditures and investments thus constituted one of the most effective instruments of state interventionist policies, by means of which the majority of east European states sought after the depression to re-activate a whole range of economic sectors, particularly domestic savings, which in turn were to contribute to the strengthening of the defence potential.

Exigencies of war therefore became an increasingly important influence in the later 1930s, accounting for up to one-third of government spending in most countries. Judging by the Czech experience, government-induced rearmament expenditure was a significant stimulating force to the economy (Pryor, 1979, pp. 236–7). On the other hand, if one looks at budgetary structures in more detail one cannot fail to entertain doubts as to their relevance to economic and social needs. Defence and civil administration (including government pensions) absorbed one-half or more on average of government spending, and if one adds debt service this left about one-third or less of the public budgets for productive purposes. The latter share may be compared with the figure of 60 per cent for contemporary Sweden (Political and Economic Planning, 1945, pp. 118–19, 164). Little wonder therefore that infrastructure facilities were tending to lag behind economic development (Ehrlich, 1973, p. 22; 1985, p. 369). Berend (1974, p. 191) reckons that the infrastructure of Eastern Europe was more backward relative to the West in 1938 than it had been in 1913.

As for the tax system itself this was highly regressive despite some attempts at reform in the 1930s. Taxation systems tended to be designed more for official convenience than for equity and economic rationale. In Yugoslavia, for example, where indirect taxes constituted three-quarters of total revenues, the principles enshrined in state fiscal policy were those

of charging its citizens as often as possible and as heavily as possible; taking the money where it could find it, and getting it from those who make the least outcry rather than according to the principle of the ability to pay. (Tomasevich, 1955, p. 688)

Income and other direct taxes constituted on average less than one-third of total revenues, whereas indirect taxes (excise and sales taxes and customs dues) accounted for two-thirds or more. The most extreme case was Bulgaria where direct taxes provided no more than 12 per cent of revenues; the least regressive was Poland where income, industrial and property taxes brought in half the revenue (Political and Economic Planning, 1945, pp. 118–22; Spigler, 1986, p. 154).

Such regressive fiscal systems, very characteristic of backward countries, were bound to hit the low income groups – primarily the peasants – hardest. In the case of the Balkan countries some 50 per cent of the total cash income of the peasantry went in taxes, an enormous burden considering their low incomes (Political and Economic Planning, 1945, p. 122; Tomasevich, 1955, p. 702). This heavy fiscal imposition undoubtedly acted as a strong disincentive to investment and improvement and was one of the major causes of backwardness and low incomes in the agrarian sector. Yet while the peasants were taxed to the hilt, other more prosperous groups, such as government officials and rent receivers, escaped fairly lightly. A glaring example was the case of owners of urban housing in Yugoslavia who incurred minimal tax liabilities on their rental income. This was one reason, together with subsidised interest rates, why so much capital formation (50 to 60 per cent) went into residential construction at the expense of investment elsewhere in the economy (Tomasevich, 1955, pp. 686–7). Yugoslavia was by no means unique in this respect, for tax anomalies were fairly widespread. The structure of taxation was ripe for reform and as one contemporary survey concluded: 'there are few spheres of public policy in which a constructive approach would yield speedier results' (Political and Economic Planning, 1945, p. 124).

The relief of agriculture

Given the size of the farm lobby and the severity of the agrarian crisis, it was a foregone conclusion that governments would be forced to intervene to ease the situation. The collapse in prices, the adverse shift in the farmers' terms of trade and the rising burden of debts left many in a state of destitution. Though farm output in physical terms was often well maintained, its real value was very much reduced. In Hungary for example, output was little changed between 1929 and 1934, but in real terms its value was almost halved (Zauberman, 1976, p. 598). Consequently at the depth of the crisis returns on farm capital were totally inadequate and often non-existent, and recovery was painfully slow (League of Nations, 1939a, p. 22). True, many smallholders consumed much of what they produced so that the real impact was less disastrous than the low returns on capital would seem to imply, but even the poorest peasant could scarcely live by bread alone. Clothing, shelter, repairs, farm implements and tools, fuel and many other supplies had to be paid for at a time when the farmer's terms of exchange had moved against him. For the larger commercial growers trading on the external market the prospects were no less bleak in a world glutted with food at a time when former customers were anxious to protect their own agrarian interests. Moreover, Eastern European exporters suffered an additional handicap in terms of price because of their low levels of efficiency compared with Western producers and their overvalued official exchange rates.

Indeed, the poverty of agriculture had deeper roots than the immediate deterioration in the terms of trade. It was also the product of unyielding agrarian structures based on traditional ownership patterns and practices, exacerbated in some cases by a sheer shortage of decent land. A good case in point is that of Slovenia where widespread small-scale ownership, coupled with a shortage of fertile land, set limits to improvements in efficiency. Because of the adverse man–land ratio, investment in agriculture to raise productivity only really made sense if it could substitute for labour, but the rate at which the latter could be drawn off the land depended ultimately on the availability of alternative employment outside the agrarian sector. Non-agrarian employment, though increasing after 1933, was never sufficient to cope with the potential excess labour on the land, and so, in the absence of strong and positive measures to achieve resource reallocation, the most that could be accomplished were marginal improvements in agrarian practices such as seed selection, improved manuring practices, better livestock breeding and the like (Hocevar, 1965, pp. 131, 148–54, 166).

Various attempts were of course made to relieve the situation: the measures included protection, debt and taxation relief, subsidies and export premia, price support schemes, concessions on payment of rent arrears, marketing boards, and incentives to reduce costs, diversify and encourage technical improvement (League of Nations, 1939a, pp. 29, 93–4, 98–9; 1939b, pp. 15–17, 27–30). Yet for the most part the measures were too limited and incoherent to provide a long-term solution to the basic agrarian problems of the region. They may have helped to stave off complete disaster, but they did little to transform the agrarian structure. Consequently investment in agriculture stagnated, incomes remained low, relative efficiency declined further, and the surplus agrarian population remained as large as ever. Post-war land reforms of varying extent, based as they were primarily on tenurial rights rather than on economic logic, had done little to ensure the viability of many of the small peasant farms that subsequently emerged, so that underemployment remained a pressing problem throughout the period. In theory, a substantial part of the agrarian manpower, especially in the Balkans and Poland, could have been eliminated without loss of output since marginal productivity was zero or negative. In practice however this solution was a non-starter for the very simple reason that there was nowhere for the surplus labour to go (Zauberman, 1976, pp. 594–5). Yet without such a transformation there was little prospect of raising efficiency in this sector and as a consequence agriculture could not perform the role it had done in the West, as a source of accumulation and a market for industrial goods (Teichova, 1989, pp. 900–904). It was the inherent limitations of the agrarian sector coupled with the social and political pressures of millions of under-employed rural workers that prompted governments to turn their attention towards industrialisation as a way out of the impasse.

Most governments readily acknowledged the farm debt problem

and took action to impose moratoria and to negotiate a general scaling down of indebtedness. For the Romanian peasant, the most heavily indebted in south-east Europe with smallholders of less than 10 hectares accounting for over 70 per cent of agrarian debt, a government moratorium on debt repayment was proclaimed in 1932, and two years later the principal was reduced by 50 per cent at a low rate of interest (Lampe and Jackson, 1982, p. 451; Seton-Watson, 1946, p. 83). Some 70 per cent of farm debtors benefited from these provisions which were accompanied by a large-scale programme of agricultural reconstruction (League of Nations, 1939b, pp. 15–16). Bulgaria in 1933 granted a five year moratorium, rates of interest were reduced, while debts of small farms – less than 10 hectares – were halved (Berend, 1985, p. 178). Rather more extensive relief was provided in Yugoslavia between 1932 and 1936, with an initial moratorium, reduced taxation and the liquidation of the debts of many smallholders which benefited some 654,000 farms (Berend, 1985, p. 178). Similar debt relief policies were also passed in Poland and Hungary in addition to measures to ease the burden of paying tax arrears (League of Nations, 1939a, pp. 29, 98–9; 1939b, p. 16).

A second method of assistance was through the use of subsidies. These took various forms including direct production subsidies, administered prices and export incentives. They were most widely used in Czechoslovakia, the only importer of agrarian products in Eastern Europe. Here the state encouraged a policy of import substitution by a combination of strict control on imports and heavy subsidisation. By 1937 subsidies, negligible in 1929, amounted to 12.9 per cent of total agrarian production (Pryor and Pryor, 1975, p. 509). This gave such a boost to agricultural output that it led to severe over-production in wheat and so the policy had to be modified. Moreover, it gave a stimulus to a sector in which Czechoslovakia had a marked comparative disadvantage in terms of international trade (Pryor and Pryor, 1975, p. 531).

In other countries subsidies were mainly confined to exports, either directly or through the use of special export premia to offset the overvalued exchange rates. By the mid-1930s most countries had introduced export premia ranging between 20 and 50 per cent (Lampe and Jackson, 1982, pp. 465–6; Royal Institute of International Affairs, 1939, p. 145). Additional support for prices and exports came with the establishment of state purchasing and marketing boards which were set up for a variety of products, especially cereals, sugar and potatoes, in all countries. Some of these virtually monopolised the marketing of certain agrarian products, usually at guaranteed prices, and they became a useful instrument in the barter trade agreements concluded with

Germany for the export of agrarian products. One of the most notable was the Czecho-Slovak Cereals Company, established in July 1934, with powers to buy all home-grown cereals at a fixed price for resale in the market and which conducted all transactions with foreign countries (League of Nations, 1939b, pp. 27–30). Romania and Poland also adopted price support measures, not without some degree of success (League of Nations, 1939a, pp. 93, 98). In so far as such policies tended to encourage crop production by virtue of the more favourable prices offered, it could be argued that they simply accentuated the over-production problem.

Assistance designed to effect cost reductions, technical improvements and product diversification were somewhat more limited. Here the Balkan countries, especially Bulgaria, took the lead by encouraging the shift away from cereals (already under way before the crisis) towards stock-breeding, industrial crops, dairy and poultry production, fruit farming and market gardening. The policy met with some degree of success (Lampe and Jackson, 1982, pp. 368–9; Royal Institute of International Affairs, 1939, p. 145). Technical improvements such as crop rotation, new strains of crops and stable feeding of livestock were also promoted. In Hungary the government also tried to secure reductions in the cost of standardised agricultural implements and machines (League of Nations, 1939b, p. 17). However, probably the major relief in this respect was in the cost of wage labour which in Poland fell by nearly two-thirds from 1927–30 to 1934–35 (League of Nations, 1939a, p. 99).

Such policies helped to alleviate the crisis and brought about a limited measure of improvement in the later 1930s as markets slowly improved. But agrarian incomes remained depressingly low, in some cases below pre-war levels, as did agricultural practices, while the burden of taxation on agriculture remained a constant source of grievance. Agrarian interests felt that they were unduly penalised financially for the benefit of industry and rearmament, and that exports were being subsidised at the expense of domestic consumption (Basch, 1944, pp. 101–2; Hertz, 1947, pp. 102–3). On both counts they may well have been right, but in its traditional form peasant farming had by then reached the end of the road.

State intervention and the promotion of industry

During the 1930s there was a more concerted effort to push forward industrialisation than ever before. The Depression, by exposing the poverty of the agrarian sector, acted as a catalyst in this respect, while the absence of capital inflows made it imperative that

Eastern Europe harness its own resources for development. The prevailing political and economic ideology also prompted a shift in direction. With liberal capitalism now discredited the forces of nationalism and nostrification intensified and the emergence of autocratic forms of government facilitated the advance of more autarkic methods of control and state ownership and direction of industry, especially in sectors of strategic importance (Turnock, 1986, p. 59). It is doubtful, however, whether there was sufficient coherence in the exercise to warrant the term 'planning' to be used in any meaningful sense (Ranki and Tomaszewski, 1986, pp. 40–41).

Many of the measures employed to foster industry were not, of course, new. Subsidies, tax exemptions, tariffs, public works, for example, had all been used well before the 1930s, while state ownership of infrastructures such as railways, ports and forests had a long lineage. What was really different about the 1930s was the much greater intensity with which controls were used to encourage import substitution and promote industrial development and the much enlarged role of the state in industrial activities. The need to erect stringent controls to protect external accounts and currencies in the early 1930s also gave an added dimension to the drive for greater self-sufficiency. From 1935 onwards many of the projects for industrial expansion were closely associated with rearmament (Singleton and Carter, 1982, p. 61; Tomasevich, 1949, p. 179).

The extent of state ownership varied considerably among the different countries. It was extensive in Poland, least so in Czechoslovakia, with other countries falling in between (Spulber, 1959, p. 268). State ownership in Poland was probably more extensive than in any other European country outside the USSR. Apart from the traditional infrastructure holdings, the Polish state, by the end of the 1930s, employed about one million people (excluding the armed forces) and owned around 100 industrial enterprises with over 1,000 establishments. The supply of military equipment was dominated by the state which also owned 80 per cent of the chemical industry, 40 per cent of the iron and steel, 50 per cent of the metallurgical industry, 20 per cent of the oil refineries, most of the main transport services, together with five state monopolies in alcohol, matches, tobacco, salt and a state lottery (Spulber, 1966, p. 35; Taylor, 1952, pp 93–4). State industries and monopolies were also quite extensive in Yugoslavia where they accounted for some 15 per cent of the country's industrial investment in 1938, mainly in metals, chemicals and food processing. The figure rises to 22 per cent if cartels, which were placed under the control of the Ministry of Commerce and Industry in 1935, are included (Lampe and Jackson, 1982, p. 500). In the case of Bulgaria, where expansion of state activity was prompted by the need to make up tax shortfalls, state-owned enterprises numbered 169 by 1939 and accounted for 8 to 9 per cent of total industrial production, and 15 per cent if cooperatives are included (Lampe, 1986, pp. 100–110). On the other hand, the spread of state enterprise was rather less extensive in Hungary, accounting for only about 5 per cent of industrial investment in the late 1930s (Berend, 1974, p. 189). Romania was closer to the Polish model.

In conjunction with state enterprises, cartels became an integral part of government economic policy in all Eastern European countries. By the latter part of the decade they accounted for well over 40 per cent of Hungary's industrial production, 66 per cent of the Polish, most of the Czech and 23 per cent of Romanian (Berend and Ranki, 1974b, p. 141; Spulber, 1959, p. 276; Teichova, 1985, pp. 958–9, 1988, pp. 44–6). Cartels, many of which were international in scope, were essentially restrictive in nature. They reduced competition by controlling prices, allocating production quotas among members, and generally regulating the conditions of trade. They therefore stifled competitive forces and encouraged industrial concentration, especially in heavy industry. During the later 1930s Germany utilised the cartel system to increase its influence in south-eastern Europe (Teichova, 1989, pp. 960–61).

A third feature of the governments' industrial strategy was the launching of major investment programmes, usually associated with public works for the relief of unemployment and later with rearmament. Whether such policies can be regarded as evidence of an eschewal of classicist budgetary principles in the genuine interests of stimulating economic activity and employment, as Zauberman (1976, p. 600) implies, is a moot point in view of the obvious social and political pressures which activated the policy-makers' stance at the time. Be that as it may, most countries embarked on substantial state-sponsored programmes during the course of the 1930s. Yugoslavia announced a large programme of public works in 1934/5. In 1936 Poland launched an ambitious six-year Defence Expansion Plan entailing the expenditure of 6,000 million zloty (later scaled down) on armament plants, military equipment and general defence. Prior to the war about half the original sum had been spent. Coterminous with this project was the plan to develop the Central Industrial District (the triangle bounded by Warsaw, Cracow and Lvov) as a major industrial region concentrating on the development of heavy industry and military equipment away from the country's frontiers (Hauner, 1986, pp. 101–2; Landau and Tomaszewski, 1985, pp. 118–19; Taylor, 1952, pp. 96–8). Two years later Hungary also announced a Five Year Plan of 1,000 million pengos with emphasis on public works and rearmament (Berend and Ranki, 1985, pp. 91–2; Royal Institute of

International Affairs, 1939, p. 118). In the case of Romania, the government, from the mid-1930s, offered two-year monopolies for the establishment of industries considered essential to the national interest, while it also contributed part of the capital cost of new arms factories with the guarantee of purchasing output at favourable prices (Royal Institute of International Affairs, 1939, pp. 129–30).

The overall results of the efforts to foster industrialisation were somewhat mixed, and certainly less impressive than the indices of manufacturing output growth through 1929 to 1938 would seem to indicate (see Table 8.3). The Balkan countries clearly achieved a much better performance than Poland, Hungary and Czechoslovakia, the last of which stagnated industrially in the 1930s. However, it should be borne in mind that the statistical data for industrial output are still far from robust for this period and consequently it is difficult to arrive at a very definitive conclusion. Jackson and Lampe (1982, pp. 408–9) give a rather more optimistic interpretation of the industrial record of the Balkan countries. They argue the case for relatively fast industrial growth in southeast Europe before World War II, with rates of growth of the following magnitudes for the years 1929 to 1938: Bulgaria 4.8 per cent, Romania 3.4 per cent and Yugoslavia 2.4 per cent. They are particularly impressed by some of the structural shifts away from artisan activities and towards modern factory production. In the case of Yugoslavia they argue that: 'Modern, mechanised production had . . . become the predominant form of industrial activity by 1939 in a territory where little statistical significance had existed before the turn of the century' (Jackson and Lampe, 1982, p. 409). Moreover, in some cases, especially textiles and food processing, import substitution registered quite significant gains.

Table 8.3   Indices of manufacturing output 1929–39 (1913 = 100)

	1929	*1938*	*% change*
Hungary	112	128	14.3
Poland	86	105	22.0
Romania	137	180	31.4
Yugoslavia	140	190	35.7
Bulgaria	179	245	36.9
Czechoslovakia	140	136	−2.9

Sources: Berend and Ranki, 1974a, pp. 299–300; United Nations, 1949c, Table 36.

Nevertheless, industrial production only achieved a very modest increase in its share in these economies. Overall, the scale and scope, as well as the timing, of the industrial changes were too limited to effect any radical transformation of the economic structure. Moreover, the efficiency of industry still fell far short of that of the advanced countries of the West.

Thus the fundamental problems of the region remained basically unchanged. The total number of people employed in industry in 1937 in the Balkan countries, for example, was still very modest and the increase in the numbers so employed was nowhere near sufficient to absorb the increasing agrarian population. In the case of Yugoslavia, to take one example, the number of industrial workers rose by about half a million between 1929 and 1937, yet over the same period the total population increased by 1.8 million (Basch, 1944, p. 241).

Despite the declared emphasis on industry during this period, the share of total investment going into this sector was quite modest, averaging 15 to 30 per cent through 1929 to 1937 (Political and Economic Planning, 1945, p. 102). Moreover, in the latter part of the period a substantial part of this was defence oriented. Berend (1974, pp. 191–2) draws attention to the weakness of industrial investment and the lag in infrastructure investment which was noted earlier. In fact the larger part of new investment, at least in the Balkans, appears to have gone into housing (40–60 per cent), stimulated in part by favourable tax treatment of rental incomes (Political and Economic Planning, 1945, p. 102; Tomasevich, 1955, p. 687).

On balance, the efforts to foster industrial development were not an unqualified success. Industry certainly proved to be the most dynamic sector in the 1930s and in most cases its share in total activity increased, albeit marginally. Even so, by 1938 industry's share of national income was still only one-quarter or less in the Balkans, one-third or so in Hungary and Poland, compared with well over one-half in the highly industrialised countries of the West. Only Czechoslovakia, with just over half its national income derived from industry, could match the latter (Berend and Ranki, 1974a, pp. 307–8). Thus it was still the state of the harvest which determined the prosperity of most of Eastern Europe.

Several aspects of the state's industrial promotion policies can be called into question. State policy tended to foster unproductive and non-economic investments. This can be seen in the large proportion of investment that went into residential construction, the concentration on defence-related industrial activities in the latter part of the period, and the fact that some state enterprises were designed for tax revenue purposes. State control and direction also led to excessive bureaucratic interference and at times an unfriendly attitude towards private enterprise. Doreen Warriner (1940, p. 16) argued that it was the bureaucrat, not the capitalist or large landowner, who exploited the worker in the Balkans. It has also been suggested that the attempts to force industrial growth were at the expense of agriculture which remained short of capital and highly taxed (Hertz, 1947, pp. 102–3).

Second, the state's financial resources were limited: it could not replace the role of foreign capital when overseas loans dried up in the 1930s, while the nostrification policy designed to discourage foreign funds and ownership did not help matters. True foreign capital still remained a significant element in Eastern Europe throughout the period, but the less congenial climate tended to discourage new enterprise and skill formation from abroad.

Third, efforts to mobilise domestic resources were frequently offset by restrictive monetary and fiscal policies including higher taxation, while the structure of taxation tended to direct resources into less essential areas of activity, for example housing.

Fourth, the direction of investment even within industry itself was not conducive to rapid development. A large proportion of industrial investment went into textiles, food processing and light industries, where the growth potential was low, to the comparative neglect of modern dynamic sectors such as chemicals, the electrical trades, telecommunications and the motor industry (Berend, 1974, pp. 192–4). The motor vehicle, for example, did not replace the railways as a force of growth as it did in the West.

The emphasis on traditional sectors was the main reason the industrial structure remained remarkably static during the period. The major gains in employment shares occurred mainly in textiles, except in Poland and Czechoslovakia, with little advance in producer goods groups (Teichova, 1981, pp. 183–4). Thus in Yugoslavia the number of textile factories rose from 30 in 1929 to 363 in 1936. One of the reasons for this outcome was that import substitution was easiest in textiles given the low domestic purchasing power and the shortage of capital and skilled labour. Protection of the home market therefore favoured import substitution in the least cost activities. Despite the greater encouragement given to heavy industry later on in the period, markets for the products (outside government procurement) was limited by the depth of demand at home and the lack of comparative advantage on the international market. Cartelisation, by bolstering product prices, also circumscribed effective demand (Teichova, 1981, pp. 181–5).

Apart from the rather lop-sided industrial structure, Eastern Europe also retained its traditional dual structure, with many small-scale inefficient firms competing with a few modern large-scale enterprises. Small businesses remained as viable as ever, partly because of the weakness of big business, the abundance of labour and the predominance of those activities in which small-scale enterprise tended to flourish. Moreover, large-scale corporations failed to make much headway in modern production and management methods. Western-style mass-production methods were something of a rarity, and the typical large company was little more than a 'general store' which supplied a multiplicity of products in small batches to limited markets within a rigid protectionist framework.

The inconsistent logic of some of the industrial policies is well illustrated by the case of Czechoslovakia, a country with by far the largest industrial sector in the region. It was badly hit in international markets during the crisis and had a very slow and chequered recovery subsequently. In part this was due to the uncoordinated domestic and foreign trade policies which resulted in relative expansion in those sectors with a comparative disadvantage, especially agriculture where a strongly subsidised import substitution policy was pursued, and a loss of share in those industries in which Czechoslovakia enjoyed a comparative advantage. The Czechs failed to capitalise on their previous industrial gains in international markets with the result that exports and production in industries with a comparative advantage remained well below the 1929 levels throughout the 1930s, whereas those sectors at a comparative disadvantage managed to regain or exceed former peak levels of activity (Pryor, 1973, p. 201; Pryor and Pryor, 1975, pp. 509, 520).

The overall balance

It is easy to paint a gloomy picture of the economies of Eastern Europe in the 1930s. The detailed accounts of industrial development, infrastructure facilities and agriculture certainly point to some modest progress in certain sectors, but they do not alter the conventional picture of an absence of fundamental change in economic structures. Apart from Czechoslovakia, they remained low income agrarian-dependent economies whose economic and social structures were not conducive to rapid economic development. In the words of Berend and Ranki (1974a, p. 318): 'East-Central Europe became an area struggling with permanent crisis and fraught with inner contradictions in a tense, explosive atmosphere where everything called for change.'

Yet despite the unfavourable background, national incomes did expand and they even managed to exceed former peaks (1929) by a reasonable margin in most cases. The real problem, however, was that much of the increase was swamped out by rapid population growth – up to three times the average for Western and Northern Europe (League of Nations, 1941, p. 50). Consequently, through 1929 to 1938 income per capita fell slightly in Yugoslavia and Czechoslovakia, was almost static in Poland, rose very modestly in Hungary and Romania, and only in Bulgaria did it increase significantly (23.5 per cent). Taking the region as a whole, average per capita income probably advanced by no more than about 5 to 6 per cent if that, which was about half the European average (Bairoch, 1976, p. 297; Lethbridge 1985, p. 538; Spulber, 1966, p. 58). This means that by the end of the 1930s the disparity in income levels between Western and Eastern Europe had widened since 1929 and probably also since 1914. In 1938 net national income per head in the Balkan countries was only one-fifth to one-quarter that of Germany, in Poland and Hungary barely one-third, and even in Czechoslovakia it was only just over one-half (Lethbridge, 1985, p. 532; see also United Nations, 1949a). In fact by every conceivable indicator Eastern Europe was less productive, less healthy and less literate than Western Europe.

Could do better no doubt. It was a potentially rich region stocked with a poor people in which the maldistribution of income was the central feature and where development had been stunted by the vicissitudes of war and the unfavourable economic climate which followed. The immediate policy reaction to the crisis of the early 1930s was predictable, given its severity and global dimensions, together with the ardent desire to avoid complete economic and financial collapse. But the strategy could be no more than a holding operation at a much reduced level of economic activity. On the other hand, when the slow improvement in economic conditions allowed some relaxation in the orthodox policy stance, the inconsistencies and incoherence of government strategies became more apparent. Tax systems were inefficient and inequitable, budgetary expenditures were largely unproductive, infrastructures were neglected, rearmament came to dominate industrial activity, while agriculture and the associated population problem were not accorded any special priority. It was the neglect of the latter in particular which effectively stifled what forces of change were present.

Notes

1 With a fifth of the area and one-quarter of the population of the former Empire, the new Republic inherited 85 per cent of the coal and lignite production, 65 per cent of the iron and steel capacity, 60 per cent of the

engineering industry, 75 per cent of textiles, over 93 per cent of sugar production, and 43 per cent of the total industrial labour force. The only really weak parts were Slovakia and Ruthenia in the East (*The Economist*, 1938a, pp. 544–5).

References

Aldcroft, D. H., 1977, *From Versailles to Wall Street, 1919–1929*, London, Allen Lane.

Aldcroft, D. H., 1980, *The European Economy, 1914–1980*, London, Croom Helm.

Aldcroft, D. H., 1988, 'Eastern Europe in an Age of Turbulence, 1919–1950', *Economic History Review*, 41: 592–602.

Aldcroft, D. H., 1989, 'The Decline of Europe: Trade and Reconstruction in the 1920s', *EUI Colloquium Papers*, 136/89. Florence, European University Institute.

Aldcroft, D. H., 1991, 'Destabilising Influences in the European Economy in the 1920s', in C. Holmes and A. Booth (eds), *Economy and Society: European Industrialisation and Its Social Consequences: Essays Presented to Sidney Pollard*, Leicester, Leicester University Press.

Alpert, P., 1951, *Twentieth Century Economic History of Europe*, New York, Schuman.

Bairoch, P., 1976, 'Europe's Gross National Product: 1800–1975', *Journal of European Economic History*, 5: 273–340.

Bandera, V. N., 1964, *Foreign Capital as an Instrument of National Economic Policy: A Study Based on the Experience of East European Countries between the Two World Wars*, The Hague, Nijhoff.

Basch, A., 1944, *The Danube Basin and the German Economic Sphere*, London, Kegan Paul, Trench, Trubner.

Berend, I. T., 1974, 'Investment Strategy in East-Central Europe', in H. Daems and H. van der Wee (eds), *The Rise of Managerial Capitalism*, The Hague, Nijhoff.

Berend, I. T., 1985, 'Agriculture', in M. C. Kaser and E. A. Radice (eds), *The Economic History of Eastern Europe 1919–1975. Vol. I. Economic Structure and Performance Between the Wars*, Oxford, Oxford University Press.

Berend, I. and Ranki, G., 1969, 'Economic Problems of the Danube Region after the Break-up of the Austro-Hungarian Monarchy', *Journal of Contemporary History*, 4: 169–84.

Berend, I. T. and Ranki, G., 1974a, *Economic Development in East Central Europe in the 19th and 20th Centuries*, New York, Columbia University Press.

Berend, I. T. and Ranki, G., 1974b, *Hungary: A Century of Economic Development*, Newton Abbot, David & Charles.

Berend, I. T. and Ranki, G., 1985, *The Hungarian Economy in the Twentieth Century*, London, Croom Helm.

Bonnell, A. T., 1940, *German Control over International Economic Relations, 1930–1940*, Urbana, Illinois, University of Illinois Press.

Condliffe, J. B., 1941, *The Reconstruction of World Trade: A Survey of International Economic Relations*, London, Allen & Unwin.

Deldlycke, T., Gelders, H. and Limbor, J. M., 1968, *The Working Population and Its Structure: International Historical Statistics*, Vol. I, Brussels, Université Libre de Bruxelles.

Dovring, F., 1960, *Land and Labour in Europe, 1900–1950*, The Hague, Nijhoff.

The Economist, 1938a, 'The Bastion of Europe', 12 March, 130: 544–5.

The Economist, 1938b, 'Germany's Trade Offensive', 5 November, 133: 262–7.

The Economist, 1939, 'The Fight for Romanian Trade', 3 June, 135: 537–8.

Ehrlich, E., 1973, 'Infrastructure and an International Comparison of Relationships with Indicators of Development in Eastern Europe, 1920–1950', *Papers in East European Economics*, 33: 1–33.

Ehrlich, E., 1985, 'Infrastructure', in M. C. Kaser and E. A. Radice (eds), *The Economic History of Eastern Europe 1919–1975*. Vol. I, *Economic Structure and Performance Between the Wars*, Oxford, Oxford University Press.

Einzig, P., 1938, *Bloodless Invasion: German Economic Penetration into the Danubian States and the Balkans*, London, Duckworth.

Ellis, H. S., 1941, *Exchange Control in Central Europe*, Cambridge, Mass., Harvard University Press.

Friedman, P., 1974, *Impact of Trade Destruction on National Incomes: A Study of Europe, 1924–1938*, Gainesville, University Presses of Florida.

Friedman, P., 1978, 'An Econometric Model of National Income, Commercial Policy and the Level of International Trade: the Open Economies of Europe, 1924–1938', *Journal of Economic History*, 38: 148–80.

Gordon, M. S., 1941, *Barriers to World Trade: a Study of Recent Commercial Policy*, New York, Macmillan.

Gorecki, R., 1935, *Poland and her Economic Development*, London, Allen & Unwin.

Harris, S. E., 1936, *Exchange Depreciation: Its Theory and its History 1931–35, With Some Consideration of Related Domestic Policies*, Cambridge, Mass., Harvard University Press.

Hauner, M., 1986, 'Military Budgets and the Armaments Industry', in M. C. Kaser and E. A. Radice (eds), *The Economic History of Eastern Europe 1919–1975*, Vol. II. *Interwar Policy, the War and Reconstruction*. Oxford, Oxford University Press.

Hertz, F., 1947, *The Economic Problem of the Danubian States: A Study in Economic Nationalism*, London, Gollancz.

Heuser, H., 1939, *Control of International Trade*, London, Routledge.

Hiden, J., 1977, *Germany and Europe 1919–1939*, London, Longman.

Hocevar, T., 1965, *The Structure of the Slovenian Economy 1848–1963*. New York, Studia Slovenica.

Jackson, M. R. and Lampe, J. R., 1982, 'The Evidence of Industrial Growth in South Eastern Europe before the Second World War', *East European Quarterly*, 16: 385–415.

Kaiser, D. E., 1980, *Economic Diplomacy and the Origins of the Second*

World War: Germany, Britain, France, and Eastern Europe, 1930–1939, Princeton, Princeton University Press.

Kaser, M. C. and Radice, E. A. (eds), 1985, *The Economic History of Eastern Europe 1919–1975*. Vol. I, *Economic Structure and Performance Between the Wars*, Oxford, Oxford University Press.

Kaser, M. C. and Radice, E. A. (eds), 1986, *The Economic History of Eastern Europe 1919–1975*. Vol. II, *Interwar Policy, the War and Reconstruction*, Oxford, Oxford University Press.

Lampe, J. R., 1986, *The Bulgarian Economy in the Twentieth Century*, London, Croom Helm.

Lampe, J. R. and Jackson, M. R., 1982, *Balkan Economic History 1550–1950*, Bloomington, Indiana University Press.

Landau, Z. and Tomaszewski, J., 1985, *The Polish Economy in the Twentieth Century*, London, Croom Helm.

League of Nations, 1932, *Conference for the Economic Restoration of Central and Eastern Europe*, Stresa, League of Nations.

League of Nations, 1933, *World Economic Survey 1932–33*, Geneva, League of Nations.

League of Nations, 1935a, *Enquiry into Clearing Agreements*, Geneva, League of Nations.

League of Nations, 1935b, *World Economic Survey 1934–35*, Geneva, League of Nations.

League of Nations, 1937, *Money and Banking 1936/37*, Geneva, League of Nations.

League of Nations, 1938, *Report on Exchange Control*, Geneva, League of Nations.

League of Nations, 1939a, *European Conference on Rural Life: Population and Agriculture with Special Reference to Agricultural Overpopulation*, Geneva, League of Nations.

League of Nations, 1939b, *European Conference on Rural Life 1939: The Capital and Income of Farms in Europe as They Appear from Farm Accounts for the Years 1927–28 to 1934–35*, Geneva, League of Nations.

League of Nations, 1941, *Europe's Trade*, Geneva, League of Nations.

League of Nations, 1942, *Commercial Policy in the Interwar Period*, Geneva, League of Nations.

League of Nations, 1943, *Trade Relations between Free-Market and Controlled Economies*, Geneva, League of Nations.

League of Nations, 1944, *International Currency Experience: Lessons of the Interwar Period*, Geneva, League of Nations.

League of Nations, 1945, *Industrialization and Foreign Trade*, Geneva, League of Nations.

Lee, C. H., 1969, 'The Effects of the Depression on Primary Producing Countries', *Journal of Contemporary History*, 4: 139–55.

Lethbridge, E., 1985, 'National Income and Product', in M. C. Kaser and E. A. Radice (eds), *The Economic History of Eastern Europe 1919–1975*, Vol. I, *Economic Structure and Performance Between the Two Wars*, Oxford, Oxford University Press.

Liepmann, K., 1938, *Tariff Levels and the Economic Unity of Europe*, London, Allen & Unwin.

Macartney, C. A., 1937, *Hungary and Her Successors: The Treaty of Trianon and Its Consequences 1919–1937*, Oxford, Oxford University Press.

Macartney, C. A. and Palmer, A. W., 1962, *Independent Eastern Europe*, London, Macmillan.

Maddison, A., 1973, *Economic Policy and Performance in Europe 1913–1970*, London, Collins/Fontana.

Momtchiloff, N., 1944, *Ten Years of Controlled Trade in South-Eastern Europe*, Cambridge, Cambridge University Press.

Moore, W. E., 1945, *Economic Demography in Eastern and Southern Europe*, Geneva, League of Nations.

Morgan, O. S. (ed.), 1933, *Agricultural Systems of Middle Europe*, New York, New York University Press.

Munting, R. and Holderness, B. A., 1991, *Crisis, Recovery and War: An Economic History of Continental Europe 1918–1945*, London, Philip Allan.

Newman, W. J., 1968, *The Balance of Power in the Interwar Years 1919–1939*, New York, Random House.

Nötel, R., 1974, 'International Capital Movements and Finance in Eastern Europe, 1919–1941', *Vierteljahrschrift für Sozial-und Wirtschafts-geschichte*, 61: 65–112.

Nötel, R., 1984, 'Money, Banking and Industry in Interwar Austria and Hungary', *Journal of European Economic History*, 13(2): 137–202.

Nötel, R., 1986, 'International Credit and Finance', in M. C. Kaser and E. A. Radice (eds), *The Economic History of Eastern Europe 1919–1975. Vol. II, Interwar Policy, the War and Reconstruction*, Oxford, Oxford University Press.

Pasvolsky, L., 1928, *Economic Nationalism of the Danubian States*, London, Allen & Unwin.

Political and Economic Planning, 1945, *Economic Development in S. E. Europe*, London, PEP.

Pollard, S., 1981, *Peaceful Conquest: The Industrialization of Europe 1760–1970*, Oxford, Oxford University Press.

Polonsky, A., 1975, *The Little Dictators: the History of Eastern Europe since 1918*, London, Routledge & Kegan Paul.

Pryor, Z. P., 1973, 'Czechoslovak Economic Development in the Interwar Period', in V. S. Mamatey and R. Luza (eds), *A History of the Czechoslovak Republic 1918–1948*, Princeton, Princeton University Press.

Pryor, Z. P., 1979, 'Czechoslovak Fiscal Policies in the Great Depression', *Economic History Review*, 32: 228–40.

Pryor, Z. P. and Pryor, F. L., 1975, 'Foreign Trade and Interwar Czechoslovak Economic Development 1918–1938', *Vierteljahrschrift für Sozial-und Wirtschaftsgeschichte*, 62: 500–533.

Ranki, G., 1983, *Economic and Foreign Policy: The Struggle of the Great Powers for the Hegemony in the Danube Valley, 1919–1939*, New York, Columbia University Press.

Ranki, G. and Tomaszewski, J., 1986, 'The Role of the State in Industry, Banking and Trade', in M. C. Kaser and E. A. Radice (eds), *The Economic History of Eastern Europe 1919–1975*, Vol. II, *Interwar Policy, the War and Reconstruction*, Oxford, Oxford University Press.

Raupach, H., 1969, 'The Impact of the Great Depression on Eastern Europe', *Journal of Contemporary History*, 4: 75–86.

Rosenstein-Rodan, P. N., 1943, 'Problems of Industrialisation of Eastern and South-Eastern Europe', *Economic Journal*, 53: 202–11.

Ross, G., 1983, *The Great Powers and the Decline of the European States System 1914–1945*, London, Longman.

Rothschild, J., 1974, *East Central Europe between the two World Wars*, Seattle, University of Washington Press.

Royal Institute of International Affairs, 1936, *The Balkan States: Economic: a Review of the Economic and Financial Development of Albania, Bulgaria, Greece, Roumania and Yugoslavia since 1919*, Oxford, Oxford University Press.

Royal Institute of International Affairs, 1937, *The Problem of International Investment*, Oxford, Oxford University Press.

Royal Institute of International Affairs, 1939, *South Eastern Europe: a Political and Economic Survey*, Oxford, Oxford University Press.

Royal Institute of International Affairs, 1940, *South-Eastern Europe: A Brief Survey*, Oxford, Oxford University Press.

Schönfeld, R., 1975, 'Die Balkanlander in der Weltwirtschaftskrise', *Vierteljahrschrift für Sozial-und Wirtschaftsgeschichte*, 62: 179–213.

Seton-Watson, H., 1946, *Eastern Europe between the Wars 1918–1941*, Cambridge, Cambridge University Press.

Singleton, F. and Carter, B., 1982, *The Economy of Yugoslavia*, London, Croom Helm.

Smith, L., 1936, 'The Zloty, 1924–35', *Journal of Political Economy*, 44: 145–83.

Spigler, I., 1986, 'Public Finance', in M. C. Kaser and E. A. Radice (eds), *The Economic History of Eastern Europe 1919–1975. Vol. II, Interwar Policy, the War and Reconstruction*, Oxford, Oxford University Press.

Spulber, N., 1959, 'The Role of the State in Economic Growth in Eastern Europe since 1860', in H. G. J. Aitken (ed.), *The State and Economic Growth*, New York, Social Science Research Council.

Spulber, N., 1966, *The State and Economic Development in Eastern Europe*, New York, Random House.

Svennilson, I., 1954, *Growth and Stagnation in the European Economy*, Geneva, United Nations.

Taylor, J., 1952, *The Economic Development of Poland 1919–1950*, Ithaca, NY, Cornell University Press.

Teichova, A., 1981, 'Structural Changes and Industrialization in Interwar Central-East Europe' in P. Bairoch and M. Levy-Leboyer (eds), *Disparities in Economic Development since the Industrial Revolution*, London, Macmillan.

Teichova, A., 1985, 'Industry' in M. C. Kaser and E. A. Radice (eds), *The Economic History of Eastern Europe 1919–1975*, Vol. I, *Economic Structure and Performance Between the Wars*, Oxford, Oxford University Press.

Teichova, A., 1988, *The Czechoslovak Economy 1918–1980*, London, Routledge.

Teichova, A., 1989, 'East-Central and South-East Europe 1919–39', in P. Mathias and S. Pollard (eds), *The Cambridge Economic History of Europe*, Vol. VIII. *The Industrial Economies: the Development of Economic and Social Policies*, Cambridge, Cambridge University Press.

Tiltman, H., 1935, *Peasant Europe*, London, Benn.

Tomasevich, J., 1949, 'Foreign Economic Relations', in R. J. Kerner (ed.), *Yugoslavia*, Berkeley, University of California Press.

Tomasevich, J., 1955, *Peasants, Politics and Economic Change in Yugoslavia*, Stanford, Stanford University Press.

Turnock, D., 1986, *The Romanian Economy in the Twentieth Century*, London, Croom Helm.

United Nations, 1949a, *Economic Survey of Europe 1948*, Geneva, United Nations.

United Nations, 1949b, *International Capital Movements during the Interwar Period*, New York, United Nations.

United Nations, 1949c, *Statistical Yearbook 1948*, New York, United Nations.

Warriner, D., 1939, *Economics of Peasant Farming*, Oxford, Oxford University Press.

Warriner, D., 1940, *Eastern Europe after Hitler*, Fabian Research Series 50, London, Gollancz.

Woytinsky, W. S. and Woytinsky, E. S., 1953, *World Population and Production: Trends and Outlook*, New York, Twentieth Century Fund.

Yates, P. L., 1959, *Forty Years of Foreign Trade*, London, Allen & Unwin.

Zauberman, A., 1976, 'Russia and Eastern Europe 1920–1970', in C. M. Cipolla (ed.), *The Fontana Economic History of Europe: Contemporary Economies, Part Two*, London, Collins/Fontana.

Zweig, F., 1944, *Poland between the Wars*, London, Secker & Warburg.

Index